taste of home
new
church
supper
cookbook

taste of home
BOOKS

REIMAN MEDIA GROUP, LLC • GREENDALE, WI

taste of home

Reader's Digest

Editor-in-Chief: Catherine Cassidy

Vice President, Executive Editor/Books:
Heidi Reuter Lloyd

Creative Director: Howard Greenberg

North American Chief Marketing Officer:
Lisa Karpinski

Food Director: Diane Werner, RD

Senior Editor/Retail Books: Faithann Stoner

Editor: Sara Rae Lancaster

Associate Creative Director: Edwin Robles Jr.

Layout Designer: Catherine Fletcher

Project Art Director: Julianne Schnuck

Content Production Manager: Julie Wagner

Copy Chief: Deb Warlaumont Mulvey

Proofreader: Victoria Soukup Jensen

Recipe Asset System Manager: Coleen Martin

Recipe Testing & Editing: Taste of Home Test Kitchen

Food Photography: Taste of Home Photo Studio

Administrative Assistant: Barb Czysz

The Reader's Digest Association, Inc.

President and Chief Executive Officer: Robert E. Guth

President, North America: Dan Lagani

President/Publisher, Trade Publishing: Harold Clarke

Associate Publisher: Rosanne McManus

Vice President, Sales & Marketing: Stacey Ashton

International Standard Book Number
(10): 1-61765-016-1
International Standard Book Number
(13): 978-1-61765-016-1
Library of Congress Control Number: 2012930472

Cover Photography

Photographer: Jim Wieland
Food Stylist: Kathryn Conrad
Set Stylist: Pam Stasney

Pictured on front cover:
Ambrosia Cupcakes, page 183
Chocolate Macaroon Bars, page 192
Grilled Three-Potato Salad, page 102
Pork Sandwiches with Root Beer Sauce, page 155
Grilled Vegetable Medley, page 104
Fresh Peach Lemonade, page 185

Printed in China.
3 5 7 9 10 8 6 4

Table of Contents

Introduction 4

Appetizers 6

Comforting Classics 30

Slow Cooker Favorites 48

Breakfast & Brunch 74

Salads & Sides 96

Hearty Main Dishes 120

Soups & Sandwiches 144

Delightful Desserts 168

Seasonal Fare 196

Feeding A Crowd 224

Indexes 250

Savor a Little *Piece of Heaven.*

Over 300 Potluck Favorites!

Some of the best cooks around sit next to you each Sunday. Now, make their very best recipes your own with the **Taste of Home New Church Supper Cookbook.**

Inside this brand-new addition to the **Church Supper Cookbook family**—brought to you by Taste of Home, the world's #1 food & entertaining magazine—you'll discover **346 family-inspired, congregation-approved** recipes fit for any size occasion.

Enjoy a hearty helping of:

VARIETY: Includes **300+ recipes for every meal** and potluck occasion...appetizers, main dishes, casseroles, salads and sides, desserts and even brunch specialties! **All serve 8 or more** and **more than 200 recipes** are shown with **full-color photos**.

TEST-KITCHEN APPROVED: Not only does **each recipe come from a home cook** who knows the importance of good food that's simple yet appealing, **every recipe is tested in the Taste of Home Test Kitchen**. You never have to wonder if your family and friends will **enjoy your potluck offering**.

SEASONAL SPECIALTIES: From the the most **sacred holidays** to **good ol' seasonal fun**, the **New Church Supper Cookbook** features festive recipes for **an entire year of special celebrations**.

MEALTIME BLESSINGS IDEAS: Each chapter **opens with inspirational scripture or a friendly, nostalgic mealtime blessing** that's sure to **bring back memories** of Sunday dinner at Grandma's.

SPECIALTY CHAPTERS: Planning for a **group of 40 or more?** No sweat. The bonus **"Feeding a Crowd"** section features dozens of high-yield recipes, **from cookies and cupcakes to snacks and main dishes**, that are **sure to satisfy crowds of 20, 30, 50...even 100!** To keep things fuss-free, flip to the **"Slow Cooker Favorites"** chapter. Here, busy cooks will find **classic potluck fare** that can be prepared, transported and served in a slow cooker.

HAVE A GREAT RECIPE? Would you like to share your great **Church Supper** recipe for future editions of the Taste of Home family cookbooks? **Send them to: tasteofhome.com/submit**

LAST MINUTE IDEAS: Need something **really quick?** Look for the "last minute" icon. It identifies **dozens of tasty, crowd-pleasing recipes** you can **whip up in about 20 minutes!** Pleasing a crowd has never been **so easy**.

With **so many effortless dishes** specifically tailored to large-group gatherings, you'll be **first in line** to add your name to the **potluck signup sheet**.

buffet meatballs, pg. 9

smoky potato rounds, pg. 17

Appetizers

Thank you for the food we eat, thank you for the
friends we meet. Thank you for another day,
to pass your love along the way. Amen.

SAVORY MUSHROOM TARTLETS

My husband dares guests to eat just one of these tasty morsels. The savory snacks are perfect for gatherings.
JUDI VREELAND, ALAMO, CALIFORNIA

48	thin slices white bread, cut into 3-inch rounds
1/2	cup butter, softened, divided
3	tablespoons finely chopped green onions
1/2	pound fresh mushrooms, finely chopped
2	tablespoons all-purpose flour
1	cup heavy whipping cream
2	tablespoons minced chives
1	tablespoon minced fresh parsley
1/2	teaspoon lemon juice
1/2	teaspoon salt
	Dash cayenne pepper
2	tablespoons Parmesan cheese, optional

1. Spread one side of bread rounds with 1/4 cup butter; place buttered side up in lightly greased miniature muffin cups. Bake at 400° for 10 minutes or until lightly browned. Cool for 2 minutes before removing to wire racks.

2. In a saucepan, saute onions in the remaining butter for 3 minutes. Add mushrooms; saute for 10-12 minutes or until mushroom liquid has evaporated. Remove from the heat; stir in flour and cream until blended. Bring to a boil; boil and stir for 2 minutes or until thickened. Add chives, parsley, lemon juice, salt and cayenne; mix well. Cool slightly.

3. Place bread cups on a baking sheet; fill with mushroom mixture. Sprinkle with Parmesan cheese if desired. Bake at 350° for 10 minutes. Broil 4 in. from the heat for 2 minutes or until lightly browned.

Yield: 4 dozen.

LIME CUCUMBER SALSA

This special salsa is not only great served with tortilla chips. We also love it atop a baked potato or over fish or chicken.
MARCIA KWIECINSKI, CORREGIDOR, PHILIPPINES

1	large cucumber, seeded and diced
1	to 2 garlic cloves, minced
1	jalapeno pepper, finely chopped
3	green onions, sliced
2	tablespoons minced fresh cilantro
2	tablespoons lime juice
2	tablespoons olive oil
1	teaspoon grated lime peel
1/2	teaspoon salt, optional
1/4	teaspoon pepper

1. In a large bowl, combine all the ingredients. Refrigerate for at least 2 hours before serving.

Yield: 2-1/2 cups.

Editor's Note: Wear disposable gloves when cutting hot peppers; the oils can burn skin. Avoid touching your face.

BUFFET MEATBALLS

These popular bites come together with just a handful of items, including convenient packaged meatballs. Grape juice and apple jelly are the simple secret ingredients behind the sweet yet tangy sauce.

JANET ANDERSON, CARSON CITY, NEVADA

1	cup grape juice
1	cup apple jelly
1	cup ketchup
1	can (8 ounces) tomato sauce
1	package (64 ounces) frozen fully cooked Italian meatballs

1. In a small saucepan, combine the juice, jelly, ketchup and tomato sauce. Cook and stir over medium heat until jelly is melted; remove from the heat.

2. Place meatballs in a 5-qt. slow cooker. Pour sauce over the top and gently stir to coat. Cover and cook on low for 4-5 hours or until heated through.

Yield: about 11 dozen.

NUTTY CARAMEL CORN

Plain microwave popcorn becomes irresistible when it's jazzed up with molasses, peanut butter and nuts. This awesome snack never lasts long around our house.

JACQUE CASTILLO, BROOKINGS, OREGON

3	packages (3-1/2 ounces each) microwave popcorn
1	cup salted peanuts
1	cup salted roasted almonds
1	cup packed brown sugar
3/4	cup butter, cubed
3/4	cup corn syrup
3/4	cup peanut butter
1/2	cup molasses
1	teaspoon vanilla extract
1/2	teaspoon baking soda
1	cup pecan halves

1. Pop popcorn according to manufacturer's directions. Meanwhile, in a large heavy saucepan, combine the peanuts, almonds, brown sugar, butter, corn syrup, peanut butter and molasses. Bring to a boil over medium heat; cook and stir for 5 minutes.

2. Remove from the heat; stir in vanilla and baking soda (mixture will foam). In a very large bowl, combine popcorn and pecans. Add hot syrup mixture and toss to coat. Spread onto greased baking sheets.

3. Bake at 250° for 1 hour or until dry, stirring every 15 minutes. Remove from pans to waxed paper to cool. Break into clusters. Store in airtight containers or plastic bags.

Yield: 6 quarts.

HOT WING DIP

Since I usually have all the ingredients on hand, this is a great go-to recipe when I'm expecting guests.
COLEEN CORNER, GROVE CITY, PENNSYLVANIA

2	cups shredded cooked chicken
1	package (8 ounces) cream cheese, cubed
2	cups (8 ounces) shredded cheddar cheese
1	cup ranch salad dressing
1/2	cup Louisiana-style hot sauce

Tortilla chips and/or celery sticks
Minced fresh parsley, optional

1. In a 3-qt. slow cooker, combine the chicken, cream cheese, cheddar cheese, salad dressing and hot sauce. Cover and cook on low for 1-2 hours or until cheese is melted. Serve with chips and/or celery. Sprinkle with parsley if desired.

Yield: 4-1/2 cups.

CRISPY CHICKEN WONTONS

(pictured at right)
Served with a choice of sauces, these crunchy appetizers are a big hit at parties and potlucks. They're so popular that my family has even requested them as a main dish for dinner.
CONNIE BLESSE, AUBERRY, CALIFORNIA

3	cups finely chopped cooked chicken
1/2	cup shredded carrots
1/4	cup finely chopped water chestnuts
2	teaspoons cornstarch
1	tablespoon water
1	tablespoon soy sauce
1/2	to 1 teaspoon ground ginger
1	package (16 ounce) wonton wrappers
2	tablespoons butter, melted
1	tablespoon canola oil

Plum or sweet-and-sour sauce

1. In a large bowl, combine the chicken, carrots and water chestnuts. In a small bowl, combine the cornstarch, water, soy sauce and ginger until smooth. Add to chicken mixture; toss to coat.

2. Position a wonton wrapper with one point toward you. (Keep remaining wrappers covered with a damp paper towel until ready to use.) Place 1 teaspoon of filling in the center of wrapper. Fold bottom corner over filling; fold sides toward center over filling. Roll toward the remaining point. Moisten top corner with water; press to seal. Repeat with remaining wrappers and filling.

3. Place on greased baking sheets. Combine butter and oil; brush over wontons. Bake at 375° for 10-12 minutes or until golden brown. Serve with plum or sweet-sour sauce.

Yield: about 4 dozen.

SPICY MAPLE CHICKEN WINGS

My girls and I often ask my husband to make us his "famous" chicken wings. Their sweet, yet spicy flavor make them a favorite at our house, and also at family gatherings and potlucks.
DONNA HOFFMAN, ADDISON, ILLINOIS

3	pounds chicken wings
Oil for deep-fat frying	
1/2	cup butter, cubed
1/2	cup each maple syrup and Louisiana-style hot sauce
1/4	cup packed brown sugar
1/2	teaspoon salt
1/4	teaspoon pepper
2	tablespoons water
1-1/2	teaspoons cornstarch

1. Cut chicken wings into three sections; discard wing tip sections.

2. In an electric skillet or deep-fat fryer, heat oil to 375°. Fry chicken, a few pieces at a time, for 8 minutes or until golden brown and juices run clear, turning occasionally. Drain on paper towels.

3. In a small saucepan, melt butter. Stir in the syrup, hot sauce, brown sugar, salt and pepper. Combine water and cornstarch; stir into sauce. Bring to a boil; cook and stir for 2 minutes or until thickened.

4. Place wings in a large bowl; pour sauce over and toss to coat.

Yield: about 2 dozen.

Editor's Note: Uncooked chicken wing sections (wingettes) may be substituted for whole chicken wings.

APRICOT-RICOTTA STUFFED CELERY

This healthful, protein-rich filling can double as a dip for sliced apples. I often make a batch to keep on hand so it's ready as an impromptu snack.
DOROTHY REINHOLD, MALIBU, CALIFORNIA

3	dried apricots
1/2	cup part-skim ricotta cheese
2	teaspoons brown sugar
1/4	teaspoon grated orange peel
1/8	teaspoon salt
5	celery ribs, cut into 1-1/2 inch pieces

1. Place apricots in a food processor. Cover and process until finely chopped. Add the ricotta cheese, brown sugar, orange peel and salt; cover and process until blended. Stuff or pipe into celery. Chill until serving.

Yield: about 2 dozen.

CUCUMBER-STUFFED CHERRY TOMATOES

This is a wonderful appetizer that you can make ahead. I like to triple the recipe because they disappear fast.
CHRISTI MARTIN, ELKO, NEVADA

24	cherry tomatoes
1	package (3 ounces) cream cheese, softened
2	tablespoons mayonnaise
1/4	cup finely chopped peeled cucumber
1	tablespoon finely chopped green onion
2	teaspoons minced fresh dill

1. Cut a thin slice off the top of each tomato. Scoop out and discard pulp; invert tomatoes onto paper towels to drain.

2. In a small bowl, combine cream cheese and mayonnaise until smooth; stir in the cucumber, onion and dill. Spoon into tomatoes. Refrigerate until serving.

Yield: 2 dozen.

MINI PHYLLO TACOS

For a winning appetizer, serve crispy phyllo cups filled with taco-seasoned ground beef and zesty shredded cheese. The handheld munchies are sure to be a popular item on any menu.

ROSEANN WESTON, PHILIPSBURG, PENNSYLVANIA

1	pound lean ground beef (90% lean)
1/2	cup finely chopped onion
1	envelope taco seasoning
3/4	cup water
1-1/4	cups shredded Mexican cheese blend, divided
2	packages (1.9 ounces each) frozen miniature phyllo tart shells

1. In a small skillet, cook beef and onion over medium heat until meat is no longer pink; drain. Stir in taco seasoning and water. Bring to a boil. Reduce heat; simmer, uncovered for 5 minutes. Remove from the heat; stir in 1/2 cup cheese blend.

2. Place tart shells in an ungreased 15-in. x 10-in. x 1-in. baking pan. Fill with taco mixture.

3. Bake at 350° for 6 minutes. Sprinkle with remaining cheese blend; bake 2-3 minutes longer or until cheese is melted.

Yield: 2-1/2 dozen.

VEGGIE TORTILLA PINWHEELS

These terrific bite-size appetizers are always a hit wherever I take them. They're easy to make ahead of time, and are a great addition to other party fare!

LORI KOSTECKI, WAUSAU, WISCONSIN

LAST MINUTE!

2	packages (8 ounces each) cream cheese, softened
1	envelope ranch salad dressing mix
5	green onions, chopped
1	can (4 ounces) chopped green chilies, drained
1	can (3.8 ounces) sliced ripe olives, drained
1	celery rib, chopped
1/4	cup chopped sweet red pepper
2	to 3 tablespoons real bacon bits
8	flour tortillas (10 inches)

1. In a small bowl, beat cream cheese and dressing mix until blended. Beat in the onions, green chilies, olives, celery, red pepper and bacon. Spread over tortillas. Roll up. Cut each into 1-in. slices. Refrigerate leftovers.

Yield: about 5 dozen.

CRAB-STUFFED MUSHROOMS

Ever since I found this recipe years ago, these seafood-stuffed morsels have been making frequent appearances at family get-togethers.
HARRIET STICHTER, MILFORD, INDIANA

36	large fresh mushrooms (about 3 pounds)
1/2	cup butter, divided
1-1/2	cups finely chopped onions
3	cans (6 ounces each) crabmeat, drained, flaked and cartilage removed
3	tablespoons lemon juice
1/2	cup mayonnaise
1/4	cup minced fresh parsley
1	teaspoon Worcestershire sauce
1/2	teaspoon salt
1/4	teaspoon pepper
1/4	cup grated Parmesan cheese

1. Remove stems from mushrooms; set caps aside. Finely chop stems. In a skillet, melt 1/4 cup butter; saute stems and onions until tender.

2. In a bowl, combine crab and lemon juice. Add onion mixture, mayonnaise, parsley, Worcestershire sauce, salt and pepper; mix well. Stuff into mushroom caps; sprinkle with Parmesan cheese.

3. Place in a greased 15-in. x 10-in. x 1-in. baking pan. Melt remaining butter; drizzle over mushrooms. Bake, uncovered, at 350° for 20-25 minutes or until heated through. Serve warm.

Yield: 3 dozen.

Think Ahead
Instead of assembling Crab-Stuffed Mushrooms as guests arrive, stuff them in the morning and place on a baking sheet. Cover with a damp paper towel and refrigerate until baking time.

BLT BRUSCHETTA

I like to dress up traditional bruschetta with popular BLT sandwich fixin's. The maple bacon adds a tasty dimension. You could also substitute mesquite-flavored bacon.
PAT STEVENS, GRANBURY, TEXAS

LAST MINUTE!

5	maple-flavored bacon strips, cooked and crumbled
1/2	cup finely chopped seeded tomato
1/2	cup finely chopped leaf lettuce
1/2	cup prepared pesto, divided
2	tablespoons minced fresh basil
1/4	teaspoon salt
1/4	teaspoon pepper
1	loaf (10-1/2 ounces) French bread baguette
3	tablespoons olive oil

1. In a large bowl, combine the bacon, tomato, lettuce, 2 tablespoons pesto, basil, salt and pepper; set aside.

2. Cut baguette into 36 slices; place on ungreased baking sheets. Brush with oil.

3. Bake at 400° for 9-11 minutes or until golden brown. Spread with remaining pesto; top each slice with 2 teaspoons bacon mixture.

Yield: 3 dozen.

CRANBERRY JALAPENO CHEESE SPREAD

This easy spread is based on several different relishes and spreads I've tasted or made before. I love the sweet and spicy combination of flavors!

DIANE NEMITZ, LUDINGTON, MICHIGAN

1	cup dried cranberries
1/2	cup packed brown sugar
1/2	cup orange juice
4	teaspoons chopped seeded jalapeno pepper
1	tablespoon lemon juice
1	teaspoon grated orange peel
1/4	teaspoon Chinese five-spice powder
1	package (8 ounces) reduced-fat cream cheese
	Assorted crackers

1. In a small saucepan, combine the first seven ingredients. Bring to a boil. Reduce heat; simmer, uncovered, for 10 minutes or until thickened. Remove from the heat; cool completely.

2. In a bowl, beat cream cheese until fluffy. Beat in cranberry mixture until blended. Serve with crackers.

Yield: 2 cups.

Editor's Note: Wear disposable gloves when cutting hot peppers; the oils can burn skin. Avoid touching your face.

SMOKY POTATO ROUNDS

(pictured at left)

I love potato skins but decided to top them with barbecue sauce to kick up the flavor a notch. Once the potatoes are baked, these appetizers come together in a hurry.

REBECCA DOZIER, KOUTS, INDIANA

2	large baking potatoes
1/3	cup barbecue sauce
1/2	cup shredded cheddar cheese
6	bacon strips, cooked and crumbled
1/2	cup sour cream
3	green onions, thinly sliced

1. Scrub and pierce potatoes. Bake at 375° for 45 minutes or until almost tender.

2. When cool enough to handle, cut each potato widthwise into 1/2-in. slices. Place on a greased baking sheet. Brush with barbecue sauce; sprinkle with cheese and bacon.

3. Bake for 8-10 minutes or until potatoes are tender and cheese is melted. Top potato rounds with sour cream and onions.

Yield: 1-1/2 dozen.

1. In a small bowl, combine cracker crumbs and butter. Press onto the bottom of a greased 9-in. springform pan. Sprinkle with cheddar cheese. In a large skillet, saute the zucchini, mushrooms, onion and red pepper in oil until tender. Spoon over cheese.

2. In a large bowl, beat cream cheese until smooth. Add eggs; beat on low speed just until combined. Stir in bacon. Pour over vegetable mixture. Sprinkle with Parmesan cheese.

3. Place pan on a baking sheet. Bake at 375° for 30-35 minutes or until center is almost set. Cool on a wire rack for 10 minutes. Carefully run a knife around edge of pan to loosen; remove sides of pan. Serve warm or chilled. Refrigerate leftovers.

Yield: 16 servings.

SWEET & SOUR CHICKEN WINGS

Enjoy these lip-smacking wings at Christmas parties, but keep the recipe in mind for your summertime cookouts, too. The saucy appetizer is great year-round!
CONNIE VANDER PLOEG, SIOUX CENTER, IOWA

2	cups sugar
2	cups water
2	cups reduced-sodium soy sauce
1	cup unsweetened pineapple juice
1/2	cup canola oil
2	teaspoons garlic powder
2	teaspoons ground ginger
8	pounds frozen chicken wingettes and drumettes, thawed

1. In a large resealable plastic bag, combine the first seven ingredients. Add the chicken wings; seal bag and toss to coat. Refrigerate for 8 hours or overnight.

2. Drain and discard marinade. Place wings in two greased 15-in. x 10-in. x 1-in. baking pans. Cover and bake at 350° for 40-45 minutes or until juices run clear.

Yield: about 5-1/2 dozen.

CHEDDAR-VEGGIE APPETIZER TORTE

A line forms quickly behind this quiche-like torte at any gathering. The cheesy wedges are easy to eat as finger food.
BARBARA ESTABROOK, RHINELANDER, WISCONSIN

1-1/3	cups finely crushed multigrain crackers
1/4	cup butter, melted
2	cups (8 ounces) shredded sharp cheddar cheese
1	small zucchini, finely chopped
5	small fresh mushrooms, sliced
1/3	cup finely chopped red onion
1/4	cup finely chopped sweet red pepper
1	tablespoon olive oil
1	carton (8 ounces) spreadable garlic and herb cream cheese
4	eggs, lightly beaten
2	tablespoons crumbled cooked bacon
2	tablespoons grated Parmesan cheese

JALAPENOS WITH OLIVE-CREAM FILLING

Whenever I need something for a get-together or potluck, I take these yummy jalapenos. They're ready in minutes!

KRISTAL & SEAN PETERSON, WALKER, LOUISIANA

LAST MINUTE!

1	package (8 ounces) cream cheese, softened
1/4	cup chopped pimiento-stuffed olives
2	tablespoons olive juice
16	large jalapeno peppers, halved lengthwise and seeded

1. In a small bowl, combine the cream cheese, olives and olive juice. Spoon about 2 teaspoons into each jalapeno half. Serve immediately or refrigerate.

Yield: 32 appetizers.

Editor's Note: Wear disposable gloves when cutting hot peppers; the oils can burn skin. Avoid touching your face.

Pepper Pointers
If you have to cut a large number of peppers, try this: first cut off the tops, then slice them in half lengthwise. Use the small end of a melon baller to easily scrape out the seeds and membranes.

MINI CHICKEN EMPANADAS

Refrigerated pie pastry makes quick work of assembling these bite-sized appetizers loaded with chicken and cheese. I've made the hearty bites several times since I first received the recipe from a friend many years ago.

BETTY FULKS, ONIA, ARKANSAS

LAST MINUTE!

1	cup finely chopped cooked chicken
2/3	cup shredded Colby-Monterey Jack cheese
3	tablespoons cream cheese, softened
4	teaspoons chopped sweet red pepper
2	teaspoons chopped seeded jalapeno pepper
1	teaspoon ground cumin
1/2	teaspoon salt
1/8	teaspoon pepper
1	package (15 ounces) refrigerated pie pastry

1. In a small bowl, combine the first eight ingredients. On a lightly floured surface, roll each pastry into a 15-inch circle. Cut pastry with a floured 3-in. round biscuit cutter. Place a heaping teaspoonful of filling on one side of each circle. Brush edges of pastry with water; fold circles in half.

2. Place on greased baking sheets. With a fork, press edges to seal. Bake at 400° for 12-15 minutes or until golden brown. Serve warm.

Yield: about 2-1/2 dozen.

Editor's Note: Wear disposable gloves when cutting hot peppers; the oils can burn skin. Avoid touching your face.

SWEET 'N' SOUR APPETIZER MEATBALLS

A friend shared the recipe for these crowd-pleasing meatballs with me several years ago, and I've prepared it many times since. The sassy bites also make a great main dish when served with potatoes.

LUCRETIA BURT, TALLASSEE, ALABAMA

1	egg
1/2	cup quick-cooking oats
1	envelope onion soup mix
2	pounds ground beef
2	cans (5-1/2 ounces each) apricot nectar
3/4	cup packed brown sugar
3/4	cup ketchup
1/3	cup cider vinegar
2	tablespoons prepared mustard
1	tablespoon prepared horseradish
	Minced fresh parsley

1. In a large bowl, combine the egg, oats and soup mix. Crumble beef over mixture and mix well. Shape meat mixture into 1-in. balls.

2. Place 1 in. apart on a greased rack in a shallow baking pan. Bake at 400° for 18-20 minutes or until no longer pink. Drain on paper towels.

3. In a large skillet, combine the apricot nectar, brown sugar, ketchup, vinegar, mustard and horseradish. Bring to a boil. Reduce heat; simmer, uncovered, for 10 minutes. Add meatballs; simmer 15 minutes longer or until heated through. Sprinkle with parsley.

Yield: 4 dozen.

HOMEMADE GUACAMOLE

My daughters sometimes call my guacamole "five-finger" guacamole because it requires just five ingredients. I love the fact that this is so simple to make and that the flavor of the avocado is not overpowered by any other ingredient! I especially like the chunky avocado and lime!

NANETTE HILTON, LAS VEGAS, NEVADA

3	medium ripe avocados, peeled
1/4	cup finely chopped onion
1/4	cup minced fresh cilantro
2	tablespoons lime juice
1/8	teaspoon salt
	Tortilla chips

1. In a small bowl, mash avocado with a fork. Stir in the onion, cilantro, lime juice and salt. Refrigerate until serving. Serve with chips.

Yield: 2 cups.

MEDITERRANEAN TOMATO BITES

My friend Mary served these lovely appetizers at a summer gathering several years ago, and I adapted it a bit to my taste. It's a great August recipe when tomatoes and herbs are at their freshest!

SUSAN WILSON, MILWAUKEE, WISCONSIN

1	package (17.3 ounces) frozen puff pastry, thawed
1-1/2	cups (6 ounces) shredded Gouda cheese
6	plum tomatoes, cut into 1/4-inch slices
1/4	cup pitted ripe olives, coarsely chopped
1	cup (4 ounces) crumbled feta cheese
	Minced fresh basil and oregano

1. Unfold puff pastry; cut each sheet into 16 squares. Transfer squares to greased baking sheets. Sprinkle with Gouda cheese; top with tomatoes, olives and feta cheese.

2. Bake at 400° for 14-18 minutes or until golden brown; sprinkle with herbs. Serve warm or at room temperature.

Yield: 32 appetizers.

PRETTY STUFFED SPRING PEAS

These stuffed peas are the perfect way to welcome spring and sail right through summer. I serve them on a platter surrounded by juicy strawberries.

PHYLLIS COOPER, YARMOUTH PORT, MASSACHUSETTS

1	package (8 ounces) cream cheese, softened
2	teaspoons minced chives
1	teaspoon dried basil
1	garlic clove, minced
1/2	teaspoon caraway seeds
1/2	teaspoon dill weed
1/4	teaspoon lemon-pepper seasoning
36	fresh snow peas (about 1/4 pound), trimmed

1. In a large bowl, combine the first seven ingredients. Cover and refrigerate overnight.

2. Let the filling stand at room temperature for 30 minutes. Meanwhile, in a large saucepan, bring 6 cups water to a boil. Add snow peas; cover and boil for 1-2 minutes. Drain and immediately place peas in ice water. Drain and pat dry.

3. Gently split peas open; pipe about 1 teaspoonful of filling into each pod.

Yield: 3 dozen.

NACHO RICE DIP

Spanish rice mix adds an interesting twist to this effortless starter. Every time I serve this dip at get-togethers, my guests gobble it up.

AUDRA HUNGATE, HOLT, MISSOURI

1	package (6.8 ounces) Spanish rice and pasta mix
2	tablespoons butter
2	cups water
1	can (14-1/2 ounces) diced tomatoes, undrained
1	pound ground beef
1	pound (16 ounces) process cheese (Velveeta), cubed
1	can (14-1/2 ounces) stewed tomatoes
1	jar (8 ounces) process cheese sauce
	Tortilla chips

1. In a large saucepan, cook rice mix in butter until golden brown. Stir in water and diced tomatoes; bring to a boil. Reduce heat; cover and simmer for 15-20 minutes or until rice is tender.

2. Meanwhile, in a large skillet, cook beef until no longer pink. Drain and add to the rice. Stir in the cheese, stewed tomatoes and cheese sauce; cook and stir until cheese is melted.

3. Keep warm. Serve with tortilla chips.

Yield: about 8 cups.

MANDARIN CHICKEN BITES

Instead of a big meal, our family often enjoys nibbling on an all-day appetizer buffet at special gatherings. Each year we present tempting new dishes alongside our favorites. This is one of those tried-and-true dishes that's a "must."

SUSANNAH YINGER, CANAL WINCHESTER, OHIO

1	cup all-purpose flour
1/2	teaspoon salt
1/4	teaspoon pepper
1	pound boneless skinless chicken breasts, cut into 2-inch cubes
2	tablespoons butter
1	can (11 ounces) mandarin oranges, drained
2/3	cup orange marmalade
1/2	teaspoon dried tarragon

1. In a large resealable plastic bag, combine the flour, salt and pepper. Add chicken, a few pieces at a time, and shake to coat.

2. In a skillet, brown chicken in butter until no longer pink. In a small saucepan, combine the oranges, marmalade and tarragon; bring to a boil. Pour over chicken; stir gently to coat. Serve warm with toothpicks.

Yield: 12-15 servings.

CRAB SALAD TARTS

These little bites are as easy as they are elegant. Guests will never know you made and froze them weeks ago!

DONNA ROBERTS, SHUMWAY, ILLINOIS

1	can (6 ounces) lump crabmeat, drained
1/3	cup shredded reduced-fat Swiss cheese
1/4	cup Miracle Whip Light
2	tablespoons finely chopped celery
2	tablespoons finely chopped red onion
1	teaspoon dried parsley flakes
1/4	teaspoon pepper
1	package (1.9 ounces) frozen miniature phyllo tart shells

1. In a small bowl, combine the crabmeat, cheese, Miracle Whip Light, celery, onion, parsley and pepper.

2. Spoon filling into tart shells. Cover and freeze for up to 3 months. Or, place tart shells on an ungreased baking sheet. Bake at 350° for 10-12 minutes or until shells are lightly browned. Serve warm.

To use frozen tarts: Place on an ungreased baking sheet. Bake at 350° for 13-15 minutes or until lightly browned.

Yield: 15 appetizers.

Working with Phyllo
Because phyllo dries out quickly, keep it covered with plastic wrap, then a damp kitchen towel. Work with one sheet at a time and keep the other sheets covered. And always have all the other ingredients assembled and ready to go before you unwrap the dough.

GUACAMOLE APPETIZER SQUARES

This cold appetizer pizza has appeared at family functions for many years. I know you'll love it, too.
LAURIE PESTER, COLSTRIP, MONTANA

- 2 tubes (8 ounces each) refrigerated crescent rolls
- 1-1/2 teaspoons taco seasoning
- 1 package (1 pound) sliced bacon, diced
- 1 package (8 ounces) cream cheese, softened
- 1-1/2 cups guacamole
- 3 plum tomatoes, chopped
- 1 can (3.8 ounces) sliced ripe olives, drained

1. Unroll both tubes of crescent dough and pat into an ungreased 15-in. x 10-in. x 1-in. baking pan; seal seams and perforations. Build up edges. Prick dough with a fork; sprinkle with taco seasoning. Bake at 375° for 10-12 minutes or until golden brown. Cool completely on a wire rack.

2. In a large skillet, cook bacon over medium heat until crisp. Using a slotted spoon, remove to paper towels. In a small bowl, beat cream cheese and guacamole until smooth.

3. Spread cream cheese mixture over crust. Sprinkle with bacon, tomatoes and olives. Refrigerate until serving. Cut into squares.

Yield: about 3 dozen.

FRUIT SALSA

(pictured at right)

Fruit salsa is a nice change of pace from the traditional tomato-based salsa. Kids of all ages love the sweet fruit served with graham crackers.
KELLY HARBAUGH, YORK, PENNSYLVANIA

LAST MINUTE!

- 1 quart fresh strawberries, hulled and chopped
- 2 medium apples, peeled and chopped
- 2 medium kiwifruit, peeled and chopped
- 2 tablespoons brown sugar
- 2 tablespoons apple jelly
- 1/4 cup orange juice
- Graham crackers

1. In a large bowl, combine the strawberries, apples and kiwi. In a small bowl, combine the brown sugar, jelly and orange juice; drizzle over fruit and toss gently to coat. Serve with graham crackers.

Yield: 6 cups.

Better Bacon
Instead of frying bacon, lay strips on a jelly roll pan and bake at 350° for about 30 minutes. Bacon comes out crisp and flat. Plus, the pan cleans easily, and there's no stove-top spattering.

4. Place in an ungreased 15-in. x 10-in. x 1-in. baking pan. Bake at 375° for 12-18 minutes or until heated through.

Yield: 2 dozen.

FRESH SUMMER SALSA

This fresh-tasting combination is great with chips or grilled salmon, chicken or pork chops. It's so good, I'll sometimes eat it with a spoon!

BESSYSUE581, TASTE OF HOME.COM COMMUNITY

4	medium tomatoes, chopped
1	medium mango, peeled and chopped
1	medium ripe avocado, peeled and cubed
3/4	cup fresh or frozen corn, thawed
1/2	cup minced fresh cilantro
1/2	cup canned black beans, rinsed and drained
1/4	cup chopped red onion
1	jalapeno pepper, seeded and chopped
3	tablespoons lime juice
1	tablespoon olive oil
2	garlic cloves, minced
1/4	teaspoon salt
	Baked tortilla chip scoops

1. In a large bowl, combine the first 12 ingredients. Chill until serving. Serve with tortilla chips.

Yield: 4 cups.

Editor's Note: Wear disposable gloves when cutting hot peppers; the oils can burn skin. Avoid touching your face.

STUFFED BABY RED POTATOES

This recipe just says "party!" The ingredients are basic, but the finished appetizer looks like you worked a lot harder than you did.

CAROLE BESS WHITE, PORTLAND, OREGON

24	small red potatoes (about 2-1/2 pounds)
1/4	cup butter, cubed
1/2	cup shredded Parmesan cheese, divided
1/2	cup crumbled cooked bacon, divided
2/3	cup sour cream
1	egg, lightly beaten
1/2	teaspoon salt
1/8	teaspoon pepper
1/8	teaspoon paprika

1. Scrub potatoes; place in a large saucepan and cover with water. Bring to a boil. Reduce heat; cover and cook for 15-20 minutes or until tender. Drain.

2. When cool enough to handle, cut a thin slice off the top of each potato. Scoop out pulp, leaving a thin shell. (Cut thin slices from potato bottoms to level if necessary.)

3. In a large bowl, mash the potato tops and pulp with butter. Set aside 2 tablespoons each of cheese and bacon for garnish; add remaining cheese and bacon to potatoes. Stir in the sour cream, egg, salt and pepper. Spoon mixture into potato shells. Top with remaining cheese and bacon; sprinkle with paprika.

NACHO PARTY CHEESECAKE

Delicious cheesecake is not always a sweet dessert, as this savory version with a zesty crust proves!

MELINDA MESSER, BENSON, NORTH CAROLINA

1-3/4	cups crushed nacho tortilla chips
1/3	cup butter, melted
3	packages (8 ounces each) cream cheese, softened
1/2	cup mayonnaise
1	envelope taco seasoning
2	tablespoons all-purpose flour
4	eggs, lightly beaten
1-1/2	cups finely chopped cooked chicken breasts
1-1/2	cups (6 ounces) shredded Mexican cheese blend
1/3	cup finely chopped green onions
1	cup (8 ounces) sour cream

Whole kernel corn, cubed avocado, chopped tomato and sliced ripe olives

Salsa, optional

Assorted crackers or additional nacho tortilla chips, optional

1. Combine crushed tortilla chips and butter; press onto the bottom of a greased 9-in. springform pan.

2. In a large bowl, beat the cream cheese, mayonnaise, taco seasoning and flour until smooth. Add eggs; beat on low speed just until combined. Stir in the chicken, cheese blend and onions. Pour over crust. Place pan on a baking sheet.

3. Bake at 325° for 60-70 minutes or until center is almost set. Gently spread sour cream over the top; bake 10 minutes longer or until set.

4. Cool on a wire rack for 10 minutes. Carefully run a knife around edge of pan to loosen; cool 1 hour longer. Refrigerate for 8 hours or overnight.

5. Just before serving, remove sides of pan. Garnish with corn, avocado, tomato and olives. Serve with salsa and crackers if desired.

Yield: 24 servings.

CORNY CHOCOLATE CRUNCH

This sweet treat tastes almost like candy, and it's gone just about as fast!

DELORES WARD, DECATUR, INDIANA

3	quarts popped popcorn
3	cups Corn Chex
3	cups broken corn chips
1	package (10 to 11 ounces) butterscotch chips
12	ounces dark chocolate candy coating, coarsely chopped

1. In a large bowl, combine the popcorn, cereal and corn chips; set aside. In a microwave, melt butterscotch chips and candy coating; stir until smooth.

2. Pour over popcorn mixture and toss to coat. Spread into two greased 15-in. x 10-in. x 1-in. baking pans. When cool enough to handle, break into pieces.

Yield: about 5 quarts.

2. Meanwhile, in a large bowl, combine beef and steak seasoning. Shape into 16 patties. Cook in a large skillet until a meat thermometer reads 160° and juices run clear, turning once.

3. For sauce, in a double boiler or metal bowl over simmering water, constantly whisk the egg yolks, lemon juice and water until mixture reaches 160° or is thick enough to coat the back of a metal spoon. Reduce heat to low. Slowly drizzle in warm melted butter, whisking constantly.

4. Top each waffle fry with a burger and cheese. Broil 4-5 in. from the heat for 1-2 minutes or until cheese is melted. Top with onions and sauce.

Yield: 16 appetizers.

Editor's Note: This recipe was tested with McCormick's Montreal Steak Seasoning. Look for it in the spice aisle.

MINI-BURGER POTATO BITES

The caramelized onions and creamy sauce make these yummy bites a huge hit at parties. People say they're even better than the mini burger appetizers that are so popular at restaurants.
MARIBETH CONDO, LINDENHURST, ILLINOIS

16	frozen waffle-cut fries
2	medium onions, cut into 1/8-inch slices
1	tablespoon butter
1	tablespoon olive oil
1	teaspoon sugar
1/2	teaspoon salt
1/8	teaspoon pepper
1	pound ground beef
2	teaspoons steak seasoning
3	egg yolks
4-1/2	teaspoons lemon juice
1-1/2	teaspoons water
1/2	cup butter, melted
4	slices cheddar cheese, quartered

1. Bake waffle fries according to package directions. In a large skillet, cook onions in butter and oil over medium heat for 10 minutes. Add the sugar, salt and pepper; cook 3-5 minutes longer or until onions are golden brown, stirring frequently.

CHICKEN ARTICHOKE PIZZAS

Your guests will love the cheesy goodness of this pleasing and different pizza. Pepper Jack cheese and green chilies give each bite a kick.
PAULA GYLLAND, BROOKFIELD, WISCONSIN

1	can (14 ounces) water-packed artichoke hearts, rinsed, drained and chopped
3	cups (12 ounces) shredded pepper Jack cheese, divided
1-1/2	cups cubed cooked chicken breast
1	can (4 ounces) chopped green chilies
1/4	cup mayonnaise
1/4	cup sour cream
1	envelope Italian salad dressing mix
2	prebaked 12-inch thin pizza crusts

1. In a large bowl, combine the artichokes, 1 cup cheese, chicken, chilies, mayonnaise, sour cream and salad dressing mix. Place crusts on pizza pans; spread with artichoke mixture. Sprinkle with remaining cheese.

2. Bake at 450° for 10-14 minutes or until bubbly.
Yield: 2 pizzas (12 slices each).

PINEAPPLE-PECAN CHEESE SPREAD

This creamy cheese spread is packed with red pepper, green chilies and crunchy pecans. Instead of serving it in a dish, I like to shape it into a ball and roll it in the pecans.

CYNDE SONNIER, MONT BELVIEU, TEXAS

2	packages (8 ounces each) cream cheese, softened
1-1/2	cups (6 ounces) shredded cheddar cheese
1	cup chopped pecans, toasted, divided
3/4	cup crushed pineapple, drained
1	can (4 ounces) chopped green chilies, drained
2	tablespoons chopped roasted sweet red pepper
1/2	teaspoon garlic powder

Assorted fresh vegetables

1. In a large bowl, beat cream cheese until smooth. Add the cheddar cheese, 3/4 cup pecans, pineapple, chilies, red pepper and garlic powder; beat until combined. Transfer to a serving dish. Cover and refrigerate until serving.

2. Sprinkle with remaining pecans just before serving. Serve with assorted fresh vegetables.

Yield: 3-3/4 cups.

FRUIT SALSA WITH CINNAMON CHIPS

I first made this fresh, fruity salsa for a family baby shower. Now, someone makes this juicy snack for just about every family gathering.

JESSICA ROBINSON, INDIAN TRAIL, NORTH CAROLINA

1	cup finely chopped fresh strawberries
1	medium navel orange, peeled and finely chopped
3	medium kiwifruit, peeled and finely chopped
1	can (8 ounces) unsweetened crushed pineapple, drained
1	tablespoon lemon juice
1-1/2	teaspoons sugar

CINNAMON CHIPS:

10	flour tortillas (8 inches)
1/4	cup butter, melted
1/3	cup sugar
1	teaspoon ground cinnamon

1. In a small bowl, combine the first six ingredients. Cover and refrigerate until serving.

2. For chips, brush tortillas with butter; cut each into eight wedges. Combine sugar and cinnamon; sprinkle over tortillas. Place on ungreased baking sheets.

3. Bake at 350° for 5-10 minutes or just until crisp. Serve with fruit salsa.

Yield: 2-1/2 cups salsa (80 chips).

chicken & sausage manicotti, pg. 41

creamy chicken-rice casserole, pg. 43

Comforting Casseroles

For food that stays our hunger, for rest that brings us
ease, for homes where memories linger,
We give our thanks for these.

BEEF & TATER BAKE

The entire family will enjoy this heartwarming, all-in-one dinner. Cleanup is easy because only two dishes are used to make it!

MIKE TCHOU, PEPPER PIKE, OHIO

4	cups frozen Tater Tots
1	pound ground beef
1	package (16 ounces) frozen chopped broccoli, thawed
1	can (10-3/4 ounces) condensed cream of broccoli soup, undiluted
1	medium tomato, chopped
1	can (2.8 ounces) french-fried onions, divided
1	cup (4 ounces) shredded Colby-Monterey Jack cheese, divided
1/3	cup 2% milk
1/4	teaspoon garlic powder
1/8	teaspoon pepper

1. Place Tater Tots in an ungreased 13-in. x 9-in. baking dish. Bake, uncovered, at 400° for 10 minutes.

2. Meanwhile, in a large skillet, cook beef over medium heat until no longer pink; drain. Stir in the broccoli, soup, tomato, 3/4 cup french-fried onions, 1/2 cup cheese, milk, garlic powder and pepper; heat through. Pour over Tater Tots.

3. Cover and bake for 20 minutes. Uncover; sprinkle with remaining onions and cheese. Bake 5-10 minutes longer or until cheese is melted.

Yield: 12 servings.

LASAGNA CORN CARNE

My grandkids always ask me to make this dish, which is sort of like chili in a pan. I came up with the recipe one day using just ingredients I had on hand. It was an instant hit.

MARY LOU WILLS, LA PLATA, MARYLAND

1	pound ground beef
1	jar (16 ounces) salsa
1	can (16 ounces) kidney beans, rinsed and drained
1	can (14-3/4 ounces) cream-style corn
1	large onion, chopped
1	medium green pepper, chopped
1	celery rib, chopped
3	garlic cloves, minced
1	tablespoon minced fresh basil or 1 teaspoon dried basil
1	teaspoon salt
1	teaspoon chili powder
12	lasagna noodles, cooked and drained
2	cups (8 ounces) shredded part-skim mozzarella cheese
1/2	cup grated Parmesan cheese

1. In a large skillet, cook beef over medium heat until no longer pink; drain. Add the salsa, beans, vegetables, garlic and seasonings. Bring to a boil. Reduce heat; cover and simmer for 15 minutes.

2. Spread a fourth of the meat sauce in a greased 13-in. x 9-in. baking dish; top with four noodles. Repeat the layers once. Layer with half of the remaining sauce; sprinkle with half of the cheeses. Layer with the remaining noodles, sauce and cheeses.

3. Cover and bake at 350° for 30 minutes. Uncover; bake 15-20 minutes longer or until heated through. Let stand for 15 minutes before cutting.

Yield: 12 servings.

Leftover Lasagna
Leftover lasagna noodles? Cut the extra noodles into 1/4- or 1/2-inch strips and put them in a heavy-duty resealable plastic bag. They freeze well and make quick, hearty additions to soups.

SAUSAGE FETTUCCINE BAKE

Rich and loaded with meat, veggies and cheese, this all-in-one wonder will soon become a favorite.

LISA VARNER, CHARLESTON, SOUTH CAROLINA

1-1/2	pounds uncooked fettuccine
2	pounds bulk Italian sausage
2	large onions, chopped
1	medium green pepper, chopped
2	cans (28 ounces each) diced tomatoes, undrained
2	jars (4-1/2 ounces each) sliced mushrooms, drained
4	teaspoons Italian seasoning
4	cups (1 pound) shredded part-skim mozzarella cheese, divided
2	cans (10-3/4 ounces each) condensed cream of mushroom soup, undiluted
1/2	cup beef broth
1	cup grated Parmesan cheese

1. Cook fettuccine according to package directions. Meanwhile, in a Dutch oven, cook the sausage, onions and green pepper over medium heat until meat is no longer pink; drain. Add the tomatoes, mushrooms and Italian seasoning. Bring to a boil. Reduce heat; simmer, uncovered, for 5 minutes.

2. Drain fettuccine; stir into meat mixture. Transfer half of the sausage mixture to two greased 13-in. x 9-in. baking dishes. Sprinkle each with 1 cup mozzarella cheese; top with remaining sausage mixture.

3. In a small bowl, whisk soup and broth; spread over casseroles. Sprinkle with Parmesan and remaining mozzarella.

4. Cover and freeze one casserole for up to 3 months. Cover and bake the remaining casserole at 350° for 20 minutes. Uncover; bake 5-10 minutes longer or until bubbly and cheese is melted. Let stand for 10 minutes before serving.

To use frozen casserole: Remove from the freezer 30 minutes before baking (do not thaw). Cover and bake at 350° for 70 minutes. Uncover; bake 5-10 minutes longer or until heated through. Let stand for 10 minutes before serving.

Yield: 2 casseroles (6 servings each).

SCALLOPED POTATOES WITH HAM & CHEESE

Everyone will love this comforting casserole packed with cheesy red potatoes and ham. It's so rich and delectable, it'll have them coming back for seconds.
ALISA HANSON, DULUTH, MINNESOTA

1	can (10-3/4 ounces) condensed cream of mushroom soup, undiluted
1	cup milk
2/3	cup condensed cream of potato soup, undiluted
1/2	cup chopped onion
1/4	cup butter, melted
1/2	teaspoon minced garlic
1/2	teaspoon pepper
1/4	teaspoon seasoned salt
8	medium red potatoes, peeled and thinly sliced
3	cups cubed fully cooked ham
1-1/2	cups (6 ounces) shredded part-skim mozzarella cheese

1. In a large bowl, combine the first eight ingredients. Add the potatoes, ham and cheese; toss to coat. Transfer to a greased 13-in. x 9-in. baking dish.

2. Bake, uncovered, at 350° for 65-70 minutes or until bubbly and potatoes are tender. Let stand for 10 minutes before serving.

Yield: 10 servings.

SOUTHWEST TURKEY CASSEROLE

(pictured at right)
Here's the delicious, though sneaky, way I get my nieces and husband to eat their spinach. This creamy, spicy main dish will fill you up fast.
CRYSTAL KOLADY, HENRIETTA, NEW YORK

2	large onions, chopped
2	jalapeno peppers, seeded and chopped
2	tablespoons butter
6	cups cubed cooked turkey
2	cans (10-3/4 ounces each) condensed cream of chicken soup, undiluted
2	cups (16 ounces) sour cream
1	package (10 ounces) frozen chopped spinach, thawed and squeezed dry
2	cups (8 ounces) shredded Monterey Jack cheese
1	package (12-1/2 ounces) nacho tortilla chips, crushed
4	green onions, sliced

1. In a Dutch oven, saute onions and jalapenos in butter until tender. Stir in the turkey, soup, sour cream and spinach. In a greased 13-in. x 9-in. baking dish, layer half of the turkey mixture, cheese and tortilla chips. Repeat layers.

2. Bake, uncovered, at 350° for 25-30 minutes or until bubbly. Let stand for 5 minutes before serving. Sprinkle with green onions.

Yield: 12 servings.

Editor's Note: Wear disposable gloves when cutting hot peppers; the oils can burn skin. Avoid touching your face.

DOUBLE-CHEESE MACARONI

A friend passed this recipe on to me and I made some changes that created this definite crowd pleaser. I make it for every family get together and I haven't found anyone, child or adult, who doesn't love this ooey, gooey macaroni and cheese.
SABRINA DEWITT, CUMBERLAND, MARYLAND

1	package (16 ounces) elbow macaroni
3	cups (24 ounces) 4% cottage cheese
1/2	cup butter, cubed
1/2	cup all-purpose flour
1	teaspoon salt
1/2	teaspoon white pepper
1/4	teaspoon garlic salt
3	cups half-and-half cream
1	cup 2% milk
4	cups (16 ounces) shredded cheddar cheese

TOPPING:

1	cup dry bread crumbs
1/4	cup butter, melted

1. Cook macaroni according to package directions. Meanwhile, place cottage cheese in a food processor; cover and process until smooth. Set aside.

2. In a large saucepan, melt butter. Stir in the flour, salt, pepper and garlic salt until smooth. Gradually add cream and milk. Bring to a boil; cook and stir for 2 minutes or until thickened.

3. Drain macaroni; transfer to a large bowl. Add the cheddar cheese, cottage cheese and white sauce; toss to coat. Transfer to a greased 13-in. x 9-in. baking dish. (Dish will be full.) Combine bread crumbs and butter; sprinkle over the top.

4. Bake, uncovered, at 400° for 20-25 minutes or until bubbly.

Yield: 12 servings (1 cup each).

CHICKEN TATER BAKE

You'll please everyone in the family with this inviting and filling dish that tastes like a chicken potpie with a Tater Tot crust.
FRAN ALLEN, ST LOUIS, MISSOURI

2	cans (10-3/4 ounces each) condensed cream of chicken soup, undiluted
1/2	cup 2% milk
1/4	cup butter, cubed
3	cups cubed cooked chicken
1	package (16 ounces) frozen peas and carrots, thawed
1-1/2	cups (6 ounces) shredded cheddar cheese, divided
1	package (32 ounces) frozen Tater Tots

1. In a large saucepan, combine the soup, milk and butter. Cook and stir over medium heat until heated through. Remove from the heat; stir in the chicken, peas and carrots and 1 cup cheese.

2. Transfer to two greased 8-in. square baking dishes. Top with Tater Tots; sprinkle with remaining shredded cheddar cheese.

3. Cover and freeze one casserole for up to 3 months. Cover and bake the remaining casserole at 350° for 35 minutes. Uncover; bake 5-10 minutes longer or until heated through.

4. To use frozen casserole: Remove from the freezer 30 minutes before baking (do not thaw). Cover and bake at 350° for 1-1/2 to 1-3/4 hours or until heated through.

Yield: 2 casseroles (6 servings each).

HAM & CHEESE POTATO CASSEROLE

This recipe makes two cheesy, delicious casseroles. Have one tonight and put the other on ice for a future busy weeknight. It's like having money in the bank when things get hectic!
KARI ADAMS, FORT COLLINS, COLORADO

2	cans (10-3/4 ounces each) condensed cream of celery soup, undiluted
2	cups (16 ounces) sour cream
1/2	cup water
1/2	teaspoon pepper
2	packages (28 ounces each) frozen O'Brien potatoes
1	package (16 ounces) process cheese (Velveeta), cubed
2-1/2	cups cubed fully cooked ham

1. In a bowl, combine the soup, sour cream, water and pepper. Stir in the potatoes, cheese and ham.

2. Transfer to two greased 11-in. x 7-in. baking dishes. Cover and freeze one casserole for up to 3 months. Cover and bake the remaining casserole at 375° for 40 minutes. Uncover and bake 10-15 minutes longer or until bubbly. Let stand for 10 minutes before serving.

To use frozen casserole: Thaw in the refrigerator overnight. Remove from the refrigerator 30 minutes before baking. Bake as directed.

Yield: 2 casseroles (5 servings each).

SOUTHWESTERN SHEPHERD'S PIE

This no-fuss meal is hearty and colorful, with a great blend of Southwest flavors and the right amount of heat!
SUZETTE JURY, KEENE, CALIFORNIA

3	pounds ground beef
1	cup chopped onion
2	cans (10 ounces each) enchilada sauce
2	tablespoons all-purpose flour
2	teaspoons chopped chipotle peppers in adobo sauce
1	teaspoon ground cumin
1	teaspoon dried oregano
2-1/2	cups water
2	cups milk
1/3	cup butter, cubed
1	teaspoon salt
4	cups mashed potato flakes
2	cans (4 ounces each) chopped green chilies, undrained
2	cups (8 ounces) shredded Mexican cheese blend, divided
2	cans (11 ounces each) Mexicorn, drained
2/3	cup chopped green onions
	Paprika

1. In a Dutch oven, cook beef and onion over medium heat until meat is no longer pink; drain. Add the enchilada sauce, flour, chipotle peppers, cumin and oregano; bring to a boil. Reduce heat; simmer, uncovered, for 5 minutes.

2. Meanwhile, in a large saucepan, combine the water, milk, butter and salt; bring to a boil. Remove from the heat. Stir in potato flakes until combined. Add chilies and 1/2 cup cheese.

3. Transfer meat mixture to two greased 11-in. x 7-in. baking dishes. Layer with corn, mashed potato mixture and remaining cheese. Sprinkle with green onions. Cover and freeze one casserole for up to 3 months.

4. Cover and bake the remaining casserole at 375° for 20 minutes. Uncover and bake 5-10 minutes longer or until bubbly. Sprinkle with paprika.

5. To use frozen casserole: Thaw casserole in the refrigerator overnight. Remove from the refrigerator 30 minutes before baking.

6. Cover and bake at 375° for 20 minutes. Uncover and bake 15-20 minutes longer or until bubbly. Sprinkle with paprika.

Yield: 2 casseroles (7 servings each).

HOT CHICKEN SALAD

Rich and creamy with lots of chicken, this casserole gets a yummy crunch from water chestnuts and toasted almonds.
RUTH BURRUS, ZIONSVILLE, INDIANA

4	cups cubed cooked chicken
8	celery ribs, sliced
2	cans (8 ounces each) sliced water chestnuts, drained
1	can (10-3/4 ounces) condensed cream of chicken soup, undiluted
1-1/2	cups mayonnaise
1-1/2	cups (12 ounces) sour cream
1	cup sliced fresh mushrooms
1/2	cup slivered almonds, toasted
2	tablespoons finely chopped onion
2	tablespoons lemon juice
1/2	teaspoon salt
1/2	teaspoon pepper
1/2	cup shredded cheddar cheese
1/2	cup soft whole wheat bread crumbs

1. In a large bowl, combine the first 12 ingredients. Transfer to a greased 13-in. x 9-in. baking dish. Sprinkle with cheese and bread crumbs. Bake, uncovered, at 350° for 30-35 minutes or until heated through.

Yield: 12 servings.

CREAMY CHICKEN CASSEROLE

I created homestyle chicken casserole when my husband was craving a dish his aunt used to make. It's a staple in our house.
MARI WARNKE, FREMONT, WISCONSIN

4	cups uncooked egg noodles
4	cups cubed cooked chicken
1	package (16 ounces) frozen peas and carrots
2	cups milk
2	cans (10-3/4 ounces each) condensed cream of celery soup, undiluted
2	cans (10-3/4 ounces each) condensed cream of chicken soup, undiluted
1	cup chopped onion
2	tablespoons butter, melted
1/2	teaspoon salt
1/2	teaspoon pepper

1. Cook noodles according to package directions. Meanwhile, in a large bowl, combine the remaining ingredients. Drain noodles; add to chicken mixture.

2. Transfer to two greased 8-in. square baking dishes. Cover and freeze one casserole for up to 3 months. Cover and bake remaining casserole at 350° for 30 minutes. Uncover and bake 10-15 minutes longer or until heated through.

To use frozen casserole: Thaw in the refrigerator overnight. Remove from the refrigerator 30 minutes before cooking. Cover and microwave on high for 10-12 minutes or until heated through, stirring twice.

Yield: 2 casseroles (5 servings each).

TACO CASSEROLES

If your gang loves tacos, then they'll devour this one-dish version of the Mexican classic! It comes together and feeds a group with very little effort.

ALISON GILMORE, GLADSTONE, OREGON

3	pounds ground beef
3	cans (16 ounces each) chili beans, undrained
3	cans (8 ounces each) tomato sauce
1/3	cup taco sauce
2	tablespoons chili powder
1	tablespoon garlic powder
6	cups coarsely crushed tortilla chips
3	cups (24 ounces) sour cream
3	tablespoons all-purpose flour
3	cups (12 ounces) shredded cheddar cheese
3	medium tomatoes, chopped
12	green onions, sliced

Shredded lettuce and additional taco sauce, optional

1. In a Dutch oven, cook beef over medium heat until no longer pink; drain. Stir in the beans, tomato sauce, taco sauce, chili powder and garlic powder.

2. Divide chips among three ungreased 2-qt. baking dishes; top with beef mixture. Combine sour cream and flour; spread over top. Sprinkle with cheese, tomatoes and onions.

3. Bake, uncovered, at 350° for 30-40 minutes or until heated through. Serve with shredded lettuce and additional taco sauce if desired.

Yield: 3 casseroles (8 servings each).

CHICKEN & SAUSAGE MANICOTTI

(pictured at left)

Here's a scrumptious meal-in-one that you can make and freeze to enjoy later. Try it with ground turkey or beef, too.

FRAN SCOTT, BIRMINGHAM, MICHIGAN

1	pound sliced fresh mushrooms
2	medium green peppers, chopped
2	medium onions, chopped
1	tablespoon olive oil
4	garlic cloves, minced
3	jars (26 ounces each) spaghetti sauce
1-1/4	cups water
1-1/2	pounds chicken tenderloins, halved lengthwise
4	teaspoons dried basil
2	teaspoons chicken seasoning
2	packages (8 ounces each) uncooked manicotti shells
1	pound fully cooked andouille or Italian sausage links, halved lengthwise and sliced
2	cups (8 ounces) shredded part-skim mozzarella cheese
2	cups (8 ounces) shredded cheddar cheese

1. In a Dutch oven, saute the mushrooms, peppers and onions in oil until tender; add garlic, cook 1 minute longer. Stir in spaghetti sauce and water.

2. Sprinkle chicken with basil and chicken seasoning. Stuff chicken into uncooked manicotti shells. Spread 1 cup sauce mixture in each of two greased 13-in. x 9-in. baking dishes. Arrange manicotti over sauce; sprinkle with sausage. Pour remaining sauce over top; sprinkle with cheeses.

3. Cover and freeze one casserole for up to 3 months. Cover and bake the remaining casserole at 375° for 55-65 minutes or until bubbly and pasta is tender. Let stand for 10 minutes before serving.

To use frozen manicotti: Thaw in the refrigerator overnight. Remove from the refrigerator 30 minutes before baking. Cover and bake at 375° for 55-65 minutes or until chicken and pasta are tender. Let stand for 10 minutes before serving.

Yield: 2 casseroles (7 servings each).

Editor's Note: This recipe was tested with McCormick's Montreal Chicken Seasoning. Look for it in the spice aisle.

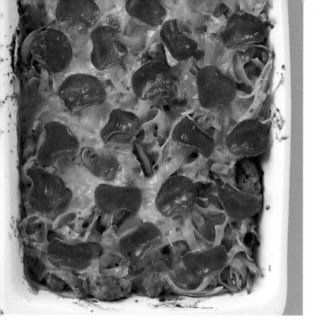

3. Transfer to two greased 13-in. x 9-in. baking dishes. Sprinkle each with mushrooms, cheeses and pepperoni.

4. Bake, uncovered, at 350° for 30-35 minutes or until heated through and cheeses have melted. Let stand for 5 minutes before serving.

Yield: 2 casseroles (6 servings each).

PEPPERONI PIZZA CASSEROLE

Loaded with popular pizza flavors, this noodle bake is sure to be a winner with all ages. You can use ground beef instead of turkey. I like to serve it with garlic bread and a salad.
DEBBIE STALEY, MOUNT VERNON, ILLINOIS

1	package (16 ounces) egg noodles
2	pounds ground turkey
1/3	cup chopped onion
1	jar (24 ounces) meatless spaghetti sauce
1	can (10 ounces) diced tomatoes and green chilies
1	can (8 ounces) mushroom stems and pieces, drained
2	cups (8 ounces) shredded part-skim mozzarella cheese
2	cups (8 ounces) shredded cheddar cheese
1	cup (4 ounces) shredded Parmesan cheese
3	ounces sliced turkey pepperoni

1. In a Dutch oven, cook noodles according to package directions; drain.

2. Meanwhile, in a large skillet, cook turkey and onion over medium heat until meat is no longer pink; drain. Stir in the spaghetti sauce and tomatoes. Bring to a boil. Reduce heat; simmer, uncovered, for 5 minutes. Stir in noodles.

LAZY PIEROGI BAKE

A favorite dish in our family is pierogi. Here, I've taken all the traditional ingredients and turned it into a tasty main dish casserole that's great for feeding a crowd.
SANDY STARKS, AMHERST, NEW YORK

1	package (16 ounces) spiral pasta
1	pound sliced bacon, diced
2	medium onions, chopped
2	garlic cloves, minced
1/2	pound fresh mushrooms, sliced
2	cans (14 ounces each) sauerkraut, rinsed and well drained
3	cans (10-3/4 ounces each) condensed cream of mushroom soup, undiluted
1/2	cup milk
1/2	teaspoon celery seed
1/8	teaspoon pepper

1. Cook pasta according to package directions. Meanwhile, in a large skillet, cook bacon over medium heat until crisp. Remove to paper towels; drain, reserving 2 tablespoons drippings.

2. In the drippings, saute onions until tender. Add garlic; cook 1 minute longer. Add mushrooms; cook until tender. Stir in sauerkraut and half of the bacon. In a large bowl, combine the soup, milk, celery seed and pepper. Drain pasta.

3. Place a fourth of the pasta in two greased 13-in. x 9-in. baking dishes. Layer each with a fourth of the sauerkraut and soup mixture. Repeat layers.

4. Cover and bake at 350° for 25 minutes. Uncover; sprinkle with remaining bacon. Bake 10-15 minutes longer or until heated through. Let stand for 5-10 minutes before serving.

Yield: 16 servings.

VERY VEGGIE LASAGNA

I concocted this quick and easy recipe to use up some of the abundant fresh produce from my garden.

BERNIECE BALDWIN, GLENNIE, MICHIGAN

2	medium carrots, julienned
1	medium zucchini, cut into 1/4-inch slices
1	yellow summer squash, cut into 1/4-inch slices
1	medium onion, sliced
1	cup fresh broccoli florets
1/2	cup sliced celery
1/2	cup julienned sweet red pepper
1/2	cup julienned green pepper
1/2	to 1 teaspoon salt
2	tablespoons canola oil
2	garlic cloves, minced
3-1/2	cups spaghetti sauce
14	lasagna noodles, cooked and drained
4	cups (16 ounces) shredded part-skim mozzarella cheese

1. In a large skillet, stir-fry vegetables and salt in oil until crisp-tender. Add garlic; cook 1 minute longer.

2. Spread 3/4 cup spaghetti sauce in the greased 13-in. x 9-in. baking dish. Arrange seven noodles over sauce, overlapping as needed. Layer with half of the vegetables, spaghetti sauce and cheese. Repeat layers.

3. Cover and bake at 350° for 60-65 minutes or until bubbly. Let stand for 15 minutes before cutting.

Yield: 12 servings.

CREAMY CHICKEN-RICE CASSEROLE

Gravy, chicken soup and sour cream make this a rich and hearty dish ideal for chilly days. Be prepared to make it often, as it fills 'em up fast and tastes fantastic!

NANCY FOUST, STONEBORO, PENNSYLVANIA

3	cups cubed cooked chicken
2-2/3	cups chicken gravy
2	cups uncooked instant rice
1	can (10-3/4 ounces) condensed cream of chicken soup, undiluted
1	cup (8 ounces) sour cream
1	can (8 ounces) mushroom stems and pieces, drained
1	medium onion, chopped
2/3	cup chopped celery
2/3	cup water
1/4	cup chopped pitted green olives
1/4	cup chopped ripe olives
2	teaspoons dried parsley flakes
1/8	teaspoon pepper

1. In a large bowl, combine all ingredients. Transfer to a greased 13-in. x 9-in. baking dish.

2. Cover and bake at 375° for 30 minutes. Uncover and stir; bake 20-25 minutes longer or until bubbly and rice and vegetables are tender.

Yield: 9 servings.

PESTO CHICKEN MOSTACCIOLI

We love pesto and mac and cheese. Who knew what a yummy combination it would be with chicken nuggets!
REBECCA STABLEIN, LAKE FOREST, CALIFORNIA

1	package (16 ounces) mostaccioli
1	package (16 ounces) frozen breaded chicken tenders
4	cups (16 ounces) shredded cheddar cheese
1	container (16 ounces) sour cream
1	carton (15 ounces) ricotta cheese
3/4	cup prepared pesto
2/3	cup heavy whipping cream
1/2	cup grated Parmesan cheese
1/2	cup dry bread crumbs
1/4	cup butter, melted

1. Cook mostaccioli and chicken according to package directions. Meanwhile, in a large bowl, combine the cheddar cheese, sour cream, ricotta, pesto, cream and Parmesan cheese.

2. Chop chicken tenders and drain mostaccioli; add to cheese mixture. Toss to coat. Transfer to two greased 11-in. x 7-in. baking dishes (dishes will be full). Combine bread crumbs and butter; sprinkle over the top.

3. Bake, uncovered, at 350° for 25-30 or until heated through and golden brown.

Yield: 2 casseroles (5 servings each).

SPAGHETTI HAM BAKE
(pictured at right)

The generous portions satisfy my hungry family, while I appreciate being able to freeze one pan for another busy day.
MARY KILLION, HERMISTON, OREGON

2	packages (7 ounces each) thin spaghetti, broken into 2-inch pieces
4	cups cubed fully cooked ham
2	cans (10-3/4 ounces each) condensed cream of chicken soup, undiluted
2	cups (16 ounces) sour cream
1/2	pound sliced fresh mushrooms
1/2	cup chopped onion
1/2	cup sliced ripe olives, optional
1-1/2	teaspoons ground mustard
1	teaspoon seasoned salt
2	teaspoons Worcestershire sauce

TOPPING:

2	cups soft bread crumbs
1/4	cup butter, melted
2	cups (8 ounces) shredded cheddar cheese

1. Cook spaghetti according to package directions; drain and place in a large bowl. Stir in the ham, soup, sour cream, mushrooms, onion, olives if desired, mustard, seasoned salt and Worcestershire sauce.

2. Transfer to two greased 11-in. x 7-in. baking dishes. In a small bowl, toss bread crumbs and butter; add cheese. Sprinkle over casseroles.

3. Cover and freeze one casserole for up to 2 months. Bake the remaining casserole, uncovered, at 325° for 30 minutes or until heated through.

To use frozen casserole: Thaw in the refrigerator overnight. Bake, uncovered, at 325° for 50-55 minutes or until heated through.

Yield: 2 casseroles (6 servings each).

CHICKEN POTPIE WITH CHEDDAR BISCUIT TOPPING

With chunks of chicken, veggies and a cheesy biscuit topping, this makes a hearty meal that will rival homey dishes from Mom.
SALA HOUTZER, GOLDSBORO, NORTH CAROLINA

4	cups cubed cooked chicken
1	package (12 ounces) frozen broccoli and cheese sauce
1	can (10-3/4 ounces) condensed cream of chicken and mushroom soup, undiluted
1	can (10-3/4 ounces) condensed cream of chicken soup, undiluted
2	medium potatoes, cubed
3/4	cup chicken broth
2/3	cup sour cream
1/2	cup frozen peas
1/4	teaspoon pepper

TOPPING:

1-1/2	cups biscuit/baking mix
3/4	cup shredded sharp cheddar cheese
3/4	cup 2% milk
3	tablespoons butter, melted

1. In a Dutch oven, combine the first nine ingredients; bring to a boil. Transfer to a greased 13-in. x 9-in. baking dish.

2. In a small bowl, combine the topping ingredients; spoon over top. Bake, uncovered, at 350° for 40-45 minutes or until bubbly and topping is golden brown. Let stand for 10 minutes before serving.

Yield: 9 servings.

ARTICHOKE CHICKEN LASAGNA

Chicken, artichokes and a rich white sauce make this lasagna more special than the usual tomato and beef variety.
DONNA BOELLNER, ANNAPOLIS, MARYLAND

2/3	cup butter, divided
1/3	cup all-purpose flour
1	teaspoon salt, divided
1/4	teaspoon ground nutmeg
1/8	teaspoon pepper
3	cups milk
1-3/4	pounds boneless skinless chicken breasts, cut into thin strips and halved
2	cans (14 ounces each) water-packed artichoke hearts, rinsed, drained and quartered
1	teaspoon dried thyme
9	lasagna noodles, cooked and drained
1	cup grated Parmesan cheese

1. In a large saucepan, melt 1/3 cup butter. Stir in the flour, 1/2 teaspoon salt, nutmeg and pepper until smooth. Gradually stir in milk. Bring to a boil; cook and stir for 2 minutes or until thickened.

2. In a large skillet, cook chicken in remaining butter until no longer pink. Stir in the artichokes, thyme and remaining salt; heat through.

3. In a greased 13-in. x 9-in. baking dish, layer about 1/3 cup white sauce, three noodles, 1/2 cup sauce, 1/3 cup Parmesan cheese and about 3 cups chicken mixture. Repeat layers. Top with remaining noodles, sauce and Parmesan cheese.

4. Bake, uncovered, at 350° for 35-40 minutes or until bubbly and golden brown. Let stand for 10 minutes before cutting.

Yield: 12 servings.

Easy Prep
To easily slice boneless skinless chicken breasts for recipes such as Artichoke Chicken Lasagna, do so when they are slightly frozen.

BROCCOLI CHICKEN SUPREME

This saucy, comforting casserole will draw compliments when it's served at your next potluck dinner. Try the sauce with leftover or cooked meats, fish or vegetables.

VI NEIDING, SOUTH MILWAUKEE, WISCONSIN

6	cups fresh broccoli florets
3	cups sliced fresh mushrooms
1	tablespoon butter
6	cups cubed cooked chicken
3	cans (8 ounces each) sliced water chestnuts, drained

SAUCE:

6	tablespoons butter, cubed
1/2	cup plus 1 tablespoon all-purpose flour
1-1/2	teaspoons seasoned salt
1/8	teaspoon pepper
3	cups chicken broth
1	cup heavy whipping cream
6	egg yolks, lightly beaten
3/4	teaspoon lemon juice
1/8	teaspoon ground nutmeg
3/4	cup slivered almonds, toasted

1. Place broccoli in a steamer basket; place in a large saucepan over 1 in. of water. Bring to a boil; cover and steam for 5-7 minutes or until crisp-tender. Meanwhile, in a large skillet, saute mushrooms in butter until tender.

2. In a greased 13-in. x 9-in. baking dish, layer 4 cups chicken, two-thirds of the mushrooms, two cans of water chestnuts and 4 cups broccoli. In a greased 8-in. square baking dish, layer the remaining chicken, mushrooms, water chestnuts and broccoli.

3. In a large saucepan over medium heat, melt butter. Stir in the flour, seasoned salt and pepper until smooth. Gradually add broth and cream. Bring to a boil; cook and stir for 2 minutes or until thickened and bubbly. Remove from the heat.

4. Stir a small amount of hot mixture into egg yolks. Return all to the pan; cook and stir until mixture reaches 160° and coats the back of a metal spoon. Remove from heat; stir in lemon juice and nutmeg.

5. Pour 3 cups sauce over the large casserole and remaining sauce over the small casserole; sprinkle with almonds. Bake, uncovered, at 375° for 20-25 minutes or until bubbly and heated through.

Yield: 12 servings.

creamy macaroni and cheese, pg. 50

hawaiian kielbasa sandwiches, pg. 55

Slow Cooker Favorites

Count your blessings, name them one by one;
Count your blessings, see what God hath done.

VEGGIE-SAUSAGE CHEESE SOUP

I took this soup to a potluck at work, where it was well received...and the only dish prepared by a guy! The great combination of textures and flavors had everyone asking for a copy of the recipe.
RICHARD GRANT, HUDSON, NEW HAMPSHIRE

- 2 medium onions, finely chopped
- 1 each medium green and sweet red peppers, chopped
- 2 celery ribs, chopped
- 1 tablespoon olive oil
- 4 garlic cloves, minced
- 1 pound smoked kielbasa or Polish sausage, cut into 1/4-inch slices
- 2 medium potatoes, diced
- 1 can (14-3/4 ounces) cream-style corn
- 1 can (14-1/2 ounces) chicken broth
- 1 can (10-3/4 ounces) condensed cream of mushroom soup, undiluted
- 2 medium carrots, sliced
- 1 cup whole kernel corn
- 1 cup sliced fresh mushrooms
- 1 tablespoon Worcestershire sauce
- 1 tablespoon Dijon mustard
- 1 tablespoon dried basil
- 1 tablespoon dried parsley flakes
- 1/2 teaspoon pepper
- 2 ups (8 ounces) shredded sharp cheddar cheese
- 1 can (12 ounces) evaporated milk

1. In a skillet, saute the onions, peppers and celery in oil until tender. Add garlic; cook 1 minute longer.

2. Transfer to a 5-qt. slow cooker. Stir in the sausage, potatoes, cream-style corn, broth, soup, carrots, corn, mushrooms, Worcestershire sauce, Dijon mustard and seasonings. Cover and cook on low for 6-8 hours or until vegetables are tender.

3. Stir in cheese and milk. Cook on low 30 minutes longer or until cheese is melted. Stir until blended.

Yield: 16 servings (4 quarts).

SPICY SAUSAGE HASH BROWNS

I love to develop my own recipes. My family members and friends from church tend to be my favorite and most honest critics. Here's one they request often.
ANGELA SHERIDAN, OPDYKE, ILLINOIS

- 1 pound bulk spicy pork sausage
- 1 package (30 ounces) frozen shredded hash brown potatoes, thawed
- 2 cups (16 ounces) sour cream
- 1 jar (16 ounces) double-cheddar cheese sauce
- 2 cans (4 ounces each) chopped green chilies
- 1/2 teaspoon crushed red pepper flakes

1. In a large skillet, cook sausage over medium heat until no longer pink; drain. Transfer to a 4-qt. slow cooker. Stir in the remaining ingredients. Cover and cook on low for 5-6 hours or until heated through.

Yield: 9 servings.

Editor's Note: This recipe was tested with Ragu double-cheddar cheese sauce.

CRUNCHY CANDY CLUSTERS

Before I retired, I would take these yummy peanut butter bites to work for special occasions. They're so simple, which is why I still make them for holidays. My family looks forward to the coated cereal and marshmallow clusters.

FAYE O'BRYAN, OWENSBORO, KENTUCKY

2	pounds white candy coating, coarsely chopped
1-1/2	cups peanut butter
1/2	teaspoon almond extract, optional
4	cups Cap'n Crunch cereal
4	cups crisp rice cereal
4	cups miniature marshmallows

1. Place candy coating in a 5-qt. slow cooker. Cover and cook on high for 1 hour. Add peanut butter. Stir in extract if desired.

2. In a large bowl, combine the cereals and marshmallows. Stir in the peanut butter mixture until well coated. Drop by tablespoonfuls onto waxed paper. Let stand until set. Store at room temperature.

Yield: 6-1/2 dozen.

HOT CRANBERRY PUNCH

I serve this rosy spiced beverage at parties and family gatherings during the winter. Friends like the zesty twist it gets from Red-Hots. It's a nice change from the usual hot chocolate.

LAURA BURGESS, BALLWIN, MISSOURI

8	cups hot water
1-1/2	cups sugar
4	cups cranberry juice
3/4	cup orange juice
1/4	cup lemon juice
12	whole cloves, optional
1/2	cup red-hot candies

1. In a 5-qt. slow cooker, combine water, sugar and juices; stir until sugar is dissolved. If desired, place cloves in a double thickness of cheesecloth; bring up corners of cloth and tie with string to form a bag. Add spice bag and red-hots to slow cooker.

2. Cover and cook on low for 2-3 hours or until heated through. Before serving, discard spice bag and stir punch.

Yield: 3-1/2 quarts.

APRICOT-APPLE CIDER

Dried apricots give this comforting cider a friendly taste twist. Cranberries, cinnamon, allspice and cloves make it a perfect way to chase away the chill from cool nights.

GINNIE BUSAM, PEWEE VALLEY, KENTUCKY

8	cups unsweetened apple juice
1	can (12 ounces) ginger ale
1/2	cup dried apricots, halved
1/2	cup dried cranberries
2	cinnamon sticks (3 inches)
1	tablespoon whole allspice
1	tablespoon whole cloves

1. In a 5-qt. slow cooker, combine apple juice and ginger ale. Place the apricots, cranberries, cinnamon sticks, allspice and cloves on a double thickness of cheesecloth; bring up corners of cloth and tie with string to form a bag. Place in slow cooker.

2. Cover and cook on high for 3-4 hours or until heated through. Discard spice bag.

Yield: 13 servings (2-1/2 quarts).

CHICAGO-STYLE BEEF SANDWICHES

(pictured at right)

I'm originally from the Windy City, so I love Chicago-style beef. These tender sandwiches are loaded with authentic flavor, and are so simple to prepare using a slow cooker.

LOIS SZYDLOWSKI, TAMPA, FLORIDA

1	boneless beef chuck roast (4 pounds)
1	teaspoon salt
3/4	teaspoon pepper
2	tablespoons olive oil
1/2	pound fresh mushrooms
2	medium carrots, cut into chunks
1	medium onion, cut into wedges
6	garlic cloves, halved
2	teaspoons dried oregano
1	carton (32 ounces) beef broth
1	tablespoon beef base
12	Italian rolls, split
1	jar (16 ounces) giardiniera, drained

1. Cut roast in half; sprinkle with salt and pepper. In a large skillet, brown meat in oil on all sides; drain. Transfer to a 5-qt. slow cooker.

2. In a food processor, combine the mushrooms, carrots, onion, garlic and oregano. Cover and process until finely chopped. Transfer to slow cooker. Combine beef broth and base; pour over the top. Cover and cook on low for 8-10 hours or until tender.

3. Remove meat and shred with two forks. Skim fat from cooking juices. Return meat to slow cooker; heat through. Using a slotted spoon, serve beef on buns; top with giardiniera.

Yield: 12 servings.

LIME CHICKEN TACOS

Lime adds zest to this easy filling for tortillas, and leftovers make a refreshing topping to any taco salad. In fact, the versatility in this recipe is so great, it's a dish fit for a casual dinner at home or a special occasion with friends.
TRACY GUNTER, BOISE, IDAHO

1-1/2	pounds boneless skinless chicken breasts
3	tablespoons lime juice
1	tablespoon chili powder
1	cup frozen corn
1	cup chunky salsa
12	flour tortillas (6 inches), warmed

Sour cream, shredded cheddar cheese and shredded lettuce, optional

1. Place the chicken in a 3-qt. slow cooker. Combine lime juice and chili powder; pour over chicken. Cover and cook on low for 5-6 hours or until chicken is tender.

2. Remove chicken; cool slightly. Shred meat with two forks and return to the slow cooker; heat through. Stir in corn and salsa.

3. Cover and cook on low for 30 minutes or until heated through. Serve in tortillas with sour cream, cheese and lettuce if desired.

Yield: 12 tacos.

HAWAIIAN KIELBASA SANDWICHES

If you are looking for a different way to use kielbasa, the sweet and mildly spicy flavor of these sandwiches is a nice change of pace.

JUDY DAMES, BRIDGEVILLE, PENNSYLVANIA

3	pounds smoked kielbasa or Polish sausage, cut into 3-inch pieces
2	bottles (12 ounces each) chili sauce
1	can (20 ounces) pineapple tidbits, undrained
1/4	cup packed brown sugar
12	hoagie buns, split

1. Place kielbasa in a 3-qt. slow cooker. Combine the chili sauce, pineapple and brown sugar; pour over kielbasa. Cover and cook on low for 3-4 hours or until heated through. Serve on buns.

Yield: 12 servings.

CRISPY SNACK MIX

This recipe proves that you can make just about anything in the slow cooker, even a delightfully crispy snack mix.

JANE (PAIR) SIMS, DE LEON, TEXAS

4-1/2	cups chow mein noodles
4	cups Rice Chex
1	can (9-3/4 ounces) salted cashews
1	cup flaked coconut, toasted
1/2	cup butter, melted
2	tablespoons reduced-sodium soy sauce
2-1/4	teaspoons curry powder
3/4	teaspoon ground ginger

1. In a 5-qt. slow cooker, combine the noodles, cereal, cashews and coconut. In a small bowl, whisk the butter, soy sauce, curry powder and ginger; drizzle over cereal mixture and mix well.

2. Cover and cook on low for 2-1/2 hours, stirring every 30 minutes. Serve snack mix warm or at room temperature.

Yield: about 2-1/2 quarts.

GREEN OLIVE DIP

Here's a cheesy dip the whole crowd will love. It's full of beef and beans, and could even be used to fill taco shells.
BETH DUNAHAY, LIMA, OHIO

1	pound ground beef
1	medium sweet red pepper, chopped
1	small onion, chopped
1	can (16 ounces) refried beans
1	jar (16 ounces) mild salsa
2	cups (8 ounces) shredded part-skim mozzarella cheese
2	cups (8 ounces) shredded cheddar cheese
1	jar (5-3/4 ounces) sliced green olives with pimientos, drained

Tortilla chips

1. In a skillet, cook the beef, pepper and onion over medium heat until meat is no longer pink; drain.

2. Transfer to a greased 3-qt. slow cooker. Add the beans, salsa, cheeses and olives. Cover and cook on low for 3-4 hours or until cheese is melted, stirring occasionally. Serve with chips.

Yield: 8 cups.

BARBECUE COUNTRY RIBS

Barbecue ribs are the perfect comfort food and, thanks to this slow cooker recipe, they're easier than ever to make!
REBECCA KNODE, MECHANICSBURG, PENNSYLVANIA

4	pounds boneless country-style pork ribs
1	bottle (12 ounces) chili sauce
1	cup ketchup
1/2	cup packed brown sugar
1/3	cup balsamic vinegar
2	tablespoons Worcestershire sauce
2	teaspoons onion powder
1	teaspoon salt
1	teaspoon garlic powder
1	teaspoon chili powder
1	teaspoon pepper
1/2	teaspoon hot pepper sauce, optional
1/4	teaspoon Liquid Smoke, optional

1. Place ribs in a 5-qt. slow cooker. Combine the chili sauce, ketchup, brown sugar, vinegar, Worcestershire sauce, seasonings and pepper sauce and Liquid Smoke if desired; pour over ribs.

2. Cover and cook on low for 5-6 hours or until meat is tender.

Yield: 10 servings.

COLORFUL CHICKEN STEW

Instead of beef stew, try this hearty chicken stew for a change. I rely on chili powder to spice up the chicken and fresh-tasting veggies. Since it simmers in a slow cooker all day, it's wonderful to have it ready when you walk in the door.
ILA MAE ALDERMAN, GALAX, VIRGINIA

1	pound boneless skinless chicken breasts, cubed
1	can (14-1/2 ounces) Italian diced tomatoes, undrained
2	medium potatoes, peeled and cut into 1/2-inch cubes
5	medium carrots, chopped
3	celery ribs, chopped
1	large onion, chopped
1	medium green pepper, chopped
2	cans (4 ounces each) mushroom stems and pieces, drained
2	low-sodium chicken bouillon cubes

Artificial sweetener equivalent to 2 teaspoons sugar

1	teaspoon chili powder
1/4	teaspoon pepper
1	tablespoon cornstarch
2	cups cold water

1. In a 5-qt. slow cooker, combine the first 12 ingredients. In a small bowl, combine cornstarch and water until smooth. Stir into chicken mixture. Cover and cook on low for 8-10 hours or until chicken and vegetables are tender.

Yield: 10 servings.

VEGGIE POTATO SOUP

Chock-full of potatoes, this vegetarian soup is as filling as it is flavorful. Serve on cold winter nights with crusty bread or take a thermos-full to work; with this in store, you'll really look forward to lunch!
HANNAH THOMPSON, SCOTTS VALLEY, CALIFORNIA

6	medium potatoes, cubed
3	cans (14-1/2 ounces each) vegetable broth
1	medium carrot, thinly sliced
1	large leek (white portion only), chopped
1/4	cup butter, cubed
1	garlic clove, minced
1	teaspoon dried thyme
3/4	teaspoon salt
1/4	teaspoon dried marjoram
1/4	teaspoon pepper
1/4	cup all-purpose flour
1-1/2	cups half-and-half cream
1	cup frozen peas, thawed

1. In a 5-qt. slow cooker, combine the first 10 ingredients. Cover and cook on low for 5-6 hours or until vegetables are tender.

2. In a small bowl, combine flour and cream until smooth; add to slow cooker. Stir in peas. Cover and cook on high for 30 minutes or until slightly thickened.

Yield: 11 servings (2-3/4 quarts).

Impromptu Vegetable "Brush"

If you don't have a vegetable brush to scrub fresh potatoes before using in a recipe, try this easy trick. Simply roll a piece of aluminum foil into a ball, use it to scrub away the dirt and then throw it away.

CREAMY MACARONI AND CHEESE

America's most popular comfort food just got better thanks to the convenience of being made in a slow cooker.
JENNIFER BABCOCK, CHICOPEE, MASSACHUSETTS

3	cups uncooked elbow macaroni
1	pound process cheese (Velveeta), cubed
2	cups (8 ounces) shredded Mexican cheese blend
2	cups (8 ounces) shredded white cheddar cheese
1-3/4	cups milk
1	can (12 ounces) evaporated milk
3/4	cup egg substitute
3/4	cup butter, melted

1. Cook macaroni according to package directions; drain. Place in a greased 5-qt. slow cooker. Stir in the remaining ingredients.

2. Cover and cook on low for 2-3 hours or until a thermometer reads 160°, stirring once.

Yield: 16 servings (3/4 cup each).

HASH BROWN EGG BREAKFAST

(pictured at left)
I love this hearty breakfast dish. It's great for potlucks because it's easy to carry and feeds a bunch.
NANCY MARION, FROSTPROOF, FLORIDA

1	package (32 ounces) frozen cubed hash brown potatoes, thawed
2	cups cubed fully cooked ham
1-1/2	cups (6 ounces) shredded cheddar cheese
1	large green pepper, chopped
1	medium onion, chopped
12	eggs, lightly beaten
1	cup 2% milk
1	teaspoon salt
1	teaspoon pepper

1. Layer with a third of the potatoes, ham, cheese, green pepper and onion in a greased 6-qt. slow cooker. Repeat layers twice.

2. In a large bowl, whisk the eggs, milk, salt and pepper; pour over top. Cover and cook on low for 3 to 4 hours or until a thermometer reads 160°.

Yield: 12 servings (1-1/3 cups each).

Keep It Hot
To keep potluck offerings hot, cover each dish with plastic wrap, then place a lid on top. Finally, wrap the dishes in warm towels for added insulation.

CHILI CHEESE DIP

After trying to create a Mexican soup, I ended up with this outstanding dip that eats like a meal. My husband and two young children love it! Now it's a popular choice for football game days or family gatherings.
SANDRA FICK, LINCOLN, NEBRASKA

1	pound lean ground beef (90% lean)
1	cup chopped onion
1	can (16 ounces) kidney beans, rinsed and drained
1	can (15 ounces) black beans, rinsed and drained
1	can (14-1/2 ounces) diced tomatoes in sauce
1	cup frozen corn
3/4	cup water
1	can (2-1/4 ounces) sliced ripe olives, drained
3	teaspoons chili powder
1/2	teaspoon dried oregano
1/2	teaspoon chipotle hot pepper sauce
1/4	teaspoon garlic powder
1/4	teaspoon ground cumin
1	package (16 ounces) reduced-fat process cheese (Velveeta), cubed

Corn chips

1. In a large skillet, cook beef and onion over medium heat until no longer pink; drain. Transfer to a 5-qt. slow cooker. Stir in the beans, tomatoes, corn, water, olives, chili powder, oregano, pepper sauce, garlic powder and cumin.

2. Cover and cook on low for 4-5 hours or until heated through; stir in cheese. Cover and cook for 30 minutes or until cheese is melted. Serve with corn chips.

Yield: 8 cups.

WARM POMEGRANATE PUNCH

If you're looking for something special to serve on a chilly evening, try this warming punch. It has a subtle tea flavor, and the juices create just the right balance of sweet and tart.
TASTE OF HOME TEST KITCHEN

4	cups pomegranate juice
4	cups unsweetened apple juice
2	cups brewed tea
1/2	cup sugar
1/3	cup lemon juice
3	cinnamon sticks (3 inches)
12	whole cloves

1. In a 4- or 5-qt. slow cooker, combine the first five ingredients. Place cinnamon sticks and cloves on a double thickness of cheesecloth; bring up corners of cloth and tie with string to form a bag. Add to slow cooker.

2. Cover and cook on low for 2-4 hours or until heated through. Discard spice bag. Serve warm.

Yield: 2-1/2 quarts.

4. Cover and cook on low for 1 hour or until heated through. Spoon beef mixture down the center of tortillas; add toppings of your choice. Roll up.

Yield: 12 servings.

Editor's Note: This recipe was tested with El Paso brand Mexican-style hot tomato sauce. If you cannot find Mexican-style hot tomato sauce, you may substitute 1/2 cup tomato sauce, 1 teaspoon hot pepper sauce, 1/8 teaspoon onion powder and 1/8 teaspoon chili powder.

SLOW COOKER SLOPPY JOES

Slow cook your way to a crowd-pleasing entree! Ground beef is transformed into a classic sandwich filling with just a few pantry staples.

JOEANNE STERAS, GARRETT, PENNSYLVANIA

2	pounds ground beef
1	cup chopped green pepper
2/3	cup chopped onion
2	cups ketchup
2	envelopes sloppy joe mix
2	tablespoons brown sugar
1	teaspoon prepared mustard
12	hamburger buns, split

1. In a large skillet, cook the beef, pepper and onion over medium heat until meat is no longer pink; drain. Stir in the ketchup, sloppy joe mix, brown sugar and mustard.

2. Transfer to a 3-qt. slow cooker. Cover and cook on low for 4-5 hours or until flavors are blended. Spoon 1/2 cup onto each bun.

Yield: 12 servings.

GREEN CHILI BEEF BURRITOS

This recipe gets rave reviews every time I make it. The shredded beef has a savory, slow-cooked flavor you can't get anywhere else.

JENNY FLAKE, NEWPORT BEACH, CALIFORNIA

1	boneless beef chuck roast (3 pounds)
1	can (14-1/2 ounces) beef broth
2	cups green enchilada sauce
1	can (4 ounces) chopped green chilies
1/2	cup Mexican-style hot tomato sauce
1/2	teaspoon salt
1/2	teaspoon garlic powder
1/2	teaspoon pepper
12	flour tortillas (12 inches)

Optional toppings: shredded lettuce, chopped tomatoes, shredded cheddar cheese and sour cream

1. Cut roast in half and place in a 3- or 4-qt. slow cooker. Add broth. Cover and cook on low for 8-9 hours or until meat is tender.

2. Remove beef. When cool enough to handle, shred meat with two forks. Skim fat from cooking liquid; reserve 1/2 cup cooking juices.

3. Return shredded beef and reserved liquid to the slow cooker. Stir in enchilada sauce, green chilies, tomato sauce, salt, garlic powder and pepper.

CREAMY ARTICHOKE DIP

Folks are sure to gather around this ooey-gooey dip (that's surprisingly light!) whenever it's placed on any buffet table. With cheese, jalapenos and a hint of lemon, it's a treasured favorite.

MARY SPENCER, GREENDALE, WISCONSIN

2	cans (14 ounces each) water-packed artichoke hearts, rinsed, drained and coarsely chopped
1	package (8 ounces) reduced-fat cream cheese, cubed
3/4	cup (6 ounces) plain yogurt
1	cup (4 ounces) shredded part-skim mozzarella cheese
1	cup reduced-fat ricotta cheese
3/4	cup shredded Parmesan cheese, divided
1/2	cup shredded reduced-fat Swiss cheese
1/4	cup reduced-fat mayonnaise
2	tablespoons lemon juice
1	tablespoon chopped seeded jalapeno pepper
1	teaspoon garlic powder
1	teaspoon seasoned salt
	Tortilla chips

1. In a 3-qt. slow cooker, combine the artichokes, cream cheese, yogurt, mozzarella cheese, ricotta cheese, 1/2 cup Parmesan cheese, Swiss cheese, mayonnaise, lemon juice, jalapeno, garlic powder and seasoned salt. Cover and cook on low for 1 hour or until heated through.

2. Sprinkle with remaining Parmesan cheese. Serve with tortilla chips.

Yield: 5 cups.

TEXAS BEEF BARBECUE

A boneless beef roast simmers for hours in a slightly sweet sauce before it's shredded and tucked into rolls to make hearty sandwiches.
JENNIFER BAUER, LANSING, MICHIGAN

1	beef sirloin tip roast (4 pounds)
1	can (5-1/2 ounces) spicy hot V8 juice
1/2	cup water
1/4	cup white vinegar
1/4	cup ketchup
2	tablespoons Worcestershire sauce
1/2	cup packed brown sugar
1	teaspoon salt
1	teaspoon ground mustard
1	teaspoon paprika
1/4	teaspoon chili powder
1/8	teaspoon pepper
16	kaiser rolls, split

1. Cut roast in half; place in a 5-qt. slow cooker. Combine the V8 juice, water, vinegar, ketchup, Worcestershire sauce, brown sugar and seasonings; pour over roast. Cover and cook on low for 8-10 hours or until meat is tender.

2. Remove meat and shred with two forks; return to slow cooker and heat through. Spoon 1/2 cup meat mixture onto each roll.

Yield: 16 servings.

CARAMEL PEAR PUDDING

Here is a deliciously different dessert that is especially good when pears are seasonally available. It's easy to fix and a comforting treat after any meal. I enjoy snacking on it in front of the fireplace.
DIANE HALFERTY, CORPUS CHRISTI, TEXAS

1	cup all-purpose flour
1/2	cup sugar
1-1/2	teaspoons baking powder
1/2	teaspoon ground cinnamon
1/4	teaspoon salt
1/8	teaspoon ground cloves
1/2	cup 2% milk
4	medium pears, peeled and cubed
1/2	cup chopped pecans
3/4	cup packed brown sugar
1/4	cup butter, softened
1/2	cup boiling water
	Vanilla ice cream, optional

1. In a large bowl, combine the flour, sugar, baking powder, cinnamon, salt and cloves. Stir in milk until smooth. Add pears and pecans. Spread evenly into a 3-qt. slow cooker coated with cooking spray.

2. In a small bowl, combine brown sugar and butter; stir in boiling water. Pour over batter (do not stir). Cover and cook on low for 3-4 hours or until pears are tender. Serve warm with ice cream if desired.

Yield: 10 servings.

SWEET-AND-SOUR CHICKEN WINGS

These wings are perfect for holiday gatherings. Because they come with plenty of sauce, I sometimes serve them over rice as a main dish. Any way you do it, this sweet and tangy dish will be a hit!

JUNE EBERHARDT, MARYSVILLE, CALIFORNIA

1	cup sugar
1	cup cider vinegar
1/2	cup ketchup
2	tablespoons reduced-sodium soy sauce
1	teaspoon chicken bouillon granules
16	chicken wings
6	tablespoons cornstarch
1/2	cup cold water

1. In a small saucepan, combine the first five ingredients. Bring to a boil; cook and stir until sugar is dissolved. Cut wings into three sections; discard wing tip sections.

2. Transfer to a 3-qt. slow cooker; add vinegar mixture. Cover and cook on low for 3 to 3-1/2 hours or until chicken juices run clear.

3. Transfer wings to a serving dish and keep warm. Skim fat from cooking juices; transfer to a small saucepan. Bring liquid to a boil.

4. Combine cornstarch and water until smooth. Gradually stir into the pan. Bring to a boil; cook and stir for 2 minutes or until thickened. Spoon over chicken. Serve with a slotted spoon.

Yield: 32 appetizers.

SLOW COOKER MEXICAN DIP

My husband and I love to entertain, and this hearty, 7-ingredient dip is always on our menu. It couldn't be much easier to put together, and using our slow cooker leaves us free to share some quality time with our guests. After all, isn't that the purpose of a party?

HEATHER COURTNEY, AMES, IOWA

1-1/2	pounds ground beef
1	pound bulk hot Italian sausage
1	cup chopped onion
1	package (8.8 ounces) ready-to-serve Spanish rice
1	can (16 ounces) refried beans
1	can (10 ounces) enchilada sauce
1	pound process cheese (Velveeta), cubed
1	package tortilla chip scoops

1. In a Dutch oven, cook the beef, sausage and onion over medium heat until meat is no longer pink; drain. Heat rice according to package directions.

2. In a 3-qt. slow cooker, combine the meat mixture, rice, beans, enchilada sauce and cheese. Cover and cook on low for 1-1/2 to 2 hours or until cheese is melted. Serve with tortilla scoops.

Yield: 8 cups.

HEARTY PASTA TOMATO SOUP

I adapted the original recipe for this flavorful soup so I could make it in the slow cooker. It's ideal for any luncheon or gathering where you won't have easy access to a stove.
LYDIA KROESE, PLYMOUTH, MINNESOTA

1	pound bulk Italian sausage
6	cups beef broth
1	can (28 ounces) stewed tomatoes
1	can (15 ounces) tomato sauce
2	cups sliced zucchini
1	large onion, chopped
1	cup sliced carrots
1	cup sliced fresh mushrooms
1	medium green pepper, chopped
1/4	cup minced fresh parsley
2	teaspoons sugar
1	teaspoon dried oregano
1	teaspoon dried basil
1	garlic clove, minced
2	cups frozen cheese tortellini
	Grated Parmesan cheese, optional

1. In a skillet, cook the sausage over medium heat until no longer pink; drain. Transfer to a 5-qt. slow cooker; add the next 13 ingredients. Cover and cook on high for 3-4 hours or until the vegetables are tender.

2. Cook tortellini according to package directions; drain. Stir into slow cooker; cover and cook 30 minutes longer. Serve with Parmesan cheese if desired.

Yield: 14 servings (about 3-1/2 quarts).

So Simple to Shred
Shredding roasts for tasty sandwiches is easy! Grab two forks and move them in opposite directions, pulling the meat into thin shreds. Return the shredded meat to the pan to warm or use as the recipe directs.

BBQ BEEF SANDWICHES

After years of searching, I found a recipe for shredded barbecue beef that's a hit with all my family and friends.
REBECCA ROHLAND, MEDFORD, WISCONSIN

2	cups ketchup
1	medium onion, chopped
1/4	cup cider vinegar
1/4	cup molasses
2	tablespoons Worcestershire sauce
2	garlic cloves, minced
1/2	teaspoon salt
1/2	teaspoon ground mustard
1/2	teaspoon pepper
1/4	teaspoon garlic powder
1/4	teaspoon crushed red pepper flakes
1	boneless beef chuck roast (3 pounds)
14	sesame seed hamburger buns, split

1. In a large bowl, combine the first 11 ingredients. Cut roast in half; place in a 5-qt. slow cooker. Pour ketchup mixture over roast. Cover and cook on low for 8-10 hours or until meat is tender.

2. Remove meat and shred with two forks. Skim fat from cooking juices. Return meat to slow cooker; heat through. Using a slotted spoon, serve beef on buns.

Yield: 14 sandwiches.

MOIST & TENDER TURKEY BREAST

Guests are sure to love the taste of this traditional entree, and you'll love how easily it comes together.
HEIDI VAWDREY, RIVERTON, UTAH

1	bone-in turkey breast (6 to 7 pounds)
4	fresh rosemary sprigs
4	garlic cloves, peeled
1	tablespoon brown sugar
1/2	teaspoon coarsely ground pepper
1/4	teaspoon salt

1. Place turkey breast in a 6-qt. slow cooker. Place rosemary and garlic around turkey. Combine the brown sugar, pepper and salt; sprinkle over turkey.

2. Cover and cook on low for 4-6 hours or until turkey is tender.

Yield: 12 servings.

HEARTY TACO CHILI

(pictured at right)
Ranch dressing mix and taco seasoning give this hearty mixture extra special flavor. Try it over baked potatoes, too!
JULIE NEUHALFEN, GLENWOOD, IOWA

2	pounds ground beef
1	can (16 ounces) kidney beans, rinsed and drained
1	can (15 ounces) pinto beans, rinsed and drained
1	can (15 ounces) black beans, rinsed and drained
1	can (14 ounces) hominy, rinsed and drained
1	can (10 ounces) diced tomatoes and green chilies, undrained
1	can (8 ounces) tomato sauce
1	small onion, chopped
1	envelope ranch salad dressing mix
1	envelope taco seasoning
1/2	teaspoon pepper
2	cans (14-1/2 ounces each) diced tomatoes, undrained
1	can (4 ounces) chopped green chilies
	Corn chips, sour cream and shredded cheddar cheese, optional

1. In a large skillet, cook beef over medium heat until no longer pink; drain. Transfer to a 5-qt. slow cooker. Add the beans, hominy, tomatoes, tomato sauce, onion, salad dressing mix, taco seasoning and pepper.

2. In a blender, combine diced tomatoes and green chilies; cover and process until smooth. Add to the slow cooker. Cover and cook on low for 6-8 hours.

3. Serve with corn chips, sour cream and cheese if desired.

Yield: 11 servings (2-3/4 quarts).

Using Fresh Garlic
Husk a garlic clove in an instant by cutting it in half lengthwise with a sharp knife. If the husk still doesn't come off, quarter the clove.

STUFFING FROM THE SLOW COOKER

If you're hosting a big Thanksgiving dinner this year, add this simple, slow-cooked stuffing to your menu to ease entertaining. This recipe comes in handy when you run out of oven space at large family gatherings.

DONALD SEILER, MACON, MISSISSIPPI

1	cup chopped onion
1	cup chopped celery
1/4	cup butter
6	cups cubed day-old white bread
6	cups cubed day-old whole wheat bread
1	teaspoon salt
1	teaspoon poultry seasoning
1	teaspoon rubbed sage
1/2	teaspoon pepper
1	can (14-1/2 ounces) reduced-sodium chicken broth or vegetable broth
1/2	cup egg substitute

1. In a small nonstick skillet over medium heat, cook onion and celery in butter until tender.

2. In a large bowl, combine the bread cubes, salt, poultry seasoning, sage and pepper. Stir in onion mixture. Combine broth and egg substitute; add to bread mixture and toss to coat.

3. Transfer to a 3-qt. slow cooker coated with cooking spray. Cover and cook on low for 3-4 hours or until heated through.

Yield: 12 servings.

SPINACH ARTICHOKE DIP

Perfect for special occasions, this rich dip tastes especially good when served warm with crackers. The red onion and spinach add flavor and flecks of color.

JAN HABERSTICH, WATERLOO, IOWA

1	can (14 ounces) water-packed artichoke hearts, rinsed, drained and chopped
1	cup fresh baby spinach, chopped
1/2	cup sour cream
1/2	cup mayonnaise
1/2	cup shredded part-skim mozzarella cheese
1/2	cup shredded Parmesan cheese
1/3	cup chopped red onion
1/4	teaspoon garlic powder
	Assorted crackers or breads

1. In a 1-1/2-qt. slow cooker, combine the first eight ingredients. Cover and cook on low for 2-3 hours or until heated through. Serve dip with crackers or breads.

Yield: 3 cups.

TROPICAL BBQ CHICKEN

One bite and you'll understand why this is my favorite slow cooker recipe. The slightly spicy sauce will win you over, too!

YVONNE MCKIM, VANCOUVER, WASHINGTON

6	chicken leg quarters, skin removed
3/4	cup ketchup
1/2	cup orange juice
1/4	cup packed brown sugar
1/4	cup red wine vinegar
1/4	cup olive oil
4	teaspoons minced fresh parsley
2	teaspoons Worcestershire sauce
1	teaspoon garlic salt
1/2	teaspoon pepper
2	tablespoons plus 2 teaspoons cornstarch
1/4	cup water

1. With a sharp knife, cut leg quarters at the joints. Place chicken in a 4-qt. slow cooker.

2. In a small bowl, combine the ketchup, orange juice, brown sugar, vinegar, oil, parsley, Worcestershire sauce, garlic salt and pepper; pour over chicken.

3. Cover and cook on low for 5-6 hours or until a meat thermometer reads 180°.

4. Remove chicken to a serving platter; keep warm. Skim fat from cooking juices; transfer 2 cups to a small saucepan. Bring liquid to a boil.

5. Combine cornstarch and water until smooth. Gradually stir into the pan. Bring to a boil; cook and stir for 2 minutes or until thickened. Serve with chicken.

Yield: 12 servings.

SLOW-COOKED REUBEN BRATS

Who knew brats could be just as delicious prepared in a slow cooker as they are prepared on the grill? Here, I've combined the hearty sausages with the flavor of a classic sandwich.

ALANA SIMMONS, JOHNSTOWN, PENNSYLVANIA

10	uncooked bratwurst links
3	cans (12 ounces each) light beer or nonalcoholic beer
1	large sweet onion, sliced
1	can (14 ounces) sauerkraut, rinsed and well drained
3/4	cup mayonnaise
1/4	cup chili sauce
2	tablespoons ketchup
4-1/2	teaspoons finely chopped onion
2	teaspoons sweet pickle relish
1	garlic clove, minced
1/4	teaspoon salt
1/8	teaspoon pepper
10	hoagie buns, split
2/3	cup butter, softened
10	slices Swiss cheese

1. In a large skillet, brown bratwurst in batches; drain. In a 5-qt. slow cooker, combine the beer, sliced onion and sauerkraut; top with bratwurst.

2. Cover and cook on low for 7-9 hours or until sausage is no longer pink.

3. In a small bowl, combine the mayonnaise, chili sauce, ketchup, chopped onion, relish, garlic, salt and pepper.

4. Spread cut sides of each bun with 1 tablespoon butter and 4-1/2 teaspoons mayonnaise mixture; top with a cheese slice, bratwurst and the sauerkraut mixture.

5. Place on an ungreased baking sheet. Bake at 350° for 8-10 minutes or until cheese is melted.

Yield: 10 servings.

SLOW-COOKED VEGETABLE SOUP

Not only is this soup hearty and filling, but it also has a unique blend of flavors and a beautiful appearance. It's nice to serve a lighter option loaded with fiber and vitamins.

CHRISTINA TILL, SOUTH HAVEN, MICHIGAN

3/4	cup chopped onion
1/2	cup chopped celery
1/2	cup chopped green pepper
2	tablespoons olive oil
1	large potato, peeled and diced
1	medium sweet potato, peeled and diced
1	to 2 garlic cloves, minced
3	cups chicken or vegetable broth
2	medium fresh tomatoes, chopped
1	can (16 ounces) kidney beans, rinsed and drained
1	can (15 ounces) garbanzo beans or chickpeas, rinsed and drained
2	teaspoons soy sauce
1	teaspoon paprika
1/2	teaspoon dried basil
1/4	teaspoon salt
1/4	teaspoon ground turmeric
1	bay leaf

Dash cayenne pepper

1. In a large skillet, saute the onion, celery and green pepper in oil until crisp-tender. Add potato, sweet potato and garlic; saute 3-5 minutes longer.

2. Transfer to a 5-qt. slow cooker. Stir in the remaining ingredients. Cover and cook on low for 9-10 hours or until vegetables are tender. Discard bay leaf.

Yield: 12 serving (about 3 quarts).

PEPPERONI PIZZA DIP

Looking for a dish that's easy to make and transport? Try this pizza-inspired dip! You won't have to keep it warm long, because it'll be gone in a flash.

LISA FRANCIS, ELBA, ALABAMA

4	cups (16 ounces) shredded cheddar cheese
4	cups (16 ounces) shredded part-skim mozzarella cheese
1	cup mayonnaise
1	jar (6 ounces) sliced mushrooms, drained
2	cans (2-1/4 ounces each) sliced ripe olives, drained
1	package (3-1/2 ounces) pepperoni slices, quartered
1	tablespoon dried minced onion

Assorted crackers

1. In a 3-qt. slow cooker, combine the cheeses, mayonnaise, mushrooms, olives, pepperoni and onion. Cover and cook on low for 1-1/2 hours; stir.

2. Cover and cook for 1 hour or until heated through. Serve with crackers.

Yield: 5 cups.

Save Time & Money

The next time you serve a veggie platter, cut the leftovers into bite-size pieces and put them all in one heavy-duty plastic bag in the freezer. When you make soup or stew, you'll have a bag of chopped veggies on hand and ready to add.

SIMMERED SMOKED LINKS

A tasty, sweet-spicy sauce glazes bite-size sausages in this simple hors d'oeuvre. It's a must at any get-together.
MAXINE CENKER, WEIRTON, WEST VIRGINIA

2	packages (16 ounces each) miniature smoked sausage links
1	cup packed brown sugar
1/2	cup ketchup
1/4	cup prepared horseradish

1. Place sausages in a 3-qt. slow cooker. Combine the brown sugar, ketchup and horseradish; pour over sausages.

2. Cover and cook on low for 4 hours.
Yield: 16-20 servings.

SHREDDED STEAK SANDWICHES

I received this recipe when I was a newlywed, and it's been a favorite since then. The saucy barbecue even tastes great served over rice, potatoes or buttered noodles.
LEE DENEAU, LANSING, MICHIGAN

3	pounds beef top round steak, cut into large pieces
2	large onions, chopped
3/4	cup thinly sliced celery
1-1/2	cups ketchup
1/2	to 3/4 cup water
1/3	cup each lemon juice and Worcestershire sauce
3	tablespoons brown sugar
3	tablespoons cider vinegar
2	to 3 teaspoons salt
2	teaspoons prepared mustard
1-1/2	teaspoons paprika
1	teaspoon chili powder
1/2	teaspoon pepper
1/8	to 1/4 teaspoon hot pepper sauce
12	to 14 sandwich rolls, split

1. Place meat in a 5-qt. slow cooker. Add onions and celery. In a bowl, combine the ketchup, water, lemon juice, Worcestershire sauce, brown sugar, vinegar, salt, mustard, paprika, chili powder, pepper and hot pepper sauce. Pour over meat.

2. Cover and cook on high for 6-8 hours. Remove meat; cool slightly. Shred meat with two forks. Return to the slow cooker and heat through. Serve on rolls.
Yield: 12-14 servings.

MOM'S SCALLOPED POTATOES AND HAM

When I have leftover ham, this is the most-requested recipe in the house! It's a fantastic dish to bring to potlucks since I can prepare and bring it in a slow cooker.
KELLY GRAHAM, ST. THOMAS, ONTARIO

10	medium potatoes, peeled and thinly sliced
3	cups cubed fully cooked ham
2	large onions, thinly sliced
2	cups (8 ounces) shredded cheddar cheese
1	can (10-3/4 ounces) condensed cream of mushroom soup, undiluted
1/2	teaspoon paprika
1/4	teaspoon pepper

1. In a greased 6-qt. slow cooker, layer half of the potatoes, ham, onions and cheese. Repeat layers. Pour soup over top. Sprinkle with paprika and pepper.

2. Cover and cook on low for 8-10 hours or until potatoes are tender.

Yield: 9 servings.

SLOW-COOKED HERBED TURKEY

(pictured at left)
When fresh herbs are plentiful, I prepare this crowd-pleasing main dish. The turkey stays moist in the slow cooker and is bursting with garden flavors.
SUE JURACK, MEQUON, WISCONSIN

2	cans (14-1/2 ounces each) chicken broth
1	cup lemon juice
1/2	cup packed brown sugar
1/2	cup minced fresh sage
1/2	cup minced fresh thyme
1/2	cup lime juice
1/2	cup cider vinegar
1/2	cup olive oil
2	envelopes onion soup mix
1/4	cup Dijon mustard
2	tablespoons minced fresh marjoram
3	teaspoons paprika
2	teaspoons garlic powder
2	teaspoons pepper
1	teaspoon salt
2	boneless skinless turkey breast halves (3 pounds each)

1. In a blender, combine the first 15 ingredients; cover and process until blended. Place turkey breasts in a gallon-size resealable plastic bag; add half of marinade. Seal bag and turn to coat; refrigerate overnight. Pour remaining marinade into a bowl; cover and refrigerate.

2. Drain and discard marinade from turkey. Transfer turkey breasts to a 5-qt. slow cooker. Add reserved marinade; cover and cook on high for 4-5 hours or a thermometer reads 170°. Let stand for 10 minutes before slicing.

Yield: 14-16 servings.

cherry coffee cake, pg. 80

pecan-raisin cinnamon rolls, pg. 87

Breakfast & Brunch

Now I awake and see the light; the Lord has kept me through the night. To You I lift my voice and pray, that You will keep me through the day.

ORANGE-CHEESECAKE BREAKFAST ROLLS

(pictured at left)

These yummy rolls, with their citrus flavor and cream cheese filling, are a nice change of pace from the usual cinnamon kind.

HANNAH COBB, OWINGS MILLS, MARYLAND

2	packages (1/4 ounce each) active dry yeast
3/4	cup warm water (110° to 115°)
1-3/4	cups warm 2% milk (110° to 115°)
1	cup sugar
2	eggs
3	tablespoons butter, melted
1-1/2	teaspoons salt
7	to 8 cups all-purpose flour

FILLING:

1	package (8 ounces) cream cheese, softened
1/2	cup sugar
1	tablespoon orange juice concentrate
1/2	teaspoon vanilla extract

GLAZE:

2	cups confectioners' sugar
3	tablespoons orange juice
1	teaspoon grated orange peel

1. In a large bowl, dissolve yeast in warm water. Add the milk, sugar, eggs, butter, salt and 5 cups flour. Beat until smooth. Stir in enough remaining flour to form a firm dough.

2. Turn onto a floured surface; knead until smooth and elastic, about 6-8 minutes. Place in a greased bowl, turning once to grease the top. Cover and let rise in a warm place until doubled, about 1 hour.

3. In a small bowl, beat the cream cheese, sugar, orange juice concentrate and vanilla until smooth. Punch dough down. Turn onto a lightly floured surface; divide in half. Roll one portion into an 18-in. x 7-in. rectangle. Spread half of the filling to within 1/2 in. of edges.

4. Roll up jelly-roll style, starting with a long side; pinch seam to seal. Cut into 12 slices; place cut side down in a greased 13-in. x 9-in. baking pan. Repeat with remaining dough and filling. Cover and let rise until doubled, about 30 minutes.

5. Bake at 350° for 25-30 minutes or until golden brown. Combine the confectioners' sugar, orange juice and peel; drizzle over the warm rolls. Refrigerate leftovers.

Yield: 2 dozen.

Editor's Note: To make ahead, prepare, shape and place rolls in baking pans as directed. Cover; refrigerate overnight. Remove rolls from the refrigerator and let stand for 30 minutes. Bake and glaze as directed.

PULL-APART STICKY BUN RING

Moist, sticky and filled with rich maple flavor, this treat tastes as delicious as it looks. The gooey cream cheese inside is sure to get mouths watering.

DOREEN WRIGHT-LAUKAITIS, OXFORD, MASSACHUSETTS

3/4	cup chopped pecans
1/2	cup butter, melted, divided
1/3	cup maple syrup
2	tubes (6 ounces each) refrigerated flaky buttermilk biscuits
1/2	cup sugar
1	teaspoon ground cinnamon
1	package (8 ounces) cream cheese

1. Sprinkle pecans into a greased 10-in. fluted tube pan. In a small bowl, combine 2 tablespoons butter and maple syrup; pour over pecans. Set aside.

2. Separate biscuits; split each in half horizontally. Place remaining butter in a shallow bowl. In another shallow bowl, combine the sugar and ground cinnamon.

3. Cut cream cheese into 20 cubes; roll in sugar mixture. Place one cube in the center of each piece of dough. Fold dough over cheese cube; pinch edges to seal tightly. Dip one side of each biscuit in butter, then sugar mixture.

4. Arrange biscuits in prepared pan, sugar side up. Pour remaining butter over top; sprinkle with remaining sugar mixture. Bake at 375° for 25-30 minutes or until golden brown. Immediately invert onto a serving platter. Serve warm. Refrigerate leftovers.

Yield: 20 servings.

2. In a small bowl, combine flour and sugar; cut in butter until mixture resembles coarse crumbs. Sprinkle over batter.

3. Bake at 350° for 20-25 minutes or until a toothpick inserted near the center comes out clean. Cool for 5 minutes before removing from pans to wire racks. In a small bowl, whisk glaze ingredients; drizzle over warm muffins. Serve warm.

Yield: 40 muffins.

PEACHES 'N' CREAM MUFFINS

Packed with cinnamon and chunks of peaches, these muffins are always a hit and ideal for potluck-style breakfasts. They are very easy to make, and there are never any left over.
CAROLE FRASER, NORTH YORK, ONTARIO

2	cups all-purpose flour
1/4	cup sugar
3	teaspoons baking powder
1	teaspoon ground cinnamon
1/2	teaspoon salt
1	can (15-1/4 ounces) sliced peaches, drained
4	ounces cream cheese
2	eggs
1-1/4	cups milk
1/3	cup honey
1/4	cup butter, melted
1	teaspoon grated lemon peel
1-1/2	cups bran flakes cereal

1. In a large bowl, combine the flour, sugar, baking powder, cinnamon and salt. Cut the peaches and cream cheese into 1/2-in. cubes; set aside.

2. In a bowl, beat eggs, milk, honey, butter and lemon peel until blended. Stir in the bran flakes, peaches and cream cheese. Stir into dry ingredients just until moistened.

3. Fill greased muffin cups three-fourths full. Bake at 400° for 18-20 minutes or until a toothpick comes out clean. Cool for 5 minutes before removing from pans to wire racks.

Yield: 1-1/2 dozen.

LEMON CRUMB MUFFINS

I love to have the dough for these muffins ready and waiting in the refrigerator when company comes. The tender bites bake up in just 20 minutes, and their cake-like texture makes them perfect for breakfast, dessert or snacking.
CLAUDETTE BROWNLEE, KINGFISHER, OKLAHOMA

6	cups all-purpose flour
4	cups sugar
3/4	teaspoon baking soda
3/4	teaspoon salt
8	eggs
2	cups (16 ounces) sour cream
2	cups butter, melted
3	tablespoons grated lemon peel
2	tablespoons lemon juice

TOPPING:

3/4	cup all-purpose flour
3/4	cup sugar
1/4	cup cold butter, cubed

GLAZE:

1/2	cup sugar
1/3	cup lemon juice

1. In a large bowl, combine the flour, sugar, baking soda and salt. In another bowl, combine the eggs, sour cream, butter, lemon peel and juice. Stir into dry ingredients just until moistened. Fill greased or paper-lined muffin cups three-fourths full.

FRUITY BAKED OATMEAL

Here's a baked twist on a breakfast classic. My husband says it's his favorite breakfast treat and the ultimate comfort food. One bite and you'll taste why. It's warm, filling and loaded with flavor. Because it's baked in a pan, it's also great for feeding a crowd.
KAREN SCHROEDER, KANKAKEE, ILLINOIS

3	cups quick-cooking oats
1	cup packed brown sugar
2	teaspoons baking powder
1	teaspoon salt
1/2	teaspoon ground cinnamon
2	eggs, lightly beaten
1	cup fat-free milk
1/2	cup butter, melted
3/4	cup chopped peeled tart apple
1/3	cup each chopped fresh or frozen peaches and fresh or frozen blueberries

Additional fat-free milk, optional

1. In a large bowl, combine the oats, brown sugar, baking powder, salt and cinnamon. Combine the eggs, milk and butter; add to the dry ingredients. Stir in the apple, peaches and blueberries.

2. Pour into an 8-in. square baking dish coated with cooking spray. Bake, uncovered, at 350° for 35-40 minutes or until a knife inserted near the center comes out clean. Cut into squares. Serve with milk if desired.

Yield: 9 servings.

Editor's Note: If using frozen blueberries, use without thawing to avoid discoloring the batter.

OMELET CASSEROLE FOR 60

Not only is this dish simple to make, it's also perfect for a church breakfast or an afternoon brunch. The Swiss cheese and diced ham add nice flavor.

RENEE SCHWEBACH, DUMONT, MINNESOTA

1	cup butter, melted
100	eggs
2-1/2	quarts 2% milk
1-1/4	teaspoons white pepper
7-1/2	cups (30 ounces) shredded Swiss cheese
7-1/2	cups cubed fully cooked ham

1. Divide the butter among five 13-in. x 9-in. baking dishes; set aside. In a large bowl, beat 20 eggs, 2 cups milk and 1/4 teaspoon pepper until blended. Stir in 1-1/2 cups cheese and 1-1/2 cups ham; pour into one prepared dish. Repeat four times.

2. Bake, uncovered, at 350° for 40-45 minutes or until a knife inserted near the center comes out clean (cover with foil if the top browns too quickly). Let stand for 5 minutes before cutting.

Yield: 60 servings.

CHERRY COFFEE CAKE

(pictured at right)

My mother taught me how to cook, and this delightful recipe is from her. Whoever tries it agrees it's the best coffee cake ever invented! It requires no kneading, and you can easily tint the icing any color you want.

GINNIE PATTERSON, TAFT, TENNESSEE

2-1/2	to 3 cups all-purpose flour
1/4	cup sugar
1	package (1/4 ounce) active dry yeast
1	teaspoon salt
1/2	cup water
1/2	cup 2% milk
1/2	cup butter, cubed
2	eggs
1	can (21 ounces) cherry pie filling
GLAZE:	
1/2	cup confectioners' sugar
1/4	teaspoon almond extract
3	to 4 teaspoons 2% milk

1. In a large bowl, combine 1-1/2 cups flour, sugar, yeast and salt. In a small saucepan, heat the water, milk and butter to 120°-130°. Add to dry ingredients; beat just until moistened. Beat in eggs until smooth.

2. Stir in enough remaining flour to form a soft dough (dough will be sticky). Cover and let rise in a warm place until doubled, about 40 minutes.

3. Stir dough down and spoon two-thirds into a greased 13-in. x 9-in. baking pan. Top with pie filling. Drop remaining dough by tablespoonfuls over pie filling. Cover and let rise in a warm place until doubled, about 30 minutes.

4. Bake at 350° for 35-40 minutes or until golden brown. Place pan on a wire rack. Combine the confectioners' sugar, extract and enough milk to achieve a drizzling consistency; drizzle over warm coffee cake.

Yield: 12 servings.

HAM 'N' CHEESE SQUARES

So easy to prepare, this appetizing egg dish is loaded with ham, Swiss cheese and caraway flavor. It cuts nicely into squares, making it an ideal addition to a brunch buffet. Serve it with a brightly colored fresh fruit salad and golden toasted bread.
SUE ROSS, CASA GRANDE, ARIZONA

1-1/2	cups cubed fully cooked ham
1	carton (6 ounces) plain yogurt
1/4	cup crushed saltines (about 6)
1/4	cup shredded Swiss cheese
2	tablespoons butter, melted
2	teaspoons caraway seeds
6	eggs

1. In a large bowl, combine the first six ingredients. In a small bowl, beat eggs until thickened and lemon-colored; fold into ham mixture. Transfer to a greased 8-in. square baking dish.

2. Bake at 375° for 20-25 minutes or until a knife inserted near the center comes out clean. Let stand for 5 minutes before cutting.

Yield: 9 servings.

CINNAMON SWIRL BREAD

A yeast bread that doesn't require kneading? You bet! The cereal in this morning loaf adds moisture and a slight crunch, and the swirled cinnamon filling looks and tastes good.

BETTY LOU WELLMAN, SILVERTON, OREGON

2	packages (1/4 ounce each) active dry yeast
1/2	cup warm water (110° to 115°)
1	cup warm milk (110° to 115°)
1/2	cup butter, softened
1	egg
1/2	cup uncooked Malt-O-Meal cereal
1/3	cup sugar
2	teaspoons salt
4	to 4-1/2 cups all-purpose flour

FILLING:

1	egg white, lightly beaten
1/2	cup sugar
1	tablespoon ground cinnamon

1. In a bowl, dissolve yeast in water. Add milk, butter, egg, cereal, sugar, salt and 2 cups flour; mix until smooth. Stir in enough remaining flour to form a soft dough. Do not knead. Cover and let rise in a warm place until doubled, about 1-1/4 hours.

2. Punch dough down; divide in half. Roll each portion into a 12-in. x 7-in. rectangle. Brush with the egg white.

3. Combine sugar and cinnamon; sprinkle over rectangles. Starting with a short side, roll up tightly and seal edges. Place each in a greased 8-in. x 4-in. loaf pan. Cover and let rise until doubled, about 30 minutes.

4. Bake at 375° for 40-45 minutes or until golden brown. Remove from pans to cool on wire racks.

Yield: 2 loaves.

GRANOLA-TO-GO BARS

This grab-and-go goodie makes a portable breakfast or a hearty snack for a long day out. Chewy and sweet, these fruity oat bars really satisfy!

SALLY HAEN, MENOMONEE FALLS, WISCONSIN

3-1/2	cups quick-cooking oats
1	cup chopped almonds
1	egg, lightly beaten
2/3	cup butter, melted
1/2	cup honey
1	teaspoon vanilla extract
1/2	cup sunflower kernels
1/2	cup flaked coconut
1/2	cup chopped dried apples
1/2	cup dried cranberries
1/2	cup packed brown sugar
1/2	teaspoon ground cinnamon

1. Combine oats and almonds in a 15-in. x 10-in. x 1-in. baking pan coated with cooking spray. Bake at 350° for 15 minutes or until toasted, stirring occasionally.

2. In a large bowl, combine the egg, butter, honey and vanilla. Stir in the sunflower kernels, coconut, apples, cranberries, brown sugar and cinnamon. Stir in oat mixture.

3. Press into a 15-in. x 10-in. x 1-in. baking pan coated with cooking spray. Bake at 350° for 13-18 minutes or until set and edges are lightly browned. Cool on a wire rack. Cut into bars. Store in an airtight container.

Yield: 3 dozen.

SUNNY MORNING DOUGHNUTS

I love doughnuts, but buying them can get expensive. This recipe is economical and so delicious. My family thinks it beats any store-bought variety.

SHERRY FLAQUEL, CUTLER BAY, FLORIDA

4-1/2	to 5 cups all-purpose flour
1-1/4	cups sugar
4	teaspoons baking powder
1	teaspoon salt
3	eggs, lightly beaten
1	cup 2% milk
1/4	cup canola oil
2	tablespoons orange juice
4	teaspoons grated orange peel

Oil for deep-fat frying
Confectioners' sugar

1. In a large bowl, combine 4-1/2 cups flour, sugar, baking powder and salt.

2. Combine the eggs, milk, oil, orange juice and peel; stir into dry ingredients just until moistened. Stir in enough remaining flour to form a soft dough. Cover and refrigerate for at least 1 hour.

3. Turn onto a floured surface; roll to 1/2-in. thickness. Cut with a floured 2-1/2-in. doughnut cutter.

4. In an electric skillet or deep-fat fryer, heat oil to 375°. Fry doughnuts, a few at a time, until golden brown on both sides. Drain on paper towels. Dust warm doughnuts with confectioners' sugar.

Yield: 20 doughnuts.

STREUSEL-TOPPED BLUEBERRY MUFFINS

My sister gave me this recipe and it has become one of my favorites. If you enjoy blueberries, don't pass it up!

BRENDA HOFFMAN, STANTON, MICHIGAN

1	cup sugar
1	tablespoon butter, softened
1	egg
1	cup (8 ounces) sour cream
2	cups all-purpose flour
1/2	teaspoon baking powder
1/2	teaspoon baking soda
1	cup fresh or frozen blueberries

TOPPING:

1/2	cup packed brown sugar
1/3	cup all-purpose flour
1/4	cup cold butter, cubed

GLAZE:

1/2	cup confectioners' sugar
1-1/2	teaspoons water
1/4	teaspoon vanilla extract

1. In a large bowl, mix sugar and butter until crumbly, about 2 minutes. Add egg and sour cream; mix well. Combine the flour, baking powder and baking soda; add to sugar mixture just until combined. Fold in blueberries.

2. Fill paper-lined muffin cups two-thirds full. For topping, combine brown sugar and flour in a small bowl; cut in butter until crumbly. Sprinkle over batter.

3. Bake at 350° for 20 minutes or until a toothpick inserted near the center comes out clean. Cool 5 minutes before removing from pan to a wire rack. Combine glaze ingredients; drizzle over muffins.

Yield: 1 dozen.

Editor's Note: If using frozen blueberries, use without thawing to avoid discoloring the batter.

LEMON RASPBERRY JUMBO MUFFINS

I work as a barista in my family's business and am also the baker in the cafe. This is one of the popular muffins I make. The customers love them.

LAURA SIEGRIST, JERMYN, PENNSYLVANIA

1/2	cup butter, softened
1-1/4	cups sugar
4	eggs
1	cup buttermilk
1	teaspoon vanilla extract
3	cups all-purpose flour
1	teaspoon baking powder
1/2	teaspoon baking soda
1/2	teaspoon salt
1-1/4	cups fresh or frozen raspberries
3	teaspoons grated lemon peel

GLAZE:

1	cup confectioners' sugar
3	to 4 tablespoons lemon juice

1. In a large bowl, cream butter and sugar until light and fluffy. Add eggs, one at a time, beating well after each addition. Stir in buttermilk and vanilla. Combine the flour, baking powder, baking soda and salt; add to creamed mixture just until moistened. Fold in raspberries and lemon peel.

2. Fill paper-lined jumbo muffin cups half full. Bake at 350° for 23-28 minutes or until a toothpick comes out clean. Cool for 5 minutes before removing from pan to a wire rack. Combine glaze ingredients; drizzle over warm muffins.

Yield: 1 dozen.

Editor's Note: If using frozen raspberries, use without thawing to avoid discoloring the batter.

PEACHES & CREAM FRENCH TOAST

Wake up your sleepyheads with the wonderfully warm aroma of peaches and brown sugar in this delectable breakfast bake.

SUSAN WESTERFIELD, ALBUQUERQUE, NEW MEXICO

1	cup packed brown sugar
1/2	cup butter, cubed
2	tablespoons corn syrup
1	can (29 ounces) sliced peaches, drained
1	loaf (1 pound) day-old French bread, cubed
1	package (8 ounces) cream cheese, cubed
12	eggs
1-1/2	cups half-and-half cream
1	teaspoon vanilla extract

1. In a small saucepan, combine the brown sugar, butter and corn syrup. Cook and stir over medium heat until sugar is dissolved; pour into a greased 13-in. x 9-in. baking dish.

2. Arrange peaches in dish. Place half of the bread cubes over peaches. Layer with cream cheese and remaining bread. Place the eggs, cream and vanilla in a blender; cover and process until smooth. Pour over top. Cover and refrigerate overnight.

3. Remove from the refrigerator 30 minutes before baking. Bake, uncovered, at 350° for 50-60 minutes or until a knife inserted near the center comes out clean.

Yield: 12 servings.

PECAN-RAISIN CINNAMON ROLLS

(pictured at left)

The tempting aroma of these freshly baked cinnamon rolls always sells them! I bake hundreds for two annual fundraising events in our community.

MARVEL IRVINE, ALTA, CALIFORNIA

11	to 12 cups all-purpose flour
3/4	cup sugar
3	packages (1/4 ounce each) active dry yeast
3	teaspoons salt
3-1/2	cups water
1	cup canola oil
3	eggs

FILLING:

1/4	cup butter, melted
1	cup sugar
3	teaspoons ground cinnamon
1	cup chopped pecans
1	cup raisins

FROSTING:

1/4	cup butter, softened
3-3/4	cups confectioners' sugar
1	teaspoon vanilla extract
1/4	teaspoon lemon extract
3	to 4 tablespoons water

1. In a very large bowl, combine 8 cups flour, sugar, yeast and salt. In a large saucepan, heat water and oil to 120°-130°. Add to dry ingredients; beat just until moistened. Add eggs; beat until smooth. Stir in enough remaining flour to form a soft dough (dough will be sticky).

2. Turn onto a floured surface; knead until smooth and elastic, about 6-8 minutes. Cover and let rest for 15 minutes.

3. Turn onto a lightly floured surface; divide in half. Roll each half into a 24-in. x 15-in. rectangle. Brush with butter to within 1/2 in. of edges. Combine sugar and cinnamon; sprinkle over dough. Sprinkle with pecans and raisins.

4. Roll up jelly-roll style, starting with the long sides; pinch seams to seal. Cut each into 24 rolls. Place rolls, cut side up, in four greased 13-in. x 9-in. baking pans.

5. Cover and let rise in a warm place until nearly doubled, about 30 minutes. Bake at 425° for 18-22 minutes until golden brown.

6. In a small bowl, combine the butter, confectioners' sugar, extracts and enough water to achieve spreading consistency. Spread over warm rolls. Cool on wire racks.

Yield: 4 dozen.

Editor's Note: Dough may need to be mixed in two batches, depending on the size of your mixing bowl. To halve the recipe, use 1 package plus 1-1/8 teaspoons yeast and 1 egg plus 2 tablespoons beaten egg. The other ingredients can easily be divided in half.

BISCUIT EGG BAKE

Determined to come up with a brunch dish that didn't keep me in the kitchen all morning, I created this casserole made with everyone's favorite ingredients.

JENNY FLAKE, NEWPORT BEACH, CALIFORNIA

1	tube (16.3 ounces) large refrigerated buttermilk biscuits
12	eggs
1	cup milk
1	cup chopped fresh tomatoes
1/2	cup chopped green onions
1	can (4 ounces) chopped green chilies
1	teaspoon salt
1/2	teaspoon pepper
1/2	teaspoon salt-free garlic seasoning blend
1	package (2.1 ounces) ready-to-serve fully cooked bacon, diced
2	cups (8 ounces) shredded cheddar cheese

1. Separate biscuits. Cut each biscuit into fourths; arrange in a greased 13-in. x 9-in. baking dish.

2. In a large bowl, whisk the eggs, milk, tomatoes, onions, chilies, salt, pepper and seasoning blend. Pour over biscuits. Sprinkle with bacon and cheese.

3. Bake, uncovered, at 350° for 40-45 minutes or until a thermometer reads 160°.

Yield: 10-12 servings.

skillet. Lift and tilt pan to coat bottom evenly. Cook until top appears dry; turn and cook 15-20 seconds longer.

4. Remove crepe to a wire rack. Repeat with remaining batter, greasing skillet as needed. When cool, stack the crepes with waxed paper or paper towels in between.

5. Line greased muffin cups with crepes; fill two-thirds full with sausage mixture. Bake at 350° for 15 minutes. Cover loosely with foil; bake 10-15 minutes longer or until a knife inserted near the center comes out clean.

Yield: 16 crepe cups.

CREPE QUICHE CUPS

I enjoy trying new recipes, especially when entertaining family and friends. These unique crepe cups hold a delicious sausage-and-egg filling that's perfect for a special brunch.
SHERYL RILEY, UNIONVILLE, MISSOURI

2	eggs
1	cup plus 2 tablespoons milk
2	tablespoons butter, melted
1	cup all-purpose flour
1/8	teaspoon salt

FILLING:

1/2	pound bulk pork sausage
1/4	cup chopped onion
3	eggs
1/2	cup milk
1/2	cup mayonnaise
2	cups (8 ounces) shredded cheddar cheese

1. For crepe batter, in a bowl, beat the eggs, milk and butter. Combine flour and salt; add to egg mixture and mix well. Cover and refrigerate for 1 hour.

2. In a small skillet, cook sausage and onion over medium heat until meat is no longer pink; drain. In a large bowl, whisk the eggs, milk and mayonnaise. Stir in sausage mixture and cheese; set aside.

3. Heat a lightly greased 8-in. nonstick skillet. Stir crepe batter; pour 2 tablespoons into center of

TURKEY SAUSAGE PATTIES

I developed this recipe as a way to deter my husband from eating pork sausage. The mixture also works well for making meatballs and burgers.
YVONNE WOODRUFF, SACRAMENTO, CALIFORNIA

2	eggs
2/3	cup seasoned bread crumbs
1	small onion, finely chopped
2	tablespoons Worcestershire sauce
3	garlic cloves, minced
2	teaspoons garlic salt
2	teaspoons dried thyme
2	teaspoons ground cumin
1/2	teaspoon crushed red pepper flakes
1/2	teaspoon pepper
1/8	teaspoon ground nutmeg
2	pounds lean ground turkey
5	teaspoons canola oil, divided

1. In a large bowl, combine the first 11 ingredients. Crumble turkey over mixture and mix well. Shape into thirty 2-1/2-in. patties.

2. Heat 1 teaspoon oil in a large skillet over medium heat. Cook patties in batches over medium heat for 2-3 minutes on each side or until a meat thermometer reads 165° and juices run clear, using remaining oil as needed.

Yield: 2-1/2 dozen.

VEGETARIAN EGG STRATA

I used to make this hearty strata with turkey or chicken sausage, but adapted it for a vegetarian friend. It was a huge hit. Since then, I serve it without meat alongside fresh breads or bagels and a big mixed salad.

DANNA ROGERS, WESTPORT, CONNECTICUT

1	medium zucchini, finely chopped
1	medium sweet red pepper, finely chopped
1	cup sliced baby portobello mushrooms
1	medium red onion, finely chopped
2	teaspoons olive oil
3	garlic cloves, minced
2	teaspoons minced fresh thyme or 1/2 teaspoon dried thyme
1/2	teaspoon salt
1/4	teaspoon pepper
1	loaf (1 pound) day-old French bread, cubed
2	packages (5.3 ounces each) fresh goat cheese, crumbled
1-3/4	cups grated Parmesan cheese
6	eggs
2	cups fat-free milk
1/4	teaspoon ground nutmeg

1. In a large skillet, saute the zucchini, red pepper, mushrooms and onion in oil until tender. Add the garlic, thyme, salt and pepper; saute 2 minutes longer.

2. In a 13-in. x 9-in. baking dish coated with cooking spray, layer half of the bread cubes, zucchini mixture, goat cheese and Parmesan cheese. Repeat layers.

3. In a small bowl, whisk the eggs, milk and nutmeg. Pour over top. Cover and refrigerate overnight.

4. Remove from the refrigerator 30 minutes before baking. Bake, uncovered, at 350° for 45-50 minutes or until a knife inserted near the center comes out clean. Let stand for 10 minutes before cutting.

Yield: 12 servings.

ANISE FRUIT BOWL

The anise flavor in this colorful medley has made it a favorite. Try serving the fruit with cake and whipped cream for dessert.

JUANITA STONE, GRAHAM, NORTH CAROLINA

2	cups water
1-1/2	cups sugar
3	tablespoons lemon juice
2	tablespoons aniseed
1/2	teaspoon salt
1	fresh pineapple, peeled and cubed
1	small cantaloupe, peeled, seeded and cubed
1/2	pound seedless red grapes
2	large bananas, sliced
2	medium nectarines, sliced
2	medium oranges, peeled and sectioned
2	medium kiwifruit, peeled and sliced
1	large pink grapefruit, peeled and sectioned

1. In a large saucepan, bring water, sugar, lemon juice, aniseed and salt to a boil. Reduce heat; simmer for 10-15 minutes or until slightly thickened. Cool slightly; cover and refrigerate until chilled.

2. In a bowl, combine the remaining ingredients. Pour syrup over fruit; toss to coat. Refrigerate until serving. Serve with a slotted spoon.

Yield: 18 servings (3/4 cup).

DELUXE BREAKFAST BAKE

My husband and three sons love this rich and creamy egg bake because it satifies their big appetites. I like it because it's so versatile, allowing me to use what I have on hand, and can be prepared ahead of time.

LAVONNE HEGLAND, SAINT MICHAEL, MINNESOTA

1	package (6 ounces) onion and garlic salad croutons
2	cups (8 ounces) shredded cheddar cheese
1-1/2	cups cubed fully cooked ham
4	eggs
2-3/4	cups milk, divided
3/4	teaspoon ground mustard
1	can (10-3/4 ounces) condensed cream of mushroom soup, undiluted
1	package (26 ounces) frozen shredded hash brown potatoes, thawed
1/2	teaspoon paprika
1/4	teaspoon pepper

1. Place croutons in a greased 3-qt. baking dish. Sprinkle with cheese and ham. In a large bowl, whisk the eggs, 2-1/4 cups milk and mustard; pour over ham and cheese. Cover and refrigerate overnight.

2. Remove from the refrigerator 30 minutes before baking. Combine soup and remaining milk until blended; spread over casserole. Top with hash browns; sprinkle with paprika and pepper.

3. Cover and bake at 350° for 30 minutes. Uncover; bake 35-40 minutes longer or until a knife inserted near the center comes out clean. Let stand for 10 minutes before serving.

Yield: 12 servings.

2. In a large bowl, combine the eggs, milk and seasonings. Pour over casserole. Cover and refrigerate overnight.

3. Remove from the refrigerator 30 minutes before baking. Bake, uncovered, at 375° for 45-55 minutes or until a knife inserted near the center comes out clean (cover loosely with foil if top browns too quickly). Let stand for 10 minutes before cutting.

Yield: 12 servings.

BROCCOLI CHEDDAR BRUNCH BAKE

This slimmed-down version of a favorite brunch recipe is hearty, wholesome and boasts all the gourmet flavor of the original!

CARLA WEEKS, INDEPENDENCE, IOWA

6	tablespoons reduced-fat butter, cubed
8	cups chopped fresh broccoli
1	cup finely chopped onion
6	eggs, beaten
1-1/2	cups egg substitute
1-1/2	cups (6 ounces) shredded sharp cheddar cheese, divided
1	cup fat-free milk
1	cup half-and-half cream
1	teaspoon salt
1	teaspoon pepper

1. In a Dutch oven, melt butter. Add broccoli and onion; saute until crisp-tender. In a large bowl, combine the eggs, egg substitute, 1 cup cheese, milk, cream, salt and pepper. Stir in broccoli mixture. Pour into a 3-qt. baking dish coated with cooking spray.

2. Bake, uncovered, at 350° for 40-45 minutes or until a knife inserted near the center comes out clean. Sprinkle with remaining cheese. Let stand for 10 minutes before serving.

Yield: 12 servings.

Editor's Note: This recipe was tested with Land O'Lakes light stick butter.

BACON SPINACH STRATA

Full of flavor, this make-ahead breakfast dish is pretty enough for any brunch buffet. It disappears in minutes. And being able to prepare it the night before makes handling hectic mornings a snap!

KRIS KEBISEK, BROOKFIELD, WISCONSIN

1	package (8 ounces) sliced mushrooms
1	bunch green onions, sliced
2	teaspoons canola oil
1	loaf (1 pound) day old bread, cut into 3/4-inch cubes, divided
1	cup (4 ounces) shredded Swiss cheese, divided
1	package (1 pound) sliced bacon, cooked and crumbled
2	cups (8 ounces) shredded cheddar cheese
1	package (10 ounces) frozen chopped spinach, thawed and squeezed dry
9	eggs
3	cups milk
1/2	teaspoon each onion powder, garlic powder and ground mustard
1/4	teaspoon salt
1/4	teaspoon pepper

1. In a large skillet, saute mushrooms and onions in oil until tender. Place half of the bread cubes and 1/2 cup Swiss cheese in a greased 13-in. x 9-in. baking dish. Layer with bacon, cheddar cheese, mushroom mixture, spinach and remaining Swiss cheese and bread cubes.

HAM AND SPINACH CREPES

(pictured at left)

Corn bread crepes hold a creamy, ham-and-cheese filling in this special brunch item. I appreciate that they're made the night before. In the morning, I just pop them in the oven!

DIANE NEMITZ, LUDINGTON, MICHIGAN

1-1/2	cups milk
1	cup water
5	eggs
1/4	cup canola oil
2	cups all-purpose flour
1	package (8-1/2 ounces) corn bread/muffin mix

FILLING:

4	green onions, chopped
2	tablespoons butter
1	pound finely chopped fully cooked ham
2	packages (10 ounces each) frozen chopped spinach, thawed and squeezed dry
2	packages (8 ounces each) reduced-fat cream cheese, cubed
2	tablespoons Dijon mustard
1/2	teaspoon ground nutmeg
1/8	teaspoon pepper

TOPPING:

3/4	cup dry bread crumbs
2	tablespoons butter, melted
2	tablespoons grated Parmesan cheese

1. In a bowl, whisk the milk, water, eggs and oil. Combine flour and corn bread mix; add to egg mixture and mix well. Cover and refrigerate for 1 hour.

2. For filling, in a large skillet, saute onions in butter until tender. Add the ham, spinach, cream cheese, mustard, nutmeg and pepper. Cook and stir until cheese is melted. Remove from the heat; keep warm.

3. Heat a lightly greased 8-in. nonstick skillet over medium heat; pour 3 tablespoons batter into center of skillet. Lift and tilt pan to evenly coat bottom. Cook until top appears dry; turn and cook 15-20 seconds longer. Remove to a wire rack. Repeat with remaining batter, greasing skillet as needed.

4. Spoon about 3 tablespoons of filling down the center of 22 crepes (save remaining crepes for another use). Roll up and place seam side down in two 13-in. x 9-in. baking dishes. Cover and refrigerate overnight.

5. Remove from the refrigerator 30 minutes before baking. Cover and bake at 350° for 20 minutes.

6. Combine topping ingredients. Remove foil; sprinkle topping over crepes. Bake 5 minutes longer or until heated through.

Yield: 11 servings.

LEMON-POPPY SEED DOUGHNUT HOLES

The tender texture and light lemon flavor of these irresistible gems make them a hit at breakfasts and brunches.

LEE ELROD, NEWNAN, GEORGIA

1-1/2	cups all-purpose flour
3	tablespoons poppy seeds
1-1/2	teaspoons baking powder
1/2	teaspoon salt
2	eggs
1/2	cup sugar
1/4	cup buttermilk
3	tablespoons butter, melted
1	tablespoon grated lemon peel
1	teaspoon vanilla extract

Oil for deep-fat frying

GLAZE:

2	cups confectioners' sugar
5	tablespoons lemon juice

1. In a large bowl, combine the flour, poppy seeds, baking powder and salt. In a small bowl, combine the eggs, sugar, buttermilk, butter, lemon peel and vanilla; stir into dry ingredients just until combined. Cover and refrigerate for at least 1 hour.

2. In an electric skillet or deep fryer, heat oil to 375°. Drop tablespoonfuls of batter, a few at a time, into hot oil. Fry until golden brown on both sides. Drain on paper towels.

3. For glaze, in a small bowl, combine confectioners' sugar and lemon juice. Drizzle over doughnut holes.

Yield: about 2 dozen.

BRUNCH PIZZA

(pictured at right)

This is one of our favorite breakfast dishes! Filling and satisfying with all the veggies, it brings raves whenever I serve it to guests. It's a sure-to-please brunch idea.

MARTY SCHWARTZ, SARASOTA, FLORIDA

1	tube (8 ounces) refrigerated crescent rolls
1/2	pound bacon strips, chopped
1/2	pound bulk pork sausage
1/2	pound sliced fresh mushrooms
1	small onion, finely chopped
1	small green pepper, finely chopped
1	tablespoon butter
8	eggs, lightly beaten
1	package (3 ounces) cream cheese, softened
1/3	cup sour cream
1	garlic clove, minced
1/4	teaspoon Italian seasoning
2	plum tomatoes, chopped
1-1/2	cups (6 ounces) shredded part-skim mozzarella cheese
	Picante sauce and additional sour cream, optional

1. Unroll crescent dough into a greased 13-in. x 9-in. baking dish; seal seams and perforations. Bake at 375° for 6-8 minutes or until golden brown.

2. Meanwhile, in a small skillet, cook bacon and sausage over medium heat until bacon is crisp and sausage is no longer pink. Using a slotted spoon, remove meat to paper towels; drain, reserving 2 tablespoons drippings. In the drippings, saute the mushrooms, onion and green pepper. Remove and set aside.

3. Heat butter in a large skillet over medium heat. Add eggs; cook and stir until almost set.

4. In a small bowl, beat the cream cheese, sour cream, garlic and Italian seasoning; spread over crust. Layer with eggs, sausage and bacon, sauteed vegetables, tomatoes and mozzarella.

5. Bake at 375° for 15-18 minutes or until cheese is melted. Serve with picante sauce and additional sour cream if desired.

Yield: 12 pieces.

FETA BREAKFAST BAKE

Guests at our family's bed-and-breakfast love this easy-prep brunch item. You can try several variations of the egg dish with your favorite types of cheese. Add a sprig of oregano as a pretty garnish.

CHERYL RUDE, WINFIELD, KANSAS

4	cups seasoned salad croutons
1-1/2	cups (6 ounces) crumbled feta cheese
8	eggs, lightly beaten
4	cups milk
1	tablespoon minced fresh basil or 1 teaspoon dried basil
1	tablespoon minced fresh oregano or 1 teaspoon dried oregano
1/4	teaspoon pepper
1-1/2	cups cubed fully cooked ham

1. In a large bowl, combine croutons and feta cheese; transfer to a greased 13-in. x 9-in. baking dish. In a large bowl, whisk the eggs, milk, basil, oregano and pepper. Slowly pour over crouton mixture. Sprinkle with ham.

2. Bake, uncovered, at 325° for 60-65 minutes or until a knife inserted near the center comes out clean. Let stand for 10 minutes before cutting.

Yield: 12-14 servings.

Bring Out the Flavor

Want to bring out the flavor in dried herbs? Put the desired amount in the palm of your hand, then rub your hands together over the pot, letting the herbs fall into the dish. This releases the oils in the herbs for best flavor.

broccoli-cauliflower cheese bake, pg. 100

southwest corn bread salad, pg. 107

Sides & Salads

God our Father, Lord and Savior, thank you for your love and favor. Bless this food and drink we pray, and all who share with us today.

FABULOUS FRUIT SALAD

I first made this fruit medley for a reunion, and now it's a request for all family gatherings. The sweet and tangy lemonade-pudding coating goes well with any fruit, so feel free to mix and match your favorites.

RHONDA EADS, JASPER, INDIANA

1	medium honeydew, peeled, seeded and cubed
1	medium cantaloupe, peeled, seeded and cubed
2	cups cubed seedless watermelon
2	medium peaches, peeled and sliced
2	medium nectarines, sliced
1	cup seedless red grapes
1	cup halved fresh strawberries
1	can (11 ounces) mandarin oranges, drained
2	medium kiwifruit, peeled, halved and sliced
2	medium firm bananas, sliced
1	large Granny Smith apple, cubed
1	can (12 ounces) frozen lemonade concentrate, thawed
1	package (3.4 ounces) instant vanilla pudding mix

1. In a large bowl, combine the first nine ingredients. Cover and refrigerate for at least 1 hour.

2. Just before serving, stir in bananas and apple. Combine lemonade concentrate and dry pudding mix; pour over fruit and toss to coat.

Yield: 20 servings (3/4 cup each).

CHEESY CARROT CASSEROLE

Carrots become everyone's favorite vegetable when they're dressed in this cheesy sauce and baked to perfection.

CAROL WILSON, DIXON, ILLINOIS

4	pounds carrots, cut into 1/2-inch slices
1-1/4	cups chopped onions
11	tablespoons butter, divided
5	tablespoons all-purpose flour
1/2	teaspoon salt
1/2	teaspoon celery salt
1/2	teaspoon ground mustard
1/8	teaspoon pepper
2-1/2	cups milk
10	ounces process cheese (Velveeta), cubed
5-1/2	cups cubed day-old bread

1. Place carrots in a Dutch oven and cover with water; bring to a boil. Reduce heat; cover and simmer until tender, about 10 minutes. Drain and set aside.

2. In a large saucepan, saute onions in 4 tablespoons butter until tender. Stir in the flour, salt, celery salt, mustard and pepper until blended. Gradually add milk. Bring to a boil; cook and stir for 2 minutes. Stir in cheese until melted. Add carrots and stir to coat.

3. Transfer to a greased 13-in. x 9-in. baking dish. Melt remaining butter; toss with bread cubes. Sprinkle over the carrots. Bake, uncovered, at 350° for 40-50 minutes or until heated through.

Yield: 18 servings.

Fruit Salad in a Flash

Save time by using an ice cream scoop or melon baller to remove the fleshy fruit from a melon. Cut the melon in half lengthwise, remove the seeds, and then start scooping. In a few minutes, you'll be finished!

BALSAMIC GREEN BEAN SALAD

Serve up green beans in a whole new way! The tangy flavors and crunch of this eye-appealing side complement any special meal or holiday potluck.
MEGAN SPENCER, FARMINGTON HILLS, MICHIGAN

2	pounds fresh green beans, trimmed and cut into 1-1/2-inch pieces
1/4	cup olive oil
3	tablespoons lemon juice
3	tablespoons balsamic vinegar
1/4	teaspoon salt
1/4	teaspoon garlic powder
1/4	teaspoon ground mustard
1/8	teaspoon pepper
1	large red onion, chopped
4	cups cherry tomatoes, halved
1	cup (4 ounces) crumbled feta cheese

1. Place beans in a Dutch oven and cover with water. Bring to a boil. Cover and cook for 8-10 minutes or until crisp-tender. Drain and immediately place beans in ice water. Drain and pat dry.

2. In a small bowl, whisk the oil, lemon juice, vinegar, salt, garlic powder, mustard and pepper. Drizzle over beans. Add the onion; toss to coat. Cover and refrigerate for at least 1 hour. Just before serving, stir in tomatoes and cheese.

Yield: 16 servings.

CREAMED GARDEN POTATOES AND PEAS

New potatoes and peas are given a creamy, delectable treatment in this special side dish.
JANE UPHOFF, CUNNINGHAM, KANSAS

2	pounds small red potatoes, quartered
3	cups fresh or frozen peas
1	cup water
2	tablespoons chopped onion
2	tablespoons butter
3	tablespoons plus 1 teaspoon all-purpose flour
1-1/2	teaspoons salt
1/4	teaspoon pepper
2	cups 2% milk
1	cup half-and-half cream

1. Place potatoes in a large saucepan and cover with water. Bring to a boil. Reduce heat; cover and simmer for 8-12 minutes or until tender. Drain.

2. Meanwhile, place peas and water in a small saucepan. Bring to a boil. Reduce heat; cover and simmer for 3-5 minutes or until tender. Drain.

3. In a large saucepan, saute onion in butter until tender. Stir in the flour, salt and pepper until blended; gradually add milk and cream. Bring to a boil; cook and stir for 2 minutes or until thickened. Stir in potatoes and peas; heat through.

Yield: 12 servings.

CRUNCHY POMEGRANATE SALAD

Here's an out-of-the-ordinary dish to complement your next meal. Add sliced banana, mandarin oranges or pineapple, too!

JAN OLPIN, SALT LAKE CITY, UTAH

2	cups heavy whipping cream
1/4	cup sugar
2	teaspoons vanilla extract
2-1/2	cups pomegranate seeds (about 2 pomegranates)
2	medium apples, peeled and cubed
1	cup chopped pecans, toasted

1. In a large bowl, beat cream until it begins to thicken. Add sugar and vanilla; beat until stiff peaks form.

2. Fold in pomegranate seeds and apples. Sprinkle with pecans. Serve immediately.

Yield: 16 servings (1/2 cup each).

BROCCOLI-CAULIFLOWER CHEESE BAKE

(pictured at right)

Creamy mozzarella and Swiss cheeses create the base for these tasty veggies, while a hint of cayenne pepper gives a delightful kick.

JENN TIDWELL, FAIR OAKS, CALIFORNIA

7	cups fresh cauliflowerets
6	cups fresh broccoli florets
3	tablespoons butter
1/3	cup all-purpose flour
1-1/2	teaspoons spicy brown mustard
3/4	teaspoon salt
1/4	teaspoon ground nutmeg
1/4	teaspoon cayenne pepper
1/4	teaspoon pepper
3-3/4	cups fat-free milk
1-1/2	cups (6 ounces) shredded part-skim mozzarella cheese, divided
1-1/2	cups (6 ounces) shredded Swiss cheese, divided

1. Place cauliflower and broccoli in a Dutch oven; add 1 in. of water. Bring to a boil. Reduce heat; cover and simmer for 3-5 minutes or until crisp-tender. Drain; transfer to a 13-in. x 9-in. baking dish coated with cooking spray.

2. In small saucepan, melt butter. Stir in the flour, mustard, salt, nutmeg, cayenne and pepper until smooth; gradually add milk. Bring to a boil; cook and stir for 1-2 minutes or until thickened.

3. Stir in 1-1/4 cups each mozzarella and Swiss cheeses until melted. Pour over vegetables. Bake, uncovered, at 400° for 15-20 minutes or until bubbly. Sprinkle with remaining cheeses. Bake 5 minutes longer or until golden brown.

Yield: 16 servings.

Waste Not, Want Not

When a recipe calls for broccoli florets, slice the stems into thin rounds, then place them in freezer bags. The next time you make vegetable soup, pull them out of the freezer and toss 'em in.

GRILLED THREE-POTATO SALAD

Everyone in our extended family loves to cook, so I put together all of our favorite recipes in a cookbook to be handed down from generation to generation. This recipe comes from the cookbook. It's a delicious twist on traditional potato salad.
SUZETTE JURY, KEENE, CALIFORNIA

3/4	pound Yukon Gold potatoes
3/4	pound red potatoes
1	medium sweet potato, peeled
1/2	cup thinly sliced green onions
1/4	cup canola oil
2	to 3 tablespoons white wine vinegar
1	tablespoon Dijon mustard
1	teaspoon salt
1/2	teaspoon celery seed
1/4	teaspoon pepper

1. Place all of the potatoes in a Dutch oven; cover with water. Bring to a boil. Reduce heat; cover and simmer for 15-20 minutes or until tender. Drain and rinse in cold water. Cut into 1-in. chunks.

2. Place the potatoes in a grill wok or basket. Grill, uncovered, over medium heat for 8-12 minutes or browned, stirring frequently. Transfer to a large salad bowl; add onions.

3. In a small bowl, whisk the oil, vinegar, mustard, salt, celery seed and pepper. Drizzle over potato mixture and toss to coat. Serve warm or at room temperature.

Yield: 6 servings.

HEARTY BAKED BEANS

This saucy and flavorful dish is chock-full of ground beef, bacon and four varieties of beans.
CATHY SWANCUTT, JUNCTION CITY, OREGON

1	pound ground beef
2	large onions, chopped
3/4	pound sliced bacon, cooked and crumbled
4	cans (15 ounces each) pork and beans
1	bottle (18 ounces) honey barbecue sauce
1	can (16 ounces) kidney beans, rinsed and drained
1	can (15-1/4 ounces) lima beans, rinsed and drained
1	can (15 ounces) black beans, rinsed and drained
1/2	cup packed brown sugar
3	tablespoons cider vinegar
1	tablespoon Liquid Smoke, optional
1	teaspoon salt
1/2	teaspoon pepper

1. In a large skillet, cook beef and onions over medium heat until meat is no longer pink; drain. Transfer to a 5-qt. Dutch oven. Stir in the remaining ingredients.

2. Cover and bake at 350° for 1 hour or until heated through.

Yield: 18 servings.

VANILLA-LIME FRUIT SALAD

Feel free to be creative with the fruits you use in this recipe. The versatile dressing is amazing tossed with fresh strawberries or even drizzled over pound cake.
KATE DAMPIER, QUAIL VALLEY, CALIFORNIA

1/2	cup sugar
1/2	cup water
1-1/2	teaspoons light corn syrup
1/2	vanilla bean
2	tablespoons lime juice
1-1/2	teaspoons grated lime peel
3	cups cubed fresh pineapple
2	large navel oranges, peeled and sectioned
1	large grapefruit, peeled and sectioned
4	cups fresh blueberries

1. In a saucepan, combine the sugar, water and corn syrup. With a sharp knife, scrape the vanilla bean to remove the seeds; stir into pan. Discard bean.

2. Bring to a boil. Reduce heat; simmer for 20 minutes or until reduced by half. Remove from the heat; cool for 10 minutes. Stir in lime juice and peel.

3. In a bowl, combine the pineapple, oranges, grapefruit and blueberries. Drizzle with vanilla-lime sauce and toss to coat. Refrigerate until chilled.

Yield: 16 servings.

2. Grill, covered, over medium heat for 20-25 minutes or until corn is tender, turning once. Open carefully to allow steam to escape.

Yield: 8 servings.

VEGGIE POTLUCK SALAD

With its slightly sweet, slightly tart flavors, this veggie medley acts as a delicious reminder of many great family reunions.

BETH BRUNSON, ELLENSBURG, WASHINGTON

6	cups fresh cauliflowerets
6	cups fresh broccoli florets
1	medium cucumber, quartered and sliced
3	green onions, sliced
1/2	cup sugar
1/2	cup cider vinegar
1/2	cup canola oil
1/3	cup cucumber ranch salad dressing

1. In a large bowl, combine the cauliflower, broccoli, cucumber and onions.

2. In a small bowl, combine sugar and vinegar; gradually whisk in oil and salad dressing. Pour over salad; toss to coat. Chill until serving.

Yield: 18 servings (3/4 cup each).

GRILLED VEGETABLE MEDLEY

This is our favorite way to fix summer vegetables. Cleanup is a breeze because the veggies cook in foil. It goes from garden to table in under an hour.

LORI DANIELS, BEVERLY, WEST VIRGINIA

1/4	cup olive oil
1	teaspoon salt
1	teaspoon dried parsley flakes
1	teaspoon dried basil
3	large ears fresh corn on the cob, cut into 3-inch pieces
2	medium zucchini, cut into 1/4-inch slices
1	medium yellow summer squash, cut into 1/4-inch slices
1	medium sweet onion, sliced
1	large green pepper, diced
10	cherry tomatoes
1	jar (4-1/2 ounces) whole mushrooms, drained
1/4	cup butter

1. In a large bowl, combine the oil, salt, parsley and basil. Add vegetables and toss to coat. Place on a double thickness of heavy-duty foil (about 28 in. x 18 in.). Dot with butter. Fold foil around vegetables and seal tightly.

PESTO PASTA MEDLEY

This was a favorite recipe at the prep school where I used to work. I always receive complements and requests for it.
BETH LEPORE, WINCHESTER, MASSACHUSETTS

- 3 packages (7 ounces each) dried cheese tortellini
- 1 package (12 ounces) tricolor spiral pasta
- 1 can (14 ounces) water-packed artichoke hearts, rinsed, drained and quartered
- 2 jars (3-1/2 ounces each) prepared pesto
- 1 jar (6 ounces) oil-packed sun-dried tomatoes, drained and chopped
- 1/2 teaspoon salt

Grated Parmesan cheese, optional

1. Cook tortellini and spiral pasta according to directions; drain and place in a serving bowl.

2. Add artichokes, pesto, tomatoes and salt. Sprinkle with cheese if desired. Serve warm.

Yield: 16 servings.

BROCCOLI SUPREME

Even those who claim they don't like broccoli will enjoy the rich, comforting flavor of this hearty side.
LUCY PARKS, BIRMINGHAM, ALABAMA

- 2 tablespoons all-purpose flour
- 2 cans (10-3/4 ounces each) condensed cream of chicken soup, undiluted
- 1 cup (8 ounces) sour cream
- 1/2 cup grated carrot
- 2 tablespoons grated onion
- 1/2 teaspoon pepper
- 3 packages (10 ounces each) frozen broccoli cuts, thawed
- 1-1/2 cups crushed seasoned stuffing
- 1/4 cup butter, melted

1. In a bowl, combine flour, soup and sour cream. Stir in carrot, onion and pepper. Fold in broccoli.

2. Transfer to a greased 2-1/2-qt. baking dish. Combine stuffing and butter; sprinkle over top. Bake, uncovered, at 350° for 50-60 minutes or until bubbly and heated through.

Yield: 12 servings.

WATERMELON AND TOMATO SALAD

You cannot beat this light and refreshing salad on hot summer days! The combination of watermelon, cilantro, lime and tasty heirloom tomatoes is just unusual enough to keep folks commenting on the great flavor.
BEV JONES, BRUNSWICK, MISSOURI

- 3 tablespoons lime juice
- 2 tablespoons white balsamic vinegar
- 2 tablespoons olive oil
- 2 tablespoons honey
- 1 medium mango, peeled and chopped
- 1 teaspoon grated lime peel
- 1 teaspoon kosher salt
- 1/4 teaspoon white pepper
- 8 cups cubed seedless watermelon
- 1-1/2 pounds yellow tomatoes, coarsely chopped (about 5 medium)
- 1-1/2 pounds red tomatoes, coarsely chopped (about 5 medium)
- 2 sweet onions, thinly sliced and separated into rings
- 2/3 cup minced fresh cilantro

1. For dressing, place the first eight ingredients in a blender; cover and process until pureed.

2. In a bowl, combine the watermelon, tomatoes, onions and cilantro. Just before serving, add dressing and toss to coat. Serve with a slotted spoon.

Yield: 12 servings.

PISTACHIO LETTUCE SALAD

This colorful salad is topped with a drizzle of delicious honey-and-ginger vinaigrette. You're sure to bring home an empty bowl.
ANNA MINEGAR, ZOLFO SPRINGS, FLORIDA

10	cups torn Bibb or Boston lettuce
1	can (11 ounces) mandarin oranges, drained
1	cup pistachios, coarsely chopped
1	cup raisins

DRESSING:

1/4	cup rice vinegar
2	tablespoons canola oil
2	teaspoons honey
1/2	teaspoon salt
1/4	teaspoon pepper
1/4	teaspoon ground ginger

1. In a large salad bowl, combine the lettuce, oranges, pistachios and raisins. In a blender, combine the dressing ingredients; cover and process until blended. Drizzle over salad; toss to coat.

Yield: 16 servings.

SOUTHWEST CORN BREAD SALAD

(pictured at left)

Here's an absolute favorite at potlucks and barbecues. The idea came to me as I was trying to think of a replacement for the typical taco salad. The corn bread replaces the tortilla chips.
STEFANIE FOSTER, WASILLA, ALASKA

2	packages (8-1/2 ounces each) corn bread/muffin mix
2	eggs, beaten
2/3	cup 2% milk
1	can (4 ounces) chopped green chilies
2	cans (15 ounces each) black beans, rinsed and drained
2	cups frozen corn, thawed
1	can (14-1/2 ounces) diced tomatoes, drained
1	medium green pepper, chopped
1/2	cup chopped red onion
3	cups (12 ounces) shredded sharp cheddar cheese, divided
1/3	cup water
1/3	cup cider vinegar
1/3	cup canola oil
1	envelope taco seasoning

1. In a large bowl, combine the corn bread mix, eggs, milk and chilies until blended. Pour into a greased 13-in. x 9-in. baking pan. Bake at 400° for 20-25 minutes or until a toothpick inserted near the center comes out clean. Cool on a wire rack.

2. In a large bowl, combine the beans, corn, tomatoes, green pepper, onion and 2 cups cheese. In a small bowl, whisk the water, vinegar, oil and taco seasoning. Pour over bean mixture; toss to coat. Cover and refrigerate for at least 2 hours.

3. Cut corn bread into 1-in. cubes. In a large serving bowl, layer the corn bread, bean mixture and remaining cheese. Serve immediately.

Yield: 18 servings.

YELLOW RICE & BLACK BEAN SALAD

Chipotle peppers turn up the heat on a colorful rice dish brimming with black beans. It can be served hot or cold.
ROSE RODWELL, BERGEN, NEW YORK

4	teaspoons ground cumin, divided
1/4	cup lime juice
2	tablespoons plus 1-1/2 teaspoons canola oil
1/2	teaspoon ground turmeric
1-1/2	cups water
1	cup uncooked basmati rice
1	teaspoon salt
4	green onions, sliced
1	can (15 ounces) black beans, rinsed and drained
1	small green pepper, chopped
1/2	cup chopped roasted sweet red peppers
1/3	cup minced fresh cilantro
1-1/2	teaspoons chopped chipotle pepper in adobo sauce

1. Place three teaspoons cumin in a small skillet; cook over medium heat for 1 minute or until aromas are released. Stir in lime juice and oil; set aside.

2. In a saucepan, combine turmeric and remaining cumin. Cook over medium heat for 1 minute or until aromatic. Add the water, rice and salt; bring to a boil. Reduce heat to low; cover and simmer 15 minutes or until water is absorbed. Cool. Stir in onions and half of the lime juice mixture.

3. In a large bowl, combine the remaining ingredients. Add the rice mixture and remaining lime juice mixture; toss to coat.

Yield: 12 servings (1/2 cup each).

SUMMER-FRESH QUINOA SALAD

This light and refreshing salad is easy to prepare and perfect for hot summer days. I often add zucchini or summer squash and use fresh tomatoes instead of sun-dried.
LIZ GADBOIS, WOODVILLE, WISCONSIN

2	cups quinoa, rinsed
1	cup boiling water
1/2	cup sun-dried tomatoes (not packed in oil)
1	medium cucumber, peeled, seeded and chopped
1	each medium green, sweet red and yellow peppers, chopped
6	green onions, thinly sliced
1	package (4 ounces) crumbled garlic and herb feta cheese
1/2	cup reduced-fat sun-dried tomato salad dressing, divided

1. Cook quinoa according to package directions. Transfer to a large bowl; cool completely.

2. In a small bowl, combine water and tomatoes; let stand for 5 minutes. Drain and chop tomatoes; add to quinoa. Stir in the cucumber, peppers, onions, cheese and 1/4 cup salad dressing.

3. Cover and refrigerate for 2 hours. Just before serving, stir in remaining salad dressing.

Yield: 14 servings.

Editor's Note: Look for quinoa in the cereal, rice or organic food aisle.

Small But Mighty
As a complete protein source also high in iron, magnesium, and fiber, quinoa (pronounced KEEN-wah) is not only one of the healthiest pantry staples, but also incredibly easy and quick to cook.

SWISS-ONION POTATO BAKE

When I was growing up, my mother told me I would starve my family because I didn't like to cook. Thankfully, I enjoy it now! This flavorful side dish goes nicely with meat loaf.

ANNETTA BALLESTEROS, KUTTAWA, KENTUCKY

1	cup finely chopped sweet onion
2	tablespoons butter
1	package (30 ounces) frozen shredded hash brown potatoes, thawed
2	cups (8 ounces) shredded Swiss cheese
1	teaspoon salt
1/4	teaspoon pepper
2	eggs
1	cup milk

Minced fresh parsley, optional

1. In a small skillet, saute onion in butter until tender. In a large bowl, combine the hash browns, cheese, salt, pepper and onion mixture.

2. Transfer to a greased 13-in. x 9-in. baking dish. In a bowl, whisk eggs and milk; pour over potato mixture.

3. Bake, uncovered, at 350° for 35-40 minutes or until a thermometer reads 160°. Let stand for 5 minutes before cutting. Sprinkle with parsley if desired.

Yield: 12 servings.

CARIBBEAN CRABMEAT SALAD

This slightly sweet salad adds a delightful blend of colors and flavors to any table.

PATRISHA THOMPSON, STERLING, COLORADO

3	cups uncooked tricolor spiral pasta
1	can (20 ounces) pineapple tidbits, drained
3/4	pound imitation crabmeat, chopped
1	large sweet red pepper, diced
1	jalapeno pepper, seeded and chopped
2	tablespoons minced fresh cilantro
3	tablespoons lime juice
2	tablespoons olive oil
1	tablespoon honey
1	teaspoon grated lime peel
1/2	teaspoon ground cumin
1/4	teaspoon salt
1/4	teaspoon ground ginger

1. Cook pasta according to package directions. Meanwhile, in a serving bowl, combine the pineapple, crab, red pepper, jalapeno pepper and cilantro.

2. Drain and rinse pasta in cold water; add to crab mixture. In a small bowl, whisk the remaining ingredients. Pour over salad and toss to coat. Chill until serving.

Yield: 13 servings (3/4 cup each).

Editor's Note: Wear disposable gloves when cutting hot peppers; the oils can burn skin. Avoid touching your face.

SAVORY MEDITERRANEAN ORZO

If you like to sample flavors from around the world, you'll love this Mediterranean creation. The yellow summer squash, roasted red peppers and spinach yield specks of eye-popping color that makes this dish festive.

KRISTI SILK, FERNDALE, WASHINGTON

4	cups reduced-sodium chicken broth
1	package (16 ounces) orzo pasta
1	medium onion, finely chopped
4	garlic cloves, minced
2	tablespoons olive oil
2	cups (8 ounces) crumbled feta cheese, divided
1	package (10 ounces) frozen chopped spinach, thawed and squeezed dry
1	jar (7-1/2 ounces) roasted sweet red peppers, drained and chopped
1	small yellow summer squash, finely chopped
1/2	teaspoon salt
1/2	teaspoon pepper

1. In a large saucepan, bring broth to a boil. Stir in orzo; cook over medium heat for 6-8 minutes. Remove from the heat.

2. In a small skillet, saute onion and garlic in oil until tender; add to orzo mixture. Stir in 1 cup cheese, spinach, red peppers, squash, salt and pepper.

3. Transfer to a greased 13-in. x 9-in. baking dish; sprinkle with remaining cheese. Bake at 350° for 20-25 minutes or until heated through.

Yield: 12 servings (2/3 cup each).

VEGGIE POTATO SALAD

At large gatherings Mom always brought her famous potato salad. Now, I'm carrying on the tasty tradition.
JAMES KORZENOWSKI, FENNVILLE, MICHIGAN

6	large potatoes (about 3 pounds)
1	cup Italian salad dressing
8	hard-cooked eggs, sliced
1	bunch green onions, thinly sliced
3	celery ribs, chopped
1	medium green pepper, chopped
2/3	cup chopped seeded peeled cucumber
1	cup frozen peas, thawed
1	cup mayonnaise
2/3	cup sour cream
2	teaspoons prepared mustard
1	teaspoon salt
1/8	to 1/4 teaspoon pepper

1. Place potatoes in a Dutch oven and cover with water. Bring to a boil. Reduce heat. Cover and cook for 15-20 minutes or until tender. Cool for 15-20 minutes or until easy to handle.

2. Peel and dice potatoes into a large bowl. Add salad dressing; gently toss to coat. Let stand for 30 minutes.

3. Stir in the eggs, green onions, celery, green pepper, cucumber and peas. Combine the remaining ingredients. Add to potato mixture; gently toss to coat.

Yield: 14 servings.

CHICKEN SALAD WITH A TWIST

This colorful salad will disappear fast at your next potluck. I got the recipe from my cousin, who always has great dishes at her parties...and this recipe is no exception!
VALERIE HOLT, CARTERSVILLE, GEORGIA

8	ounces uncooked spiral pasta
2-1/2	cups cubed cooked chicken
1	medium onion, chopped
2	celery ribs, chopped
1	medium cucumber, seeded and chopped
1/2	cup sliced ripe olives
1/3	cup zesty Italian salad dressing
1/3	cup mayonnaise
2	teaspoons spicy brown or horseradish mustard
1	teaspoon lemon juice
1/2	teaspoon salt
1/4	teaspoon pepper
3	plum tomatoes, chopped

1. Cook pasta according to package directions; drain and rinse in cold water. In a bowl, combine the pasta, chicken, onion, celery, cucumber and olives.

2. In a small bowl, whisk the Italian dressing, mayonnaise, mustard, lemon juice, salt and pepper. Pour over salad and toss to coat. Cover and refrigerate for 2 hours or until chilled. Just before serving, fold in tomatoes.

Yield: 12 servings.

CELERY ROOT AND PEAR SLAW

Juicy pears, tangy blue cheese and sweet raisins jazz up this crunchy coleslaw. The delicious combination is wonderful served with pork roast or baked ham.

ROXANNE CHAN, ALBANY, CALIFORNIA

1	medium celery root, peeled and julienned
3	cups shredded red cabbage
3	medium pears, thinly sliced
1/3	cup golden raisins
1/4	cup chopped red onion
1/4	cup minced fresh parsley
1/4	cup sliced almonds
3/4	cup sour cream
1/3	cup mayonnaise
4-1/2	teaspoons poppy seeds
4-1/2	teaspoons lemon juice
4-1/2	teaspoons prepared horseradish
2	garlic cloves, minced
1-1/2	teaspoons honey
3/4	teaspoon grated lemon peel
3/4	teaspoon pepper
1/2	cup crumbled blue cheese

1. In a large bowl, combine the first seven ingredients. Combine the sour cream, mayonnaise, poppy seeds, lemon juice, horseradish, garlic, honey, lemon peel and pepper; pour over slaw and toss to coat. Sprinkle with blue cheese.

Yield: 16 servings (3/4 cup each).

BLUE CHEESE WALDORF SALAD

Blue cheese puts a tasty spin on an all-time classic. Serve the mixture over lettuce leaves for a great lunch option.

DEB WILLIAMS, PEORIA, ARIZONA

4	large apples, chopped
2	cups green grapes, halved
1-1/3	cups chopped celery
1/2	cup raisins
1	tablespoon lemon juice
2/3	cup fat-free mayonnaise
2/3	cup buttermilk
1/3	cup crumbled blue cheese
1	tablespoon sugar
1/4	cup chopped walnuts, toasted

1. In a large bowl, combine the apples, grapes, celery, raisins and lemon juice.

2. In a small bowl, combine the mayonnaise, buttermilk, blue cheese and sugar. Pour over apple mixture and toss to coat. Cover and refrigerate for at least 1 hour. Just before serving, sprinkle walnuts over the top.

Yield: 12 servings.

FIVE-BEAN SALAD

Five kinds of beans in an oil-and-vinegar dressing make a classic salad that's great to take to picnics or potlucks.
JEANETTE SIMEC, OTTAWA, ILLINOIS

1	can (15 ounces) garbanzo beans or chickpeas, rinsed and drained
1	can (16 ounces) kidney beans, rinsed and drained
1	can (15-1/2 ounces) great northern beans, rinsed and drained
1	can (14-1/2 ounces) cut wax beans, rinsed and drained
1	package (9 ounces) frozen cut green beans, thawed
2	small onions, chopped
1	cup white vinegar
3/4	cup sugar
1/4	cup canola oil
1	teaspoon salt
1/2	teaspoon pepper

1. In a large bowl, combine the first six ingredients. In another bowl, whisk the vinegar, sugar, oil, salt and pepper.

2. Pour over bean mixture and toss to coat. Cover and refrigerate for several hours or overnight. Serve with a slotted spoon.

Yield: 15 servings.

LAYERED TORTELLINI-SPINACH SALAD

Layers of red cabbage, green spinach, cherry tomatoes and tortellini make this salad a real showstopper.
GENISE KRAUSE, STURGEON BAY, WISCONSIN

1	package (19 ounces) frozen cheese tortellini
2	packages (6 ounces each) fresh baby spinach
6	cups shredded red cabbage
1	pint cherry tomatoes, quartered
3	tablespoons thinly sliced green onions
1	package (1 pound) sliced bacon, cooked and crumbled
1	bottle (16 ounces) ranch salad dressing

1. Cook tortellini according to package directions. Meanwhile, in a large salad bowl, layer the spinach, cabbage, tomatoes and onions.

2. Drain tortellini and rinse in cold water; place over onions. Top with bacon. Drizzle with salad dressing; do not toss. Cover and refrigerate until serving.

Yield: 18 servings.

TANGY MASHED POTATOES

Green onions perk up regular mashed potatoes, while yogurt makes them extra creamy. They're always a hit!
DONNA NOEL, GRAY, MAINE

4	pounds potatoes, peeled and cubed (about 12 medium)
1-1/2	cups (12 ounces) reduced-fat plain yogurt
4	green onions, minced
2	tablespoons butter
1	teaspoon salt
1/2	teaspoon pepper

1. Place potatoes in a Dutch oven and cover with water. Bring to a boil. Reduce heat; cover and cook for 10-15 minutes or until tender. Drain potatoes; mash with yogurt, onions, butter, salt and pepper.

Yield: 13 servings.

PICNIC SWEET POTATO SALAD

A homemade vinaigrette coats this colorful salad chock-full of sweet potato cubes. It's ideal for warm-weather picnics and patio parties, but my family loves it year-round!
MARY MARLOWE LEVERETTE, COLUMBIA, SOUTH CAROLINA

4	medium sweet potatoes, peeled and cubed
3	medium apples, chopped
6	bacon strips, cooked and crumbled
1/4	cup chopped onion
3	tablespoons minced fresh parsley
1/2	teaspoon salt
1/4	teaspoon pepper
2/3	cup canola oil
2	tablespoons red wine vinegar

1. Place sweet potatoes in a Dutch oven and cover with water. Bring to a boil. Reduce heat; cover and cook for 10-15 minutes or just until tender. Drain. Transfer to a large bowl; cool to room temperature.

2. Add the apples, bacon, onion, parsley, salt and pepper to the potatoes. In a small bowl, whisk oil and vinegar. Pour over salad; toss gently to coat. Chill until serving.

Yield: 13 servings (3/4 cup each).

STRAWBERRY & GLAZED WALNUT SALAD

(pictured at right)
Everyone falls for the sweet taste of fresh strawberries and crunchy glazed walnuts in this easy and delightful salad.
KELLY ZIMPFER, SOUDERTON, PENNSYLVANIA

1	pound fresh strawberries, sliced
1	package (7 ounces) glazed walnuts
1	package (6 ounces) fresh baby spinach
1	package (5 ounces) spring mix salad greens

CREAMY POPPY SEED DRESSING:

1/3	cup mayonnaise
1/4	cup 2% milk
3	tablespoons sugar
4	teaspoons cider vinegar
2	teaspoons poppy seeds

1. In a large bowl, combine the strawberries, walnuts, spinach and salad greens. In a small bowl, whisk the dressing ingredients. Serve with salad.

Yield: 14 servings.

A Berry Fresh Idea
Strawberries stay fresh longer if they're stored unwashed, with the stems on, in a sealed container in the refrigerator.

ANTIPASTO SALAD

This beautiful, hearty salad is ideal for picnics because it's mayo-free. It's a huge hit wherever I take it.
BECKY MELTON, ORLANDO, FLORIDA

1	package (16 ounces) tricolor spiral pasta
1	jar (16 ounces) giardiniera, drained and cut
2	cans (one 3.8 ounces, one 2-1/4 ounces) sliced ripe olives, drained
1	jar (5-3/4 ounces) pimiento-stuffed olives, drained and sliced
1	jar (7 ounces) roasted sweet red peppers, drained and chopped
8	ounces summer sausage, cubed
8	ounces pepper Jack cheese, cubed
1	cup Italian salad dressing

1. Cook pasta according to package directions. Drain and rinse in cold water.

2. In a large bowl, combine the giardiniera, olives, red peppers, sausage, cheese and pasta. Add dressing; toss to coat. Cover and refrigerate for 1 hour.

Yield: 14 servings.

CAULIFLOWER AU GRATIN

A lighter version of a classic white sauce coats the cauliflower in a dish that's perfect for a potluck buffet.
TASTE OF HOME TEST KITCHEN

3	packages (16 ounces each) frozen cauliflower, thawed
1	large onion, chopped
1/3	cup butter, cubed
1/3	cup all-purpose flour
1/2	teaspoon salt
1/4	teaspoon ground mustard
1/4	teaspoon pepper
2	cups fat-free milk
1/2	cup grated Parmesan cheese

TOPPING:

1/2	cup soft whole wheat bread crumbs
2	tablespoons butter, melted
1/4	teaspoon paprika

1. Place 1 in. of water in a Dutch oven; add cauliflower.; Bring to a boil. Reduce heat; cover and cook for 4-6 minutes or until crisp-tender. Drain and pat dry.

2. Meanwhile, in a large saucepan, saute onion in butter until tender. Stir in the flour, salt, mustard and pepper until blended; gradually add milk. Bring to a boil; cook and stir for 1-2 minutes or until thickened. Remove from the heat. Add cheese; stir until melted.

3. Place cauliflower in a 13-in. x 9-in. baking dish coated with cooking spray. Pour sauce over top.

4. For topping, combine the bread crumbs, butter and paprika. Sprinkle over sauce. Bake, uncovered, at 350° for 30-35 minutes or until bubbly.

Yield: 12 servings.

ITALIAN ORZO SALAD

Here's a light pasta salad that's ideal for a summer potluck or picnic. It's great with grilled beef or chicken.
CINDY GRISCHO, DENVER, COLORADO

6	cups chicken broth
1	package (16 ounces) orzo pasta
1/3	cup olive oil
1/4	cup red wine vinegar
2	tablespoons lemon juice
1	tablespoon honey
1/2	teaspoon salt
1/2	teaspoon pepper
2	cups chopped plum tomatoes
1	cup chopped seeded peeled cucumber
1	cup fresh basil leaves, thinly sliced
4	green onions, chopped
1/2	cup fresh baby spinach, chopped
1-3/4	cups (7 ounces) crumbled feta cheese
1/2	cup pine nuts, toasted

1. In a large saucepan, bring broth to a boil; add pasta. Return to a boil. Cook, uncovered, for 10-12 minutes or until pasta is tender. Meanwhile, in a small bowl, whisk the oil, vinegar, lemon juice, honey, salt and pepper.

2. In a large bowl, combine the tomatoes, cucumber, basil, onions and spinach. Drain pasta; add to tomato mixture. Drizzle with dressing; toss to coat. Chill until serving.

3. Just before serving, stir in cheese and pine nuts.

Yield: 12 servings.

What's It Called?

Acini di pepe pasta looks like tiny beads. Italian for "peppercorns," it is also sometimes referred to as pastina and is most commonly used in Italian wedding soup.

PEARL PASTA SALAD

I was served this salad at a hotel in Sacramento and just loved it. Here's my version. It's great to take along on camping trips or picnics.
RACHAEL ZAVALA, PLEASANT HILL, CALIFORNIA

LAST MINUTE!

2	cups uncooked acini di pepe pasta
3	cups frozen corn
1	jar (14 ounces) oil-packed sun-dried tomatoes, drained and chopped
1	jar (6 ounces) prepared pesto
1/2	cup grated Parmesan cheese
1/4	cup olive oil
1/8	teaspoon salt
1/8	teaspoon pepper

1. In a large saucepan, cook pasta according to package directions, adding corn during the last 2 minutes. Drain and rinse in cold water.

2. In a large bowl, combine the tomatoes, pesto, cheese, oil, salt and pepper. Add pasta and corn; toss to coat. Refrigerate until serving.

Yield: 15 servings.

2. In a large bowl, combine the pudding mix, sour cream and pineapple. Toss banana with lemon juice; stir into pudding mixture. Stir in the oranges, marshmallows, pecans, peaches, cherries and orzo. Fold in whipped topping. Sprinkle with coconut. Cover and refrigerate for 2 hours or until chilled.

Yield: 16 servings.

LAYERED SALAD WITH CURRY DRESSING

Try my lightened-up version of the classic seven-layer salad. Curry powder adds a unique twist, while almonds give it a nice crunchy element.

KERRI PELZ, HENDERSONVILLE, NORTH CAROLINA

1	package (10 ounces) ready-to-serve salad greens
2	celery ribs, chopped
1/2	cup chopped green pepper
1/2	cup chopped cauliflower
2	green onions, thinly sliced
1	package (10 ounces) frozen peas, thawed
3/4	cup fat-free mayonnaise
3/4	cup (6 ounces) reduced-fat plain yogurt
1	tablespoon lemon juice
1	teaspoon curry powder
3/4	cup shredded reduced-fat cheddar cheese
1/2	cup sliced almonds

1. In a 3-qt. glass bowl, layer the salad greens, celery, pepper, cauliflower, green onions and peas.

2. In a small bowl, whisk the mayonnaise, yogurt, lemon juice and curry; carefully spread over salad. Sprinkle with cheese. Chill until serving. Just before serving, sprinkle with almonds.

Yield: 16 servings.

Add Some Heat
Most commonly found in Indian cuisine, curry powder imparts a distinctive flavor and rich golden color to recipes and can be found in both mild and hot versions.

ORZO CHEESECAKE FRUIT SALAD

This sweet salad features my favorite fruits, complemented by the creamy pudding mix. It even works as a dessert!

PRISCILLA GILBERT, INDIAN HARBOUR BEACH, FLORIDA

1	cup uncooked orzo pasta
1	package (3.4 ounces) instant cheesecake or vanilla pudding mix
1/3	cup sour cream
1	can (20 ounces) crushed pineapple, undrained
1	large banana, sliced
2	teaspoons lemon juice
2	cans (11 ounces each) mandarin oranges, drained
2	cups miniature marshmallows
1	cup chopped pecans, toasted
1	cup canned sliced peaches, drained and chopped
1/2	cup maraschino cherries, drained and quartered
1	carton (8 ounces) frozen whipped topping, thawed
1/2	cup flaked coconut, toasted

1. Cook orzo according to package directions. Drain and rinse in cold water; set aside.

CHERRY BAKED BEANS

Here's a perfect dish to bring to a family reunion or any get-together. It's fast and easy to prepare, and you won't ever have to worry about bringing leftovers home...because there won't be any!

MARGARET SMITH, SUPERIOR, WISCONSIN

1	pound lean ground beef (90% lean)
2	cans (15 ounces each) pork and beans
2	cups frozen pitted tart cherries, thawed
1	can (16 ounces) kidney beans, rinsed and drained
1	cup ketchup
1/2	cup water
1	envelope onion soup mix
2	tablespoons prepared mustard
2	teaspoons cider vinegar

1. In a large skillet, cook beef over medium heat until no longer pink; drain. In a large bowl, combine the remaining ingredients; stir in beef.

2. Transfer to an ungreased 2-1/2 qt. baking dish. Bake, uncovered, at 400° for 40-45 minutes or until heated through, stirring occasionally.

Yield: 12 servings.

MACARONI COLESLAW

Macaroni noodles add a yummy twist to traditional coleslaw. Watch people gobble it up at your next picnic.

SANDRA MATTESON, WESTHOPE, NORTH DAKOTA

1	package (7 ounces) ring macaroni or ditalini
1	package (14 ounces) coleslaw mix
2	medium onions, finely chopped
2	celery ribs, finely chopped
1	medium cucumber, finely chopped
1	medium green pepper, finely chopped
1	can (8 ounces) whole water chestnuts, drained and chopped

DRESSING:

1-1/2	cups Miracle Whip Light
1/3	cup sugar
1/4	cup cider vinegar
1/2	teaspoon salt
1/4	teaspoon pepper

1. Cook macaroni according to package directions; drain and rinse in cold water. Transfer to a large bowl; add the coleslaw mix, onions, celery, cucumber, green pepper and water chestnuts.

2. In a small bowl, whisk the dressing ingredients. Pour over salad; toss to coat. Cover and refrigerate for at least 1 hour.

Yield: 16 servings.

cheese enchiladas, pg. 138

cranberry glazed ham, pg. 124

Hearty Main Dishes

Let us thank God for food when others are hungry;
for drink when others are thirsty;
for friends when others are lonely. Amen.

MAKEOVER CHEESE-STUFFED SHELLS

You'll love the great flavor in these shells. Our Test Kitchen staff made them over without using any reduced-fat ingredients, yet still saved a ton on fat and calories!
BETH FLEMING, DOWNERS GROVE, ILLINOIS

3/4	pound lean ground beef (90% lean)
1	Italian turkey sausage link (4 ounces), casing removed
1	large onion, chopped
1	package (10 ounces) frozen chopped spinach, thawed and squeezed dry
1	cup ricotta cheese
1	egg, lightly beaten
1-1/2	cups (6 ounces) shredded part-skim mozzarella cheese, divided
1-1/2	cups 4% cottage cheese
1	cup grated Parmesan cheese
1	cup (4 ounces) shredded sharp cheddar cheese
1	teaspoon Italian seasoning
1/4	teaspoon pepper
1/8	teaspoon ground cinnamon, optional
24	jumbo pasta shells, cooked and drained

SAUCE:

3	cans (8 ounces each) no-salt-added tomato sauce
1	tablespoon dried minced onion
1-1/2	teaspoons dried basil
1-1/2	teaspoons dried parsley flakes
2	garlic cloves, minced
1	teaspoon sugar
1	teaspoon dried oregano
1/4	teaspoon pepper

1. Crumble beef and sausage into a large nonstick skillet; add onion. Cook and stir over medium heat until meat is no longer pink; drain.

2. Transfer to a large bowl. Stir in the spinach, ricotta and egg. Add 1 cup mozzarella cheese, cottage cheese, Parmesan cheese, cheddar cheese, Italian seasoning, pepper and cinnamon if desired; mix well.

3. Stuff pasta shells with meat mixture. Arrange stuffed shells in two 11-in. x 7-in. baking dishes coated with cooking spray. Combine the sauce ingredients; spoon over shells.

4. Cover and bake at 350° for 45 minutes. Uncover; sprinkle with remaining mozzarella cheese. Bake 5-10 minutes longer or until bubbly and cheese is melted. Let stand for 5 minutes before serving.

Yield: 12 servings.

SWEET 'N' MOIST HAM

We served 75 pounds of ham fixed this way. It could not be simpler, and it's moist and delightfully sweet.
DAUN HEMBD, WHITEHALL, WISCONSIN

1	sliced boneless fully cooked ham (about 6 pounds), tied
1	can (12 ounces) lemon-lime soda

1. Place ham on a rack in a shallow roasting pan. Pour soda over ham. Cover and bake at 325° for 2 hours or until a thermometer reads 140°.

Yield: 18-20 servings.

3. Bake at 425° for 30 minutes. Reduce heat to 375°; remove foil. Bake 55-60 minutes longer or until golden brown. Let stand for 10 minutes before cutting.

To use frozen potpie: Remove from the freezer 30 minutes before baking. Cover edges of crust loosely with foil; place on a baking sheet.

Yield: 2 pies (6 servings each).

GLAZED KIELBASA

You'll need only three ingredients to prepare this sweet sausage. Reduced-fat or turkey kielbasa can also be used.
JODY SANDS TAYLOR ED.D., RICHMOND, VIRGINIA

3	pounds smoked kielbasa or Polish sausage, cut into 1-inch chunks
1/2	cup packed brown sugar
1-1/2	cups ginger ale

1. Place sausage in a 3-qt. slow cooker; sprinkle with brown sugar. Pour ginger ale over the top. Cover and cook on low for 4-5 hours or until heated through. Serve with a slotted spoon.

Yield: 12-16 servings.

CHICKEN POTPIES

My aunt came up with this recipe, and I tweaked it to fit my family's tastes. The flaky, pastry crust really makes it special.
LYSA DAVIS, PINE BLUFF, ARKANSAS

2	cans (9-3/4 ounces each) chunk white chicken, drained
1	can (15-1/4 ounces) lima beans, drained
1	can (15 ounces) sliced carrots, drained
1	jar (4-1/2 ounces) sliced mushrooms, drained
1	can (14-1/2 ounces) sliced potatoes, drained
1	can (10-3/4 ounces) condensed cream of chicken soup, undiluted
1	can (10-3/4 ounces) condensed cream of mushroom soup, undiluted
1-1/2	teaspoons rubbed sage
1/4	teaspoon salt
1/4	teaspoon pepper
2	packages (15 ounces each) refrigerated pie pastry
1	tablespoon butter, melted

1. In a large bowl, combine the first 10 ingredients. Line two 9-in. pie plates with bottom crusts. Add filling. Roll out remaining pastry to fit tops of pies; place over filling. Trim, seal and flute edges. Cut slits in pastry; brush with butter.

2. Cover and freeze one potpie for up to 3 months. Bake the remaining potpie at 375° for 35-40 minutes or until golden brown. Let stand for 10 minutes before cutting.

CRANBERRY-GLAZED HAM

That show-stopping entree you've been hoping for is right here, and it only takes five ingredients to make. The sweet and tangy cranberry glaze pairs beautifully with succulent ham.

JONI PETERSON, WICHITA, KANSAS

1	can (14 ounces) whole-berry cranberry sauce
1/2	cup maple syrup
1/4	cup cider vinegar
1	to 1-1/2 teaspoons ground mustard
1	boneless fully cooked ham (5 pounds)

1. In a small bowl, combine the cranberry sauce, syrup, vinegar and mustard. Set aside 1 cup mixture for sauce.

2. Line a shallow roasting pan with foil. Place ham on a rack in prepared pan. Bake, uncovered, at 325° for 1 hour. Baste with some of the remaining cranberry mixture; bake 40-45 minutes longer or until a thermometer reads 140°, basting with additional mixture every 10 minutes. Heat reserved sauce; serve with ham.

Yield: 15 servings.

PRESTO CHICKEN TACOS

(pictured at right)

Slowly cooking the chicken with the seasonings is the key to perfection with this dish. The chicken mixture also makes a great salad topping.

NANETTE HILTON, LAS VEGAS, NEVADA

3	pounds boneless skinless chicken breasts, cut into strips
2	tablespoons canola oil
1	garlic clove, minced
2	cans (14-1/2 ounces each) diced tomatoes, undrained
1	teaspoon ground cumin
1	teaspoon chili powder
12	corn tortillas (6 inches), warmed

Optional toppings: shredded lettuce, shredded cheddar cheese, diced tomatoes, fresh cilantro leaves, sour cream and cubed avocado

1. In a Dutch oven, brown chicken in oil in batches. Add garlic; cook 1 minute longer. Add the tomatoes, cumin and chili powder. Bring to a boil.

2. Reduce the heat; cover and simmer for 15-20 minutes or until chicken is no longer pink, stirring occasionally.

3. Fill each tortilla with about 1/2 cup chicken mixture. Serve with toppings of your choice.

Yield: 12 servings.

SWEET BARBECUED PORK CHOPS

Because of its popularity, I often prepare a double recipe of these tangy chops. They also freeze well for a quick meal during those very busy weeks. I think it's the sweet and sassy sauce that makes them absolutely delectable.

SUSAN HOLDERMAN, FOSTORIA, OHIO

8	boneless pork loin chops (3/4 inch thick and 8 ounces each)
2	tablespoons canola oil
1/2	cup packed brown sugar
1/2	cup chopped sweet onion
1/2	cup each ketchup, barbecue sauce, French salad dressing and honey

1. In a large skillet, brown pork chops in oil in batches for 2-3 minutes on each side or until lightly browned. Return all to the pan. Combine the remaining ingredients; pour over chops. Bring to a boil. Reduce heat; cover and simmer for 4-5 minutes or until a thermometer reads 145°.

2. Let stand 5 minutes before serving, or cool before placing in a freezer container. Cover and freeze for up to 3 months.

To use frozen pork chops: Thaw in the refrigerator overnight. Place in a skillet; bring to a boil. Reduce heat; cover and simmer for 4-6 minutes or until heated through.

Yield: 8 servings.

CORNMEAL-COATED CHICKEN

The pepper really comes through in this quick and convenient coating mix for chicken. Not only is it tasty, it's certainly more economical than the store-bought kind.

ALJENE WENDLING, SEATTLE, WASHINGTON

1	cup all-purpose flour
1	cup cornmeal
4	teaspoons ground cumin
2	teaspoons onion powder
2	teaspoons garlic powder
2	teaspoons dried oregano
1	teaspoon salt, optional
1	teaspoon pepper
1/2	teaspoon cayenne pepper

ADDITIONAL INGREDIENTS:

1	broiler/fryer chicken (3 pounds), cut up and skin removed
3	tablespoons butter, melted

1. In a large resealable plastic bag, combine the first nine ingredients. Store in a cool dry place for up to 6 months.

Yield: 3 batches (2-1/4 cups total).

To prepare chicken: Place 3/4 cup coating mix in a resealable plastic bag. Dip chicken in butter; add chicken to bag, a few pieces at a time, and shake to coat. Place in a greased 15-in. x 10-in. x 1-in. baking pan. Bake, uncovered, at 375° for 45-50 minutes or until juices run clear.

Yield: 4 servings per batch.

MOIST MEAT LOAVES

When a lady from our church served this at her son's birthday party, I just had to have the recipe! Now it's the only meat loaf I make. It's great for potlucks, too.

JENNY INGRAHAM, KARLSTAD, MINNESOTA

8	eggs, lightly beaten
2-2/3	cups milk
6	cups (24 ounces) shredded cheddar cheese
12	slices white bread, cubed
2	large onions, finely chopped
2	cups shredded carrots
7-1/2	teaspoons salt
1	teaspoon pepper
8	pounds lean ground beef (90% lean)

ADDITIONAL INGREDIENTS (for each meat loaf):

1/4	cup packed brown sugar
1/4	cup ketchup
1	tablespoon prepared mustard

1. In two very large bowls, combine the eggs, milk, cheese, bread, onions, carrots, salt and pepper. Crumble beef over mixture and mix well. Pat into four ungreased 9-in. x 5-in. loaf pans.

2. Cover and freeze three meat loaves for up to 3 months. Bake the remaining loaf, uncovered, at 350° for 1 hour. Combine the brown sugar, ketchup and mustard; spread over loaf. Bake 15-20 minutes longer or until no pink remains and a meat thermometer reads 160°.

To use frozen meat loaf: Thaw in the refrigerator overnight. Remove from the refrigerator 30 minutes before baking. Bake, uncovered, at 350° for 1 hour. Combine the brown sugar, ketchup and mustard; spread over loaf. Bake 30-35 minutes longer or until no pink remains and a meat thermometer reads 160°.

Yield: 4 loaves (6 servings each).

HONEY-APPLE TURKEY BREAST

I found this recipe in a diabetics' cookbook. We really like the honey flavor. The sweetness comes through when I use the leftovers in casseroles and soups, too.

RITA REINKE, WAUWATOSA, WISCONSIN

3/4	cup thawed apple juice concentrate
1/3	cup honey
1	tablespoon ground mustard
1	bone-in turkey breast (6 to 7 pounds)

1. In a small saucepan, combine the apple juice concentrate, honey and mustard. Cook over low heat for 2-3 minutes or just until blended, stirring occasionally.

2. Place turkey breast on a rack in a foil-lined shallow roasting pan; pour honey mixture over the top.

3. Bake, uncovered, at 325° for 2 to 2-1/2 hours or until a meat thermometer reads 180°, basting with pan juices every 30 minutes. (Cover loosely with foil if turkey browns too quickly.) Cover and let stand for 15 minutes before carving.

Yield: 12-14 servings.

BRISKET 'N' BEAN BURRITOS

Smoky bacon, tender beef and slow cooker preparation make this easy Southwestern inspired dish a real winner.

RUTH WEATHERFORD, HUNTINGTON BEACH, CALIFORNIA

1	fresh beef brisket (2 pounds)
1	cup chopped onion
3	bacon strips, diced
1	can (8 ounces) tomato sauce
3/4	teaspoon pepper
1/4	teaspoon salt
1	can (16 ounces) refried beans
1/2	cup salsa
1	can (4 ounces) chopped green chilies
1-1/2	cups (6 ounces) shredded Monterey Jack cheese
10	flour tortillas (10 inches), warmed

1. Place brisket in a 5-qt. slow cooker; top with onion and bacon. Combine the tomato sauce, pepper and salt; pour over meat. Cover and cook on low for 4-1/2 to 5 hours or until meat is tender.

2. In a microwave-safe bowl, combine the refried beans, salsa and chilies. Cover and microwave on high for 2-3 minutes or until heated through. Remove meat from slow cooker; shred with two forks.

3. Layer the bean mixture, meat and cheese off-center on each tortilla. Fold sides and ends over filling and roll up.

Yield: 10 servings.

Editor's Note: This is a fresh beef brisket, not corned beef.

CHICKEN TETRAZZINI

Our son, Newley, and our daughter, Kasee, both were married within a month and a half. We served this delicious and comforting casserole to their guests. It's a recipe my mother-in-law relied on for 25 years.
ANDREA HUTCHINSON, CANTON, OKLAHOMA

1	large green pepper, chopped
1	medium onion, chopped
1/2	cup butter, cubed
2/3	cup all-purpose flour
1/2	teaspoon garlic powder
1/4	teaspoon pepper
4	cups milk
1	can (10-3/4 ounces) condensed cream of chicken soup, undiluted
10	slices process sharp cheddar cheese, cubed
10	slices process American cheese, cubed
5	cups cubed cooked chicken
1	package (16 ounces) frozen peas
1	jar (4 ounces) diced pimientos, drained
1	package (1 pound) spaghetti, cooked, rinsed and drained
1/4	cup slivered almonds, optional
1/4	cup minced fresh parsley

1. In a Dutch oven, saute green pepper and onion in butter until crisp-tender. Stir in flour, garlic powder and pepper until blended. Gradually add milk. Bring to a boil. Cook and stir for 2 minutes or until thickened. Stir in soup, cheeses and chicken; cook and stir until cheese is melted. Stir in peas, pimientos and spaghetti.

2. Transfer to two greased 13-in. x 9-in. baking dishes. Top with almonds if desired. Bake, uncovered, at 350° for 20-30 minutes or until heated through. Garnish with parsley.

Yield: 20-24 servings.

HEARTY SPAGHETTI

Hosting a spaghetti dinner for a bunch? Here's the answer for a saucy Italian favorite that is easy to transport and always goes over well.
JULIA LIVINGSTON, FROSTPROOF, FLORIDA

5	pounds ground beef
5	medium onions, chopped
1	bunch celery, chopped
8	cans (14-1/2 ounces each) diced tomatoes, drained
2	cans (6 ounces each) tomato paste
1	cup Worcestershire sauce
1/2	cup sugar
4	tablespoons salt
4	pounds uncooked spaghetti

1. In two large Dutch ovens or soup kettles, cook the beef, onions and celery over medium heat until meat is no longer pink; drain. Stir in the tomatoes, tomato paste, Worcestershire sauce, sugar and salt. Bring to a boil. Reduce heat; cover and simmer for 1 hour, stirring occasionally.

2. Cook spaghetti according to package directions; drain. Serve with meat sauce.

Yield: 25 servings (about 3/4 cup meat sauce with 3/4 cup spaghetti).

BAJA PORK TACOS

This delicious recipe is my copy-cat version of the most excellent Mexican food we ever had in Flagstaff, Arizona. The original recipe used beef instead of pork, but this comes mighty close to the same taste.
ARIELLA WINN, MESQUITE, TEXAS

1	boneless pork sirloin roast (3 pounds)
5	cans (4 ounces each) chopped green chilies
2	tablespoons reduced-sodium taco seasoning
1	tablespoon ground cumin
24	corn tortillas (6 inches), warmed
3	cups shredded lettuce
1-1/2	cups (6 ounces) shredded part-skim mozzarella cheese

1. Cut roast in half; place in a 3- or 4-qt. slow cooker. In a small bowl, combine the chilies, taco seasoning and cumin; pour over pork. Cover and cook on low for 8-10 hours or until meat is tender.

2. Remove pork; cool slightly. Skim fat from cooking juices. Shred meat with two forks; return to the slow cooker and heat through. Spoon 1/4 cup onto each tortilla; top each with 2 tablespoons lettuce and 1 tablespoon cheese.

Yield: 12 servings.

SWEET & SPICY CHICKEN DRUMMIES

(pictured at left)
We were on a camping trip, and one of our friends brought these chicken legs for dinner. They were fabulous! I was so impressed, I asked him for the recipe.
LYNETTE HANUS, FAYETTEVILLE, GEORGIA

2	cups sugar
1/4	cup paprika
2	tablespoons salt
2	teaspoons pepper
1	teaspoon garlic powder
1	teaspoon chili powder
1/2	teaspoon cayenne pepper
20	chicken drumsticks (5 ounces each)

1. In a large resealable plastic bag, combine the sugar, paprika, salt, pepper, garlic powder, chili powder and cayenne. Add drumsticks, a few at a time; seal and shake to coat.

2. Place chicken in two greased 15-in. x 10-in. x 1-in. baking pans. Cover and refrigerate for 8 hours or overnight. (A small amount of meat juices will form in the pan.)

3. Bake, uncovered, at 325° for 50-60 minutes or until chicken juices run clear and a meat thermometer reads 180°.

Yield: 20 drumsticks.

2. Meanwhile, in a large nonstick skillet, cook turkey over medium heat until no longer pink; drain. Stir in water and taco seasoning. Bring to a boil. Reduce heat; simmer, uncovered, for 5 minutes. Stir in refried beans until blended.

3. Spread turkey mixture over crust; sprinkle with cheese. Bake at 425° for 5-7 minutes or until cheese is melted. Top with tomatoes, lettuce and chips. Serve immediately.

Yield: 10 pieces.

PORK AND CABBAGE DINNER

I put on this pork roast in the morning to avoid that evening dinner rush so common on busy weeknights. All I do is fix a side of family-favorite potatoes and we can sit down to a satisfying supper.

TRINA HINKEL, MINNEAPOLIS, MINNESOTA

1	pound carrots
1-1/2	cups water
1	envelope onion soup mix
2	garlic cloves, minced
1/2	teaspoon celery seed
1	boneless pork shoulder butt roast (4 to 6 pounds)
1/2	teaspoon salt
1/4	teaspoon pepper
1-1/2	pounds, cabbage, cut into 2-inch pieces

1. Cut carrots in half lengthwise and then into 2-in. pieces. Place in a 5-qt. slow cooker. Add the water, soup mix, garlic and celery seed. Cut roast in half; place over carrot mixture. Sprinkle with salt and pepper. Cover and cook on high for 2 hours.

2. Reduce heat to low; cook for 4 hours. Add cabbage; cook 2 hours longer or until the meat and cabbage are tender.

3. Remove meat and vegetables to a serving plate; keep warm. If desired, thicken pan drippings for gravy and serve with the roast.

Yield: 8-10 servings.

KID-PLEASING TACO PIZZA

Kids will love this quick-and-easy take on both tacos and pizza. And you'll love that it's healthful, full of flavor, and lower in fat!

KIMBERLY THEOBALD, GALESBURG, ILLINOIS

1	tube (13.8 ounces) refrigerated pizza crust
1	pound lean ground turkey
3/4	cup water
1	envelope reduced-sodium taco seasoning
1	can (16 ounces) fat-free refried beans
1-1/2	cups (6 ounces) shredded pizza cheese blend
3	medium tomatoes, chopped
7	cups shredded lettuce
2	cups crushed baked tortilla chip scoops

1. Unroll crust into a 15-in. x 10-in. x 1-in. baking pan coated with cooking spray; flatten dough and build up edges slightly. Bake at 425° for 8-10 minutes or until edges are lightly browned.

GLAZED PORK CHOPS

The simple addition of rosemary really perks up the flavor in these beautifully glazed chops just right for any weeknight meal.

LOUISE GILBERT, QUESNEL, BRITISH COLUMBIA

1/2	cup ketchup
1/4	cup packed brown sugar
1/4	cup white vinegar
1/4	cup orange juice
1/4	cup Worcestershire sauce
2	garlic cloves, minced
1/2	teaspoon dried rosemary, crushed
8	bone-in pork loin chops (1/2 inch thick and 7 ounces each)

1. In a small bowl, combine the first seven ingredients. Pour 3/4 cup into a large resealable plastic bag; add the pork chops. Seal bag and turn to coat; refrigerate for 8 hours or overnight. Cover and refrigerate remaining marinade for basting.

2. Drain and discard marinade. Using long-handled tongs, moisten a paper towel with cooking oil and lightly coat the grill rack.

3. Grill pork, covered, over medium heat or broil 4-5 in. from the heat for 4-5 minutes on each side or until a thermometer reads 145°, basting occasionally with reserved marinade. Let meat stand for 5 minutes before serving.

Yield: 8 servings.

BUTTER & HERB TURKEY

My kids love a turkey meal, and this one falls off the bone. It's the ideal recipe for special family times, such as Sunday dinner.
ROCHELLE POPOVIC, SOUTH BEND, INDIANA

1	bone-in turkey breast (6 to 7 pounds)
2	tablespoons butter, softened
1/2	teaspoon dried rosemary, crushed
1/2	teaspoon dried thyme
1/4	teaspoon garlic powder
1/4	teaspoon pepper
1	can (14-1/2 ounces) chicken broth
3	tablespoons cornstarch
1	tablespoon cold water

1. Rub turkey with butter. Combine the rosemary, thyme, garlic powder and pepper; sprinkle over turkey. Place in a 6-qt. slow cooker. Pour broth over top. Cover and cook on low for 5-6 hours or until tender.

2. Remove turkey to a serving platter; keep warm. Skim fat from cooking juices; transfer to a small saucepan. Bring to a boil. Combine cornstarch and water until smooth. Gradually stir into the pan. Bring to a boil; cook and stir for 2 minutes or until thickened. Serve with turkey.

Yield: 12 servings (3 cups gravy).

PIEROGI PASTA SHELLS

(pictured at right)

My family loves pierogis, so I decided to create my own version. I took this dish to a Christmas party and received everyone's approval. Needless to say, I left with an empty bowl.
KIM WALLACE, DENNISON, OHIO

51	uncooked jumbo pasta shells
3	packages (24 ounces each) refrigerated mashed potatoes
2	tablespoons dried minced onion
1/2	teaspoon onion powder
1/2	teaspoon garlic powder
4	cups (16 ounces) shredded cheddar cheese, divided
1/2	cup chopped green onions

1. Cook pasta shells according to package directions; drain and rinse in cold water. Place mashed potatoes in a large microwave-safe bowl. Cover and microwave on high for 4 minutes, stirring once. Add the minced onion, onion powder and garlic powder. Stir in 2 cups of cheese until blended.

2. Stuff into shells. Place in two greased 13-in. x 9-in. baking dishes. Sprinkle with green onions and remaining cheese. Cover and bake at 350° for 20 minutes. Uncover; bake 10 minutes longer or until heated through.

Yield: 17 servings.

ZUCCHINI ENCHILADAS

I love this recipe because it helps me serve a healthy but tasty meal to my family. Also, zucchini is so plentiful in the garden and this dish makes a great way to use it up.

ANGELA LEINENBACH, MECHANICSVLLE, VIRGINIA

1	medium sweet yellow pepper, chopped
1	medium green pepper, chopped
1	large sweet onion, chopped
2	tablespoons olive oil
2	garlic cloves, minced
2	cans (15 ounces each) tomato sauce
2	cans (14-1/2 ounces each) no-salt-added diced tomatoes, undrained
2	tablespoons chili powder
2	teaspoons sugar
2	teaspoons dried marjoram
1	teaspoon dried basil
1	teaspoon ground cumin
1/4	teaspoon salt
1/4	teaspoon cayenne pepper
1	bay leaf
3	pounds zucchini, shredded (about 8 cups)
24	corn tortillas (6 inches), warmed
4	cups (16 ounces) shredded reduced-fat cheddar cheese
2	cans (2-1/4 ounces each) sliced ripe olives, drained
1/2	cup minced fresh cilantro
	Reduced-fat sour cream, optional

1. In a large saucepan, saute peppers and onion in oil until tender. Add garlic; cook 1 minute longer. Stir in the tomato sauce, tomatoes, chili powder, sugar, marjoram, basil, cumin, salt, cayenne and bay leaf. Bring to a boil. Reduce heat; simmer, uncovered, for 30-35 minutes or until slightly thickened. Discard bay leaf.

2. Place 1/3 cup zucchini down the center of each tortilla; top with 2 tablespoons cheese and about 1 tablespoon olives. Roll up and place seam side down in two 13-in. x 9-in. baking dishes coated with cooking spray. Pour sauce over the top; sprinkle with remaining cheese.

3. Bake, uncovered, at 350° for 30-35 minutes or until heated through. Sprinkle with cilantro. Serve with sour cream if desired.

Yield: 12 servings.

RASPBERRY-CHIPOTLE GLAZED HAM

Looking to liven up your same-old Sunday ham? Try this recipe, which features a sweet and spicy sauce.

MARY LOU WAYMAN, SALT LAKE CITY, UTAH

1	bone-in fully cooked spiral-sliced ham (9 to 10 pounds)
2-1/4	cups seedless raspberry jam
3	tablespoons white vinegar
3	chipotle peppers in adobo sauce, drained, seeded and minced
3	to 4 garlic cloves, minced
1	tablespoon coarsely ground pepper

1. Place ham on a rack in a shallow roasting pan. Bake, uncovered, at 325° for 2-1/2 hours.

2. Meanwhile, in a small saucepan, combine the jam, vinegar, peppers and garlic. Bring to a boil. Reduce heat; simmer, uncovered, for 5 minutes.

3. Brush some of the sauce over ham. Bake 30-35 minutes longer or until thermometer reads 140°, brushing twice with sauce. Sprinkle pepper over ham. Serve with remaining sauce.

Yield: 16-20 servings.

SAUCY PORK CHOPS

I serve these tender chops a couple of times a month because I know every family member will enjoy them. The tangy sauce is delicious over mashed potatoes, rice or noodles, too.

SHARON POLK, LAPEER, MICHIGAN

8	boneless pork chops (1/2 inch thick)
2	tablespoons canola oil
1/4	teaspoon salt
1/8	teaspoon pepper
2	cans (10-3/4 ounces each) condensed cream of chicken soup, undiluted
1	medium onion, chopped
1/2	cup ketchup
2	tablespoons Worcestershire sauce

Mashed potatoes or hot cooked rice

1. In a large skillet, cook pork chops in oil for 2-3 minutes on each side or until lightly browned. Sprinkle with salt and pepper. Transfer to a 3-qt. slow cooker.

2. In a large bowl, combine the soup, onion, ketchup and Worcestershire sauce; pour over chops. Cover and cook on high for 4-5 hours or until meat is tender. Serve with potatoes or rice.

Yield: 8 servings.

CHICKEN POTPIE

Chock-full of chicken, potatoes, peas and corn, this autumn favorite makes two golden pies, so you can serve one at supper and save the other for a busy night.

KAREN JOHNSON, BAKERSFIELD, CALIFORNIA

2	cups diced peeled potatoes
1-3/4	cups sliced carrots
2/3	cup chopped onion
1	cup butter, cubed
1	cup all-purpose flour
1-3/4	teaspoons salt
1	teaspoon dried thyme
3/4	teaspoon pepper
3	cups chicken broth
1-1/2	cups milk
4	cups cubed cooked chicken
1	cup frozen peas
1	cup frozen corn

Pastry for two double-crust pies (9 inches)

1. Place potatoes and carrots in a large saucepan; cover with water. Bring to a boil. Reduce heat; cover and simmer for 8-10 minutes or until crisp-tender. Drain and set aside.

2. In a large skillet, saute onion in butter until tender. Stir in the flour, salt, thyme and pepper until blended. Gradually stir in broth and milk. Bring to a boil; cook and stir for 2 minutes or until thickened. Add the chicken, peas, corn, potatoes and carrots; remove from the heat.

3. Line two 9-in. pie plates with bottom pastry; trim pastry even with edge. Fill pastry shells with chicken mixture. Roll out remaining pastry to fit top of pies. Cut slits or decorative cutouts in pastry. Place over filling; trim, seal and flute edges.

4. Bake one potpie at 425° for 35-40 minutes or until crust is lightly browned. Let stand for 15 minutes before cutting. Cover and freeze remaining potpie for up to 3 months.

To Use Frozen Pot Pie: Shield frozen pie crust edges with foil; place on a baking sheet. Bake at 425° for 30 minutes. Reduce heat to 350°; bake 70-80 minutes longer or until crust is golden brown.

Yield: 2 potpies (6-8 servings each).

POTATO-BAR CHILI

This is a creative twist on traditional chili. The potatoes make it a delicious, and filling, main dish.

ALCY THORNE, LOS MOLINOIS, CALIFORNIA

1-1/2	pounds lean ground beef (90% lean)
2	medium onions, chopped
1	medium green pepper, chopped
1	can (28 ounces) diced tomatoes, undrained
1	can (16 ounces) chili beans, undrained
2	tablespoons sugar
2	teaspoons chili powder
1/4	teaspoon salt
1/4	teaspoon pepper
Baked potatoes	

1. In a Dutch oven, cook the beef, onions and green pepper over medium heat until meat is no longer pink; drain. Add the tomatoes, beans, sugar and seasonings.

2. Bring to a boil. Reduce heat; simmer, uncovered, for 20 minutes. Serve with potatoes.

Yield: 7 cups.

CHEESE ENCHILADAS

(pictured at right)

You won't bring home leftovers when you make these easy enchiladas. With a homemade tomato sauce and cheesy filling, they always go fast. You can substitute any type of cheese you wish.

ASHLEY SCHACKOW, DEFIANCE, OHIO

2	cans (15 ounces each) tomato sauce
1-1/3	cups water
2	tablespoons chili powder
2	garlic cloves, minced
1	teaspoon dried oregano
1/2	teaspoon ground cumin
16	flour tortillas (8 inches), warmed
4	cups (16 ounces) shredded Monterey Jack cheese
2-1/2	cups (10 ounces) shredded cheddar cheese, divided
2	medium onions, finely chopped
1	cup (8 ounces) sour cream
1/4	cup minced fresh parsley
1/2	teaspoon salt
1/2	teaspoon pepper
Shredded lettuce, sliced ripe olives and additional sour cream, optional	

1. In a large saucepan, combine the first six ingredients. Bring to a boil. Reduce heat; simmer, uncovered, for 4-5 minutes or until thickened, stirring occasionally. Spoon 2 tablespoons sauce over each tortilla.

2. In a large bowl, combine the Monterey Jack, 2 cups cheddar cheese, onions, sour cream, parsley, salt and pepper. Place about 1/3 cup down the center of each tortilla. Roll up and place seam side down in two greased 13-in. x 9-in. baking dishes. Pour remaining sauce over top.

3. Bake, uncovered, at 350° for 20 minutes. Sprinkle with remaining cheddar cheese. Bake 4-5 minutes longer or until cheese is melted. Garnish with lettuce, olives and sour cream if desired.

Yield: 16 enchiladas.

COUNTRY RIBS WITH GINGER SAUCE

This recipe comes from my church kitchen. It's appeared on many menus through the years.
EVANGELINE JONES, STANFORDVILLE, NEW YORK

3	pounds boneless country-style pork ribs
1/4	cup sugar
1/2	teaspoon salt
1/2	cup each reduced-sodium soy sauce and ketchup
3	tablespoons brown sugar
2	teaspoons minced fresh gingerroot

1. Sprinkle ribs with sugar and salt; rub into both sides. Refrigerate 2 hours. In a small bowl, combine soy sauce, ketchup, brown sugar and ginger. Spoon half of the sauce over both sides of ribs; refrigerate 1 hour. Set remaining sauce aside for basting.

2. Place ribs on a greased rack in a 15-in. x 10-in. baking pan. Bake, uncovered, at 350° for 1-1/2 to 2 hours or until meat is tender, basting with remaining sauce every 15 minutes.

Yield: 8-12 servings.

MUSHROOM POT ROAST

Even if you don't usually care for mushrooms, you won't be able to resist this tender, slow-cooked roast. My recipe calls for a 1/2 pound of fresh sliced mushrooms along with onion, garlic and other seasonings and ingredients.
COLLEEN FAUSETT, PAHRUMP, NEVADA

1	boneless beef chuck roast (3 to 4 pounds)
1	teaspoon garlic powder
1/2	teaspoon pepper
2	tablespoons olive oil
4	cups water
1	large onion, chopped
1	celery rib, sliced
4	garlic cloves, peeled and sliced
4	teaspoons beef bouillon granules
2	bay leaves
1/2	pound sliced fresh mushrooms

1. Sprinkle beef with garlic powder and pepper. In a Dutch oven over medium-high heat, brown meat in oil on all sides. Add the water, onion, celery, garlic, bouillon and bay leaves; bring to a boil. Reduce heat; cover and simmer for 1 hour.

2. Add mushrooms. Cover and simmer 30 minutes longer or until meat is tender. Discard bay leaves. Thicken cooking liquid if desired; serve with beef.

Yield: 8-10 servings.

FRIED CHICKEN NUGGETS

What's the secret to this fast food favorite? Pancake mix and lemon-lime soda create the quick coating for tender chicken.
DOROTHY SMITH, EL DORADO, ARKANSAS

2-1/2	pounds boneless skinless chicken breasts, cut into 1-inch cubes
2-2/3	cups pancake mix
1-1/2	cups lemon-lime soda
1/4	cup butter, melted
	Oil for deep-fat frying

1. Place chicken in a 2-qt. microwave-safe bowl. Cover; microwave on high for 6-8 minutes. Stir every 2 minutes; drain. In a shallow bowl, combine mix, soda and butter.

2. Heat oil in an electric skillet or deep-fat fryer to 375°. Dip chicken into batter; fry in oil, in batches, for 2 minutes each side. Drain on paper towels.

Yield: 8-10 servings.

MARMALADE BAKED HAM

My family loves the flavor that orange marmalade, beer and brown sugar give this ham. Scoring the ham and inserting whole cloves gives it an appealing look with little effort.
CLO RUNCO, PUNXSUTAWNEY, PENNSYLVANIA

1	boneless fully cooked ham (3 to 4 pounds)
12	to 15 whole cloves
1	can (12 ounces) beer or beef broth
1/4	cup packed brown sugar
1/2	cup orange marmalade

1. Place ham on a rack in a shallow roasting pan. Score the surface of the ham, making diamond shapes 1/2 in. deep; insert a clove in each diamond.

2. Pour beer or broth over ham. Rub brown sugar over surface of ham. Cover and bake at 325° for 45 minutes.

3. Spread with marmalade. Bake, uncovered, for 15-25 minutes longer or until a thermometer reads 140°.

Yield: 12-14 servings.

ROAST TURKEY BREAST WITH ROSEMARY GRAVY

A velvety gravy coats this remarkably tender and juicy turkey breast. It's perfect for a holiday get-together. Rubbing the savory rosemary under the skin makes all the difference!
REBECCA CLARK, WARRIOR, ALABAMA

2	medium apples, sliced
1-1/2	cups sliced leeks (white portion only)
2-1/4	cups reduced-sodium chicken broth, divided
1	bone-in turkey breast (6 pounds)
1	tablespoon canola oil
2	teaspoons minced fresh rosemary, divided
3	tablespoons reduced-fat butter
1/4	cup all-purpose flour

1. Arrange apples and leeks in a roasting pan; add 1 cup broth. Place turkey breast over apple mixture. In a small bowl, combine oil and 1-1/2 teaspoons rosemary. With fingers, carefully loosen skin from the turkey breast; rub rosemary mixture under the skin. Secure skin to underside of breast with toothpicks.

2. Bake, uncovered, at 325° for 1-3/4 to 2-1/4 hours or until a meat thermometer reads 170°, basting every 30 minutes. Cover loosely with foil if turkey browns too quickly. Cover and let stand for 15 minutes before carving, reserving 1/4 cup pan juices. Discard apples and leeks.

3. In a small saucepan, melt butter; add flour and remaining rosemary until blended, stirring constantly. Skim fat from pan juices. Gradually add pan juices and remaining broth to saucepan. Bring to a boil. Cook and stir for 1 minute or until thickened. Serve with turkey.

Yield: 18 servings (1-1/3 cups gravy).

Editor's Note: This recipe was tested with Land O'Lakes light stick butter.

HERB 'N' SPICE TURKEY BREAST

This nicely seasoned turkey breast smells so good as it cooks. Prepare it for special occasions or throughout the year for a delicious dinner on its own.

TASTE OF HOME TEST KITCHEN

3	tablespoons canola oil
1	tablespoon brown sugar
1	teaspoon salt
1/2	teaspoon rubbed sage
1/2	teaspoon dried thyme
1/2	teaspoon dried rosemary, crushed
1/4	teaspoon pepper
1/8	to 1/4 teaspoon ground allspice
1	bone-in turkey breast (5 to 6 pounds)

1. In a small bowl, combine the oil, brown sugar, salt, sage, thyme, rosemary, pepper and allspice. With fingers, carefully loosen the skin from both sides of turkey breast.

2. Spread half of the brown sugar mixture under the skin. Secure skin to underside of breast with toothpicks. Spread the remaining brown sugar mixture over the skin.

3. Line the bottom of a large shallow roasting pan with foil. Place turkey breast side up on a rack in prepared pan.

4. Bake, uncovered, at 325° for 2 to 2-1/2 hours or until a meat thermometer reads 170°; (cover loosely with foil if turkey browns too quickly). Cover and let stand for 15 minutes before carving.

Yield: 10-14 servings.

POT ROAST WITH GRAVY

My family loves this slow-cooked beef roast with gravy. It's the perfect Sunday dinner to bring the weekend to a close.

DEBORAH DAILEY, VANCOUVER, WASHINGTON

1	beef rump roast or bottom round roast (5 pounds)
6	tablespoons balsamic vinegar, divided
1	teaspoon salt
1/2	teaspoon garlic powder
1/4	teaspoon pepper
2	tablespoons canola oil
3	garlic cloves, minced
4	bay leaves
1	large onion, thinly sliced
3	teaspoons beef bouillon granules
1/2	cup boiling water
1	can (10-3/4 ounces) condensed cream of mushroom soup, undiluted
4	to 5 tablespoons cornstarch
1/4	cup cold water

1. Cut roast in half; rub with 2 tablespoons vinegar. Combine the salt, garlic powder and pepper; rub over meat. In a large skillet, brown roast in oil on all sides. Transfer to a 5-qt. slow cooker.

2. Add the garlic, bay leaves and onion over roast. In a small bowl, dissolve bouillon in boiling water; stir in soup and remaining vinegar. Slowly pour over roast. Cover and cook on low for 6-8 hours or until meat is tender.

3. Remove roast; keep warm. Discard bay leaves. Whisk cornstarch and cold water until smooth; stir into cooking juices.

4. Cover and cook on high for 30 minutes or until gravy is thickened. Slice roast; return to slow cooker and heat through.

Yield: 10 servings.

BAKED BARBECUED BRISKET

This simple brisket recipe never fails me. I always hope there will be a few slices left over for sandwiches the next day.
JOAN HALLFORD, NORTH RICHLAND HILLS, TEXAS

1	tablespoon all-purpose flour
1	fresh beef brisket (5 pounds)
2	to 4 teaspoons Liquid Smoke, optional
1/2	teaspoon celery seed
1/4	teaspoon pepper
1	cup chili sauce
1/4	cup barbecue sauce

1. Place flour in a large oven roasting bag; shake to coat bag. Rub brisket with Liquid Smoke if desired, celery seed and pepper; place in bag. Place in a roasting pan. Combine chili sauce and barbecue sauce; pour over brisket. Seal bag.

2. With a knife, cut six 1/2-in. slits in top of bag. Bake at 325° for 3-1/2 to 4 hours or until meat is tender. Let stand for 5 minutes. Carefully remove brisket from bag. Thinly slice meat across the grain.

Yield: 16-20 servings.

Editor's Note: This is a fresh beef brisket, not corned beef.

APPLE PORK ROAST

My husband tells me this is the most delicious way to prepare a pork roast. Empty plates prove he's right.
FLORENCE LAPOINTE, DRYDEN, ONTARIO

1	boneless pork loin roast (3 pounds)
2	garlic cloves, sliced
2	tablespoons Dijon mustard
1	teaspoon red wine vinegar
3/4	teaspoon dried thyme
1/2	teaspoon rubbed sage
3/4	cup reduced-sodium beef broth
3/4	cup unsweetened apple juice
1/4	cup apricot jam
1-1/2	cups chopped peeled apples
1	tablespoon cornstarch
1	tablespoon reduced-fat sour cream

1. Cut eight to ten 1-in. slits in top of roast; insert garlic slices. In a large nonstick skillet coated with cooking spray, brown roast on all sides. Transfer to a roasting pan.

2. In a small bowl, combine the mustard, vinegar, thyme and sage; brush over roast. In a small saucepan, combine the broth, apple juice and jam. Cook and stir over medium heat until jam is melted; pour over roast. Arrange apples around roast.

3. Cover and bake at 350° for 1 to 1-1/4 hours or until a thermometer reads 145°, basting occasionally. Remove roast to a warm serving platter; let stand for 10 minutes before slicing.

4. Meanwhile, skim fat from pan juices. Set aside 1/2 cup juices; pour remaining juices and apples into a large saucepan. Combine cornstarch and sour cream until smooth; stir into reserved pan juices. Stir into saucepan.

5. Bring to a boil over medium heat; cook and stir for 2 minutes or until slightly thickened. Serve with roast.

Yield: 10 servings.

southwest bean soup, pg. 158

grilled vegetable sandwiches, pg. 213

Soups & Sandwiches

To God who gives us daily bread, a thankful song
we raise. We pray that God who gives us food,
Will fill our hearts with praise.

WALNUT-CREAM CHEESE FINGER SANDWICHES

Guests at an English tea my wife and I hosted thought these little sandwiches were fabulous. The cream cheese filling features bright flavors and delicious texture.

CHUCK HINZ, PARMA, OHIO

LAST MINUTE!

- 12   ounces cream cheese, softened
- 1/2   cup finely chopped walnuts, toasted
- 2   tablespoons minced fresh parsley
- 1   tablespoon finely chopped green pepper
- 1   tablespoon finely chopped onion
- 1   teaspoon lemon juice
- 1/4   teaspoon ground nutmeg

Dash salt and pepper

- 24   thin slices white sandwich bread, crusts removed

1. In a small bowl, beat the cream cheese, walnuts, parsley, green pepper, onion, lemon juice, nutmeg, salt and pepper until blended.

2. Spread about 2 tablespoonfuls over each of 12 bread slices; top with remaining bread. Cut each sandwich into three 1-in.-wide strips.

Yield: 3 dozen.

ROASTED VEGETABLE CHILI

I suggest serving this delicious and satisfying recipe with corn chips, cheese, sour cream and a small salad. To save time, purchase vegetables that have already been diced.

HANNAH BARRINGER, LOUDON, TENNESSEE

- 1   medium butternut squash, peeled and cut into 1-inch pieces
- 3   large carrots, sliced
- 2   medium zucchini, cut into 1-inch pieces
- 2   tablespoons olive oil, divided
- 1-1/2   teaspoons ground cumin
- 2   medium green peppers, diced
- 1   large onion, chopped
- 3   cans (14-1/2 ounces each) reduced-sodium chicken broth
- 3   cans (14-1/2 ounces each) diced tomatoes, undrained
- 2   cans (15 ounces each) cannellini or white kidney beans, rinsed and drained
- 1   cup water
- 1   cup salsa
- 3   teaspoons chili powder
- 6   garlic cloves, minced

1. Place the squash, carrots and zucchini in a 15-in. x 10-in. x 1-in. baking pan. Combine 1 tablespoon oil and cumin; drizzle over vegetables and toss to coat. Bake, uncovered, at 450° for 25-30 minutes or until tender, stirring once.

2. Meanwhile, in a stockpot, saute green peppers and onion in remaining oil for 3-4 minutes or until tender. Stir in the broth, tomatoes, beans, water, salsa, chili powder and garlic. Bring to a boil. Reduce heat; simmer, uncovered, for 10 minutes.

3. Stir in roasted vegetables. Return to a boil. Reduce heat; simmer, uncovered, for 5-10 minutes or until heated through.

Yield: 13 servings (5 quarts).

CAJUN CHICKEN & RICE SOUP

We enjoy this comforting, spicy soup frequently in our household. It's really good served with hot corn bread.
LISA HAMMOND, HIGGINSVILLE, MISSOURI

1	stewing chicken (about 6 pounds)
2	bay leaves
1	teaspoon salt
1	teaspoon poultry seasoning
1	teaspoon pepper
1	medium onion, chopped
2	celery ribs, chopped
1	tablespoon butter
12	garlic cloves, minced
1	can (10 ounces) diced tomatoes and green chilies, drained
3/4	cup orange juice
2	tablespoons minced fresh cilantro
2	teaspoons Cajun seasoning
1	teaspoon dried oregano
1/2	teaspoon dried thyme
1/2	teaspoon ground cumin
1/2	teaspoon paprika
2	cups cooked rice
1	can (15 ounces) pinto beans, rinsed and drained

1. Place chicken in a large stockpot; cover with water. Add the bay leaves, salt, poultry seasoning and pepper. Bring to a boil. Reduce heat; cover and simmer for 1-1/2 hours or until chicken is tender.

2. Remove chicken from broth; set aside to cool. Strain broth, discarding seasonings. Set aside 6 cups broth for the soup; save remaining broth for another use. Skim fat from soup broth. When cool enough to handle, remove chicken from bones; discard bones. Shred and set aside 3 cups chicken (save remaining chicken for another use).

3. In a large stockpot, saute onion and celery in butter until onion is crisp-tender. Add garlic; cook 1 minute longer. Stir in the tomatoes, orange juice, cilantro, seasonings and reserved broth. Bring to a boil. Reduce heat; cover and simmer for 15 minutes or until vegetables are tender. Stir in the rice, beans and reserved chicken; heat through.

Yield: 12 servings (3 quarts).

SMOKED SAUSAGE SOUP

Each satisfying bowl is chock-full of tasty smoked sausage, hash browns, green beans, carrots and more.
MARGE WHEELER, SAN BENITO, TEXAS

4-1/2	cups water
1	can (28 ounces) diced tomatoes, undrained
1	envelope onion soup mix
1	package (9 ounces) frozen cut green beans
3	small carrots, halved and thinly sliced
2	celery ribs, thinly sliced
1	tablespoon sugar
1/2	teaspoon salt
1/2	teaspoon dried oregano
1/8	teaspoon hot pepper sauce
1	pound smoked sausage, halved and thinly sliced
2-1/2	cups frozen shredded hash brown potatoes

1. In a Dutch oven, combine the first 10 ingredients. bring to a boil. Reduce heat; cover and simmer for 20-25 minutes or until vegetables are tender.

2. Stir in sausage and hash browns. Bring to a boil. Reduce heat; cover and cook for 5 minutes or until heated through.

Yield: 12 servings.

HEARTY SPLIT PEA SOUP

For a different spin on split pea soup, try this recipe. The flavor is peppery rather than smoky.

BARBARA LINK, RANCHO CUCAMONGA, CALIFORNIA

1	package (16 ounces) dried split peas
8	cups water
2	medium potatoes, peeled and cubed
2	large onions, chopped
2	medium carrots, chopped
2	cups cubed fully cooked lean ham
1	celery rib, chopped
5	teaspoons reduced-sodium chicken bouillon granules
1	teaspoon dried marjoram
1	teaspoon poultry seasoning
1	teaspoon rubbed sage
1/2	to 1 teaspoon pepper
1/2	teaspoon dried basil

1. In a Dutch oven, combine all ingredients; bring to a boil. Reduce heat; cover and simmer for 1-1/4 to 1-1/2 hours or until peas and vegetables are tender.

Yield: 12 servings (3 quarts).

GRILLED VEGETABLE SANDWICHES

(pictured at right)

Use some of your fresh garden bounty to build these hearty, unique subs. Basil-lemon mayo adds terrific flavor.

KATHY HEWITT, CRANSTON, RHODE ISLAND

3	large sweet red peppers
3	medium red onions
3	large zucchini
1/4	cup olive oil
3/4	teaspoon salt
3/4	teaspoon coarsely ground pepper
3/4	cup reduced-fat mayonnaise
1/3	cup minced fresh basil
2	tablespoons lemon juice
6	garlic cloves, minced
12	submarine buns, split
24	slices cheddar cheese
3	medium tomatoes, sliced
3/4	cup hummus

1. Cut the red peppers into eighths; cut onions and zucchini into 1/2-in. slices. Brush vegetables with oil; sprinkle with salt and pepper. Grill vegetables in batches, covered, over medium heat or broil 4 in. from the heat for 4-5 minutes on each side or until crisp-tender. Cool.

2. Combine the mayonnaise, basil, lemon juice and garlic; spread over bun bottoms. Layer with cheese, grilled vegetables and tomatoes. Spread hummus over bun tops; replace tops.

Yield: 12 servings.

TACO BEAN SOUP

This satisfying three-bean soup is very easy to fix. You can add a can of green chilies if you like it hotter. I increase the amount of tomatoes and beans for large get-togethers at my church.

SHARON THOMPSON, HUNTER, KANSAS

1	pound bulk pork sausage
1	pound ground beef
1	envelope taco seasoning
4	cups water
2	cans (16 ounces each) kidney beans, rinsed and drained
2	cans (15 ounces each) pinto beans, rinsed and drained
2	cans (15 ounces each) garbanzo beans or chickpeas, rinsed and drained
2	cans (14-1/2 ounces each) stewed tomatoes
2	cans (14-1/2 ounces each) Mexican diced tomatoes, undrained
1	jar (16 ounces) chunky salsa
	Sour cream, shredded cheddar cheese and sliced ripe olives, optional

1. In a stockpot, cook sausage and beef over medium heat until no longer pink; drain. Add taco seasoning and mix well. Stir in the water, beans, tomatoes and salsa. Bring to a boil. reduce heat; simmer, uncovered, for 30 minutes or until heated through, stirring occasionally. Garnish with sour cream, cheese and olives if desired.

Yield: 12-14 servings.

ITALIAN PULLED PORK SANDWICHES

Enjoy all the flavors of Italian sausage sandwiches with this healthier alternative.
LIA DELLARIO, MIDDLEPORT, NEW YORK

1 tablespoon fennel seed, crushed
1 tablespoon steak seasoning
1 teaspoon cayenne pepper, optional
1 boneless pork shoulder butt roast (3 pounds)
1 tablespoon olive oil
2 medium green or sweet red peppers, thinly sliced
2 medium onions, thinly sliced
1 can (14-1/2 ounces) diced tomatoes, undrained
12 whole wheat hamburger buns, split

1. In a small bowl, combine the fennel seed, steak seasoning and cayenne if desired. Rub over pork. In a large skillet, brown roast in oil on all sides. Place in a 4- or 5-qt slow cooker. Add the peppers, onions and tomatoes; cover and cook on low for 8-10 hours or until meat is tender.

2. Remove roast; cool slightly. Skim fat from cooking juices. Shred pork with two forks and return to

slow cooker; heat through. Using a slotted spoon, place 1/2 cup meat mixture on each bun.
Yield: 12 servings.

FIESTA TUNA SALAD SANDWICHES

Sometimes I make a tuna melt out of this sandwich and serve warm. The tuna salad spread is also yummy as a dip.
KATHY HEWITT, CRANSTON, RHODE ISLAND

LAST MINUTE!

6 cans (5 ounces each) white water-packed tuna, drained and flaked
1 large red onion, chopped
2 medium tomatoes, chopped
2/3 cup reduced-fat mayonnaise
2 jalapeno peppers, seeded and finely chopped
1/4 cup lemon juice
2 garlic cloves, minced
1 teaspoon seafood seasoning
1 teaspoon coarsely ground pepper
2 loaves (14 ounces each) ciabatta bread, split
3/4 pound sliced pepper Jack cheese
12 lettuce leaves

1. In a bowl, combine the first nine ingredients; spread over bread bottoms. Layer with cheese and lettuce. Replace bread tops. Cut each loaf into six slices.
Yield: 12 servings.

CRANBERRY BBQ TURKEY SANDWICHES

This slightly sweet sandwich is a great way to use up leftover turkey. Keep the meat warm in a slow cooker at your next potluck for a fuss-free, crowd-pleasing offering.
SUSAN MATTHEWS, ROCKFORD, ILLINOIS

1	can (14 ounces) jellied cranberry sauce
1	cup reduced-sodium beef broth
1/4	cup sugar
1/4	cup ketchup
2	tablespoons cider vinegar
1	tablespoon Worcestershire sauce
1	teaspoon yellow mustard
1/4	teaspoon garlic powder
1/8	teaspoon seasoned salt
1/8	teaspoon paprika
6	cups shredded cooked turkey breast
12	sandwich buns, split

1. In a saucepan, combine the first 10 ingredients. Bring to a boil. Reduce heat; simmer, uncovered, for 20 minutes or until sauce is thickened.

2. Stir in turkey; simmer 4-5 minutes longer or until heated through. Spoon 1/2 cup onto each bun.
Yield: 12 servings.

HEARTY CHILI MAC

Luckily, this recipe makes a lot, since everyone is apt to want another bowl. It freezes well and makes excellent leftovers.
FANNIE WEHMAS, SAXON, WISCONSIN

2	pounds ground beef
1	medium onion, chopped
1	can (46 ounces) tomato juice
1	can (28 ounces) diced tomatoes, undrained
2	celery ribs, chopped
3	tablespoons brown sugar
2	tablespoons chili powder
1	teaspoon salt
1	teaspoon prepared mustard
1/4	teaspoon pepper
2	cans (16 ounces each) kidney beans, rinsed and drained
1/2	cup uncooked elbow macaroni

1. In a Dutch oven, cook beef and onion over medium heat until meat is no longer pink; drain. Stir in the tomato juice, tomatoes, celery, brown sugar, chili powder, salt, mustard and pepper. Bring to a boil. Reduce heat; simmer, uncovered, for 1 hour, stirring occasionally.

2. Add the beans and macaroni; simmer 15-20 minutes longer or until macaroni is tender.
Yield: 10-12 servings.

BACON CHEESEBURGER BUNS

This is a fun way to serve bacon cheeseburgers without all the fuss of assembling the sandwiches to serve a gang. These convenient packets can be dipped into ketchup or barbecue sauce as you eat them.

MARJORIE MILLER, HAVEN, KANSAS

2	packages (1/4 ounce each) active dry yeast
2/3	cup warm water (110° to 115°)
2/3	cup warm milk (110° to 115°)
1/4	cup sugar
1/4	cup shortening
2	eggs
2	teaspoons salt
4-1/2	to 5 cups all-purpose flour

FILLING:

1	pound sliced bacon, diced
2	pounds ground beef
1	small onion, chopped
1-1/2	teaspoons salt
1/2	teaspoon pepper
1	pound process cheese (Velveeta), cubed
3	to 4 tablespoons butter, melted
	Ketchup or barbecue sauce, optional

1. In a large bowl, dissolve yeast in warm water. Add the milk, sugar, shortening, eggs, salt and 3-1/2 cups flour; beat until smooth. Stir in enough remaining flour to form a soft dough.

2. Turn onto a floured surface; knead until smooth and elastic, about 6-8 minutes. Place in a greased bowl, turning once to grease top. Cover and let rise in a warm place until doubled, about 1 hour.

3. Meanwhile, in a large skillet, cook bacon over medium heat until crisp. Using a slotted spoon, remove to paper towels. In a Dutch oven, cook the beef, onion, salt and pepper over medium heat until meat is no longer pink; drain. Add bacon and cheese; cook and stir until cheese is melted. Remove from the heat.

4. Punch dough down. Turn onto a lightly floured surface; divide into fourths. Roll each portion into an 12-in. x 8-in. rectangle; cut each into six squares.

Place 1/4 cup meat mixture in the center of each square. Bring corners together in the center and pinch to seal.

5. Place 2 in. apart on greased baking sheets. Bake at 400° for 9-11 minutes or until lightly browned. Brush with butter. Serve warm with ketchup if desired.

Yield: 2 dozen.

Leaner Ground Beef

To help eliminate fat from ground beef, cook it in a microwave-safe strainer or colander in a microwave-safe bowl. Break up the ground beef with a fork and stir it frequently as it's cooking until it's no longer pink. The fat will collect at the bottom of the bowl, and the beef is ready to be used.

PORK SANDWICHES WITH ROOT BEER SAUCE

This tasty recipe is sure to please a crowd! I love the subtle kick and hint of sweetness in this dish. Try serving these sandwiches with coleslaw and pickles.

KAREN CURRIE, KIRKWOOD, MISSOURI

1	boneless pork sirloin roast (2 pounds)
1	medium onion, sliced
2	tablespoons dried minced garlic
3	cups root beer, divided
1	bottle (12 ounces) chili sauce
1/8	teaspoon hot pepper sauce
8	kaiser rolls, split

1. Place roast in a 3-qt. slow cooker. Add the onion, garlic and 1 cup root beer. Cover and cook on low for 9-10 hours or until meat is tender.

2. In a small saucepan, combine the chili sauce, hot pepper sauce and remaining root beer. Bring to a boil. Reduce heat; simmer, uncovered, for 20-25 minutes or until thickened.

3. Remove meat from slow cooker; cool slightly. Discard cooking juices. Shred pork with two forks and return to slow cooker. Stir in barbecue sauce. Cover and cook on low for 30 minutes or until heated through. Serve on rolls.

Yield: 8 servings.

TURKEY, GOUDA & APPLE TEA SANDWICHES

(pictured at left)

These fun mini sandwiches from our home economists are a tasty addition to an afternoon tea gathering. The cranberry mayo lends a unique flavor twist, and the apples add a nice crunch.

TASTE OF HOME TEST KITCHEN

2/3	cup reduced-fat mayonnaise
2	tablespoons whole-berry cranberry sauce
24	very thin slices white bread, crusts removed
12	slices deli turkey
2	medium apples, thinly sliced
12	thin slices smoked Gouda cheese
4	cups fresh baby spinach

1. Place mayonnaise and cranberry sauce in a small food processor. Cover and process until blended. Spread over each bread slice.

2. Layer the turkey, apples, cheese and spinach over each of 12 bread slices; top with remaining bread. Cut each sandwich into quarters.

Yield: 4 dozen.

To Make Ahead: Cranberry spread can be prepared a day in advance; cover and store in the refrigerator.

CHICKEN LITTLE SLIDERS

Fruity salsa dresses up these tiny chicken burgers, which are perfect for feeding a crowd. The fun name reminds kids of the fable and makes them eager to try one.

LAURA MCALLISTER, MORGANTON, NORTH CAROLINA

SALSA:

3	plum tomatoes, seeded and chopped
1/4	cup minced fresh basil or 1 tablespoon dried basil
1/4	cup canned crushed pineapple
1/4	cup chopped red onion
1	jalapeno pepper, seeded and finely chopped
2	tablespoons lemon juice
1	teaspoon grated lemon peel
1/8	teaspoon salt
1/8	teaspoon pepper

MAYO:

1/3	cup reduced-fat mayonnaise
2	tablespoons chopped roasted sweet red pepper
1/2	teaspoon grated lemon peel
	Dash salt

BURGERS:

1	egg, beaten
1/2	cup finely chopped roasted sweet red peppers
2	tablespoons plus 2 teaspoons fat-free milk
1-1/2	teaspoons Dijon mustard
1-1/3	cups soft bread crumbs
3/4	teaspoon salt
1/4	teaspoon pepper
1-1/2	pounds ground chicken

SERVING:

1/2	cup crumbled feta cheese
18	heat-and-serve rolls, split
18	small lettuce leaves

1. In two small bowls, combine the salsa and mayo ingredients; chill until serving.

2. In a large bowl, combine the egg, peppers, milk, mustard, bread crumbs, salt and pepper. Crumble chicken over mixture and mix well. Shape into 18 patties.

3. If grilling the burgers, coat grill rack with cooking spray before starting the grill. Grill burgers, covered, over medium heat or broil 4 in. from the heat for 3-4 minutes on each side or until a meat thermometer reads 165° and juices run clear.

4. Stir cheese into salsa. Spread rolls with mayo; top each with a lettuce leaf, burger and 2 tablespoons salsa mixture.

Yield: 1-1/2 dozen.

BEEF BARBECUE

When we're not in the mood for pot roast, I fix these sandwiches instead. The meat cooks in a tasty sauce while I'm at work.

KAREN WALKER, STERLING, VIRGINIA

1	boneless beef chuck roast (3 pounds)
1	cup barbecue sauce
1/2	cup apricot preserves
1/3	cup chopped green or sweet red pepper
1	small onion, chopped
1	tablespoon Dijon mustard
2	teaspoons brown sugar
12	sandwich rolls, split

1. Cut the roast into quarters; place in a greased 5-qt. slow cooker. In a large bowl, combine the barbecue sauce, preserves, green pepper, onion, mustard and brown sugar; pour over roast. Cover and cook on low for 6-8 hours or until meat is tender.

2. Remove roast and thinly slice; return meat to slow cooker and stir gently. Cover and cook 20-30 minutes longer. Skim fat from sauce. Serve beef and sauce on rolls.

Yield: 12 servings.

CREAMY LEEK SOUP WITH BRIE

Bits of Brie add something special to this soup from our home economists. Soup is a satisfying addition to a buffet table. Use a slow cooker to keep it warm.
TASTE OF HOME TEST KITCHEN

5	cups chopped leeks (white portion only)
1/4	cup butter
5	cups chicken broth
4-1/2	cups half-and-half cream, divided
1/2	cup all-purpose flour
1	teaspoon salt
1/4	teaspoon white pepper
3	rounds (8 each) Brie cheese, rind removed
3	tablespoons minced chives

1. In a Dutch oven, saute leeks in butter until tender. Add broth; bring to a boil. Reduce heat; cover and simmer for 25 minutes.

2. Strain, reserving broth in pan. Place leeks in a blender with 1/2 cup of broth; cover and process until smooth.

3. Return to the pan. Stir in 3 cups cream. Combine the flour, salt, pepper and remaining cream until smooth; stir into soup. Bring to a boil; cook and stir for 2 minutes. Reduce heat to medium.

4. Cut Brie into small pieces; add to soup in batches, stirring until most of the cheese is melted. Garnish with chives.

Yield: 12 servings (2-1/2 quarts).

DELI BEEF HEROS

Marinated artichokes, caramelized onions and green olives add loads of flavor to these crusty roast beef sandwiches. They're also good with pastrami or corned beef.
CAMERON BYRNE, RIVERTON, WYOMING

2	large onions, chopped
1/4	cup olive oil
6	ounces cream cheese, softened
3/4	cup ricotta cheese
3/4	cup pimiento-stuffed olives
2	garlic cloves, peeled
2	French bread baguettes (10-1/2 ounces each), split
1	pound sliced deli roast beef
2	jars (7-1/2 ounces each) roasted sweet red peppers, drained and julienned
2	jars (7-1/2 ounces each) marinated quartered artichoke hearts, drained and chopped

1. In a skillet, cook onions in oil over low heat for 15-20 minutes or until golden brown, stirring occasionally.

2. Meanwhile, place the cream cheese, ricotta cheese, olives and garlic in a food processor. Cover and process until blended. Spread over baguettes. Layer bread bottoms with roast beef, peppers, artichokes and caramelized onions; replace tops. Cut each into six slices.

Yield: 12 servings.

SOUTHWEST BEAN SOUP

I made up this recipe to help me safely lose weight. Even my friends who aren't calorie-conscious say it's the best soup they've ever eaten! Cilantro and veggies make it yummy and fresh.
MARIANNE BROWN, GLENDALE, ARIZONA

1	large onion, chopped
1	medium green pepper, chopped
3	garlic cloves, minced
3	cans (14-1/2 ounces each) reduced-sodium beef broth
2	cans (15 ounces each) black beans, rinsed and drained
1	can (28 ounces) diced tomatoes, undrained
2	cans (4 ounces each) chopped green chilies
1	cup frozen corn
1-1/2	teaspoons chili powder
1	teaspoon ground cumin
1/2	cup minced fresh cilantro

1. In a large nonstick saucepan coated with cooking spray, cook and stir onion and green pepper over medium heat until almost tender. Add garlic; cook 1 minute longer.

2. Stir in the broth, beans, tomatoes, chilies, corn, chili powder and cumin. Bring to a boil. Reduce heat; cover and simmer for 20 minutes. Stir in cilantro.

Yield: 13 servings (3-1/4 quarts).

SLOW-COOKED TURKEY SANDWICHES

These sandwiches have been such a hit at office potlucks that I keep copies of the recipe in my desk to hand out.
DIANE TWAIT NELSEN, RINGSTED, IOWA

6	cups cubed cooked turkey
2	cups cubed process cheese (Velveeta)
1	can (10-3/4 ounces) condensed cream of chicken soup, undiluted
1	can (10-3/4 ounces) condensed cream of mushroom soup, undiluted
1/2	cup finely chopped onion
1/2	cup chopped celery
22	wheat sandwich buns, split

1. In a 3-qt. slow cooker, combine the first six ingredients. Cover and cook on low for 3-4 hours or until onion and celery are tender and cheese is melted. Stir mixture before spooning 1/2 cup onto each bun.

Yield: 22 servings.

MINI BURGERS WITH THE WORKS

I started preparing these mini burgers several years ago as a way to use up bread crusts. The small size of these sandwiches makes them perfect for an appetizer table, too.
LINDA LANE, BENNINGTON, VERMONT

1/4	pound ground beef
3	slices process American cheese
4	slices white bread (heels of loaf recommended)
2	tablespoons prepared Thousand Island salad dressing
2	pearl onions, thinly sliced
4	baby dill pickles, thinly sliced
3	cherry tomatoes, thinly sliced

1. Shape beef into twelve 1-in. patties. Place on a microwave-safe plate lined with paper towels. Cover with another paper towel; microwave on high for 1 minute until a meat thermometer reads 160° and juices run clear. Cut each slice of cheese into fourths; set aside.

2. Using a 1-in. round cookie cutter, cut out six circles from each slice of bread. Spread half of the bread circles with dressing. Layer with burgers, cheese, onions, pickles and tomatoes. Top with remaining bread circles; secure with toothpicks.

Yield: 1 dozen.

ADDITIONAL INGREDIENTS (for each batch):

1/2	cup water
1	cup uncooked ziti or small tube pasta

1. In a Dutch oven, cook the pork, celery and onion over medium heat until meat is no longer pink. Add garlic; cook 1 minute longer. Drain.

2. Stir in the tomatoes, beans, tomato juice, tomato sauce, broth, carrots, zucchini, Italian seasoning, salt, sugar if desired and pepper. Bring to a boil. Reduce heat; cover and simmer for 30-35 minutes or until carrots are tender.

3. Transfer 6 cups of soup to a freezer container; freeze for up to 3 months. Add water and pasta to remaining soup; bring to a boil. Cover and cook until pasta is tender.

To use frozen soup: Thaw in the refrigerator; transfer to a large saucepan. Stir in water. Bring to a boil; reduce heat. Add pasta; cover and cook until tender.

Yield: 2 batches (6 servings each).

HEARTY MINESTRONE

This is my all-time favorite soup. I love to make big batches and freeze some for later. This hearty dish reminds me of spaghetti and sauce—in soup form!
KATIE KOZIOLEK, HARTLAND, MINNESOTA

1	pound ground pork
1/2	cup chopped celery
1/2	cup chopped onion
1/2	teaspoon minced garlic
1	can (28 ounces) crushed tomatoes
1	can (16 ounces) kidney beans, rinsed and drained
1	can (15 ounces) garbanzo beans or chickpeas, rinsed and drained
2	cups tomato juice
1	can (15 ounces) tomato sauce
1	can (14-1/2 ounces) beef broth
3	medium carrots, chopped
1	medium zucchini, halved lengthwise and thinly sliced
1	tablespoon Italian seasoning
1	to 1-1/2 teaspoons salt
1/2	teaspoon sugar, optional
1/8	teaspoon pepper

CHICKEN SALAD CROISSANTS

Fresh dill is the secret to the success of these slightly upscale looking sandwiches. I like to use miniature croissants when serving them as an appetizer.
JESSIE YATES, MONETTE, ARKANSAS

3	cups diced grilled chicken
1	can (11 ounces) mandarin oranges, drained and halved
1	cup halved seedless red grapes
2	celery ribs, finely chopped
1/2	cup mayonnaise
1/4	cup sunflower kernels
2	tablespoons minced fresh dill or 2 teaspoons dill weed
7	croissants or 21 miniature croissants, split

1. In a bowl, combine the first seven ingredients. Spoon onto croissants; replace tops. If using large croissants, cut into thirds. Serve immediately.

Yield: 21 servings.

CHICKEN BEAN SOUP

This easy soup is tasty and nutritious, though you'd never guess it thanks to its robust flavor. I like to top individual bowls with a few sprigs of fresh parsley. Freshly baked rolls or bread are an added treat.

PHYLLIS SHAUGHNESSY, LIVONIA, NEW YORK

1	pound boneless skinless chicken breasts, cubed
2	cans (14-1/2 ounces each) chicken broth
2	cans (14-1/2 ounces each) Italian diced tomatoes, undrained
1	can (16 ounces) kidney beans, rinsed and drained
1	can (15-1/4 ounces) whole kernel corn, drained or 1-1/2 cups frozen corn
1	can (15 ounces) lima beans, rinsed and drained or 1-1/2 cups frozen lima beans
1	cup frozen peas and pearl onions
1	tablespoon snipped fresh dill or 1 teaspoon dill weed
1/2	teaspoon ground ginger, optional

1. In a 5-qt. slow cooker, combine all ingredients. Cover and cook on low for 4 hours or until chicken juices run clear.

Yield: 12 servings (3 quarts).

EGGPLANT MUFFULETTA

I often rely on this recipe when hosting a casual holiday party. It's a marvelous meatless sandwich that makes each gathering special.

ELIZABETH DUMONT, BOULDER, COLORADO

1	jar (8 ounces) roasted sweet red peppers, drained
1	cup pimiento-stuffed olives
1	cup pitted ripe olives
1	cup giardiniera
3/4	cup olive oil, divided
1/4	cup packed fresh parsley sprigs
3	tablespoons white wine vinegar
4	garlic cloves, halved
1-1/2	teaspoons salt, divided
1/2	teaspoon pepper, divided
1	pound sliced fresh mushrooms
1	large onion, thinly sliced
2	tablespoons butter
1	cup all-purpose flour
1	medium eggplant, cut into nine slices
3	loaves (10 ounces each) focaccia bread
2	large tomatoes, sliced
9	slices provolone cheese
9	slices part-skim mozzarella cheese

1. In a food processor, combine the red peppers, olives, giardiniera, 1/4 cup oil, parsley, vinegar, garlic, 1 teaspoon salt and 1/4 teaspoon pepper. Cover and process until blended; set aside.

2. In a large skillet, saute mushrooms and onion in butter and 1/4 cup oil. Remove and keep warm.

3. In a large resealable plastic bag, combine flour and remaining salt and pepper. Add eggplant, a few slices at a time, and shake to coat. In the same skillet, cook eggplant in remaining oil for 2-3 minutes on each side or until golden brown.

4. Split each loaf of focaccia in half lengthwise. Spread reserved olive mixture over each focaccia bottom; top with eggplant, mushroom mixture, tomatoes and cheeses.

5. Place on a baking sheet. Broil 2-3 in. from the heat for 2-4 minutes or until cheese is melted. Replace focaccia tops. Cut each loaf into six wedges.

Yield: 18 servings.

MINI BARBECUED HAM SANDWICHES

These flavorful sandwiches make a perfect mini snack or appetizer. Your guests won't be able to eat just one!

SUSANNE ROUPE, EAST FAIRFIELD, VERMONT

1	cup chili sauce
1/2	cup water
2	tablespoons sugar
2	tablespoons cider vinegar
1	tablespoon Worcestershire sauce
1	teaspoon onion powder
1	pound fully cooked ham, very thinly sliced
24	dinner rolls, split

1. In a large saucepan, combine the first six ingredients. Bring to a boil. Reduce heat; simmer, uncovered, for 6-8 minutes or until slightly thickened. Stir in ham; heat through. Serve on rolls.

Yield: 2 dozen.

TOMATO GARLIC SOUP

(pictured at right)

I like to make this simple soup when I'm expecting a crowd for dinner. It makes a lot and always satisfies.

LYNN THOMPSON, RESTON, VIRGINIA

10	whole garlic bulbs
1/2	cup olive oil
4	cans (one 14-1/2 ounces, three 28 ounces) diced tomatoes, undrained
1	medium onion, diced
3	cans (14-1/2 ounces each) stewed tomatoes
2/3	cup heavy whipping cream
1	to 3 tablespoons chopped pickled jalapeno peppers
2	teaspoons garlic pepper blend
2	teaspoons sugar
1-1/2	teaspoons salt

Croutons and shredded Parmesan cheese, optional

1. Remove papery outer skin from garlic (do not peel or separate cloves). Cut top off of garlic bulb. Drizzle with oil. Wrap each bulb in heavy-duty foil. Bake at 425° for 30-35 minutes or until softened.

Cool for 10-15 minutes. Squeeze softened garlic into a blender. Add the 14-1/2-oz. can of diced tomatoes; cover and process until smooth. Set aside.

2. Transfer 1/4 cup oil from the foil to a Dutch oven or soup kettle (discard the remaining oil). Saute onion in oil over medium heat until tender.

3. Stir in the stewed tomatoes, cream, jalapenos, garlic pepper, sugar, salt, pureed tomato mixture and remaining diced tomatoes. Bring to a boil. Reduce heat; cover and simmer for 1 hour. Garnish with croutons and cheese if desired.

Yield: 18-20 servings (4-1/2 quarts).

Substitution Secrets

When a recipe calls for a clove of garlic and you have no fresh bulbs, substitute 1/4 teaspoon of garlic powder for each clove. Or use 1/2 teaspoon of jarred fresh minced garlic for each clove.

1. In a large Dutch oven, cook bacon until crisp; remove to paper towels to drain. Reserve 3 tablespoons drippings.

2. Brown beef in drippings. Add onion; cook until onions are tender. Add garlic; cook 1 minute longer. Return bacon to pan. Stir in the next 12 ingredients.

3. Bring to a boil. Reduce heat; cover and simmer until meat is tender, about 3 hours.

4. Add beans and heat through. Discard bay leaf. Garnish with cheese if desired.

Yield: 4 quarts.

THICK & CHUNKY BEEF CHILI

Hearty, flavorful ingredients and a thick, rich sauce make this a satisfying chili that's sure to win compliments on your cooking. It's a great way to serve a crowd during the big game or to warm up on a chilly evening.
TASTE OF HOME TEST KITCHEN

12	ounces center-cut bacon, diced
2	pounds beef stew meat, cut into 1/4-inch cubes
2	medium onions, chopped
4	garlic cloves, minced
3	cans (14-1/2 ounces each) no-salt-added diced tomatoes, undrained
1	cup barbecue sauce
1	cup chili sauce
1/2	cup honey
4	teaspoons reduced-sodium beef bouillon granules
1	bay leaf
1	tablespoon chili powder
1	tablespoon baking cocoa
1	tablespoon Worcestershire sauce
1	tablespoon Dijon mustard
1-1/2	teaspoons ground cumin
1/4	teaspoon cayenne powder, optional
3	cans (16 ounces each) kidney beans, rinsed and drained
	Shredded reduced-fat cheddar cheese, optional

PIZZAWICHES

People of all ages like these pizza-flavored sandwiches, which can be made ahead of time and stored in the freezer.
JENNIFER SHORT, OMAHA, NEBRASKA

2	pounds ground beef
1	medium onion, chopped
2	cans (10-3/4 ounces each) condensed tomato soup, undiluted
1	teaspoon dried oregano
1	teaspoon chili powder
1/2	teaspoon garlic salt
1	cup (4 ounces) shredded cheddar cheese
1	cup (4 ounces) shredded part-skim mozzarella cheese
12	hamburger buns, split
3	to 4 tablespoons butter, melted

1. In a large skillet, cook beef and onion over medium heat until meat is no longer pink; drain. Stir in the soup, oregano, chili powder and garlic salt. Bring to a boil. Remove from the heat; stir in cheeses. Place about 1/3 cup meat mixture on each bun. Brush tops of buns with butter.

2. Place on an ungreased baking sheet. Bake at 375° for 7-9 minutes or until cheese is melted. Or wrap sandwiches in foil and freeze for up to 3 months.

To use frozen sandwiches: Place foil-wrapped buns on an ungreased baking sheet. Bake at 375° for 35-40 minutes or until heated through.

Yield: 12 sandwiches.

SLOW-COOKED CHICKEN NOODLE SOUP

This satisfying homemade soup with a hint of cayenne is brimming with vegetables, chicken and noodles. The recipe came from my father-in-law, but I made some adjustments to give it my own spin.

NORMA REYNOLDS, OVERLAND PARK, KANSAS

12	fresh baby carrots, cut into 1/2-inch pieces
4	celery ribs, cut into 1/2-inch pieces
3/4	cup finely chopped onion
1	tablespoon minced fresh parsley
1/2	teaspoon pepper
1/4	teaspoon cayenne pepper
1-1/2	teaspoons mustard seed
2	garlic cloves, peeled and halved
1-1/4	pounds boneless skinless chicken breast halves
1-1/4	pounds boneless skinless chicken thighs
4	cans (14-1/2 ounces each) chicken broth
1	package (9 ounces) refrigerated linguine

1. In a 5-qt. slow cooker, combine the first six ingredients. Place mustard seed and garlic on a double thickness of cheesecloth; bring up corners of cloth and tie with kitchen string to form a bag. Place in slow cooker. Add chicken and broth. Cover and cook on low for 5-6 hours or until meat is tender.

2. Discard spice bag. Remove chicken; cool slightly. Stir linguine into soup; cover and cook on high for 30 minutes or until tender. Cut chicken into pieces and return to soup; heat through.

Yield: 12 servings (3 quarts).

CUCUMBER TEA SANDWICHES

My children wanted to plant a garden, and we ended up with buckets of cucumbers. When I tired of making pickles, I came up with these pretty, little sandwiches. We made 200 of them for a family gathering, and everyone wanted the recipe.

KIMBERLY SMITH, BRIGHTON, TENNESSEE

1	package (8 ounces) cream cheese, softened
1/4	cup mayonnaise
1	tablespoon snipped fresh dill
1	tablespoon lemon juice
1/2	teaspoon Worcestershire sauce
1/4	teaspoon salt
1/8	teaspoon cayenne pepper
1/8	teaspoon pepper
2	large cucumbers, seeded and chopped
1/2	cup chopped sweet red pepper
1/4	cup chopped onion
1/4	cup pimiento-stuffed olives, chopped
1/4	cup minced fresh parsley
12	slices whole wheat bread

Cucumber slices and fresh dill sprigs, optional

1. In a small bowl, combine the first eight ingredients; beat until blended. Stir in the cucumbers, red pepper, onion, olives and parsley. Cover and refrigerate for up to 2 hours.

2. Remove crusts from bread; cut each slice into four triangles. Spread with cream cheese mixture. Garnish with cucumber slices and dill sprigs if desired.

Yield: 4 dozen.

1. In a Dutch oven, combine the first 14 ingredients. Bring to a boil. Reduce heat; cover and simmer for 20-25 minutes or until tender. Discard bay leaves. Cool slightly.

2. In a blender, process soup in batches until smooth. Return all to the pan; add cream and heat through. Garnish with additional cooked vegetables and/or apples and chives.

Yield: 13 servings (3-1/4 quarts).

MEAT 'N' CHEESE STROMBOLI

This tasty Italian-style sandwich can be served warm or at room temperature, and it heats up nicely in the microwave.
SUE SHEA, DEFIANCE, OHIO

1	medium onion, sliced and separated into rings
1	medium green pepper, sliced into rings
1	tablespoon butter
2	loaves (16 ounces each) frozen bread dough, thawed
1/2	pound thinly sliced hard salami
1/2	pound thinly sliced deli ham
8	ounces sliced part-skim mozzarella cheese
1/2	pound sliced mild cheddar cheese
1/2	teaspoon Italian seasoning
1/4	teaspoon garlic powder
1/8	teaspoon pepper
1	egg, lightly beaten
1	teaspoon poppy seeds

1. In a large skillet, saute onion and green pepper in butter until crisp-tender; set aside.

2. On two greased baking sheets, roll each loaf of dough into a 15-in. x 12-in. rectangle. Arrange the salami, ham and cheeses lengthwise over half of each rectangle to within 1/2 in. of edges. Top with onion mixture; sprinkle with the Italian seasoning, garlic powder and pepper. Fold dough over filling; pinch edges to seal.

3. Brush with egg and sprinkle with poppy seeds. Bake at 400° for 15-20 minutes or until golden brown. Cool for 5 minutes before slicing.

Yield: 2 loaves (8 servings each).

RUSTIC AUTUMN SOUP

If you're looking for a great soup fit for chilly fall days, this is it! The flavors of root vegetables really shine with the subtle sweetness of apple.
GREG HAGELI, ELMHURST, ILLINOIS

5	medium parsnips, chopped
5	medium carrots, chopped
2	medium onions, chopped
1	medium sweet potato, peeled and chopped
1	medium turnip, peeled and chopped
1/2	medium tart apple, peeled and chopped
2	tablespoons chopped roasted sweet red pepper
2	celery ribs, chopped
3	cans (14-1/2 ounces each) reduced-sodium chicken broth
2	bay leaves
1	garlic clove, minced
1	teaspoon dried tarragon
1/2	teaspoon salt
1/2	teaspoon pepper
2	cups half-and-half cream

Optional garnish: additional cooked finely chopped carrots, parsnips and/or apples, fresh chives

the heat for 3-4 minutes or until toasted. Brush bottom halves with dressing; layer with ham, turkey and provolone cheese. Spread top halves with olive mixture; layer with roast beef and Colby-Monterey Jack cheese.

3. Broil 2-3 minutes longer or until cheese is melted. Layer bottom halves with tomatoes, lettuce and onion; replace tops. Cut each loaf into six slices.

Yield: 12 servings.

SPICY BLACK BEAN SOUP

A splash of sherry enhances this hearty, easy-to-make soup. For a milder flavor, remove the ribs and seeds from the jalapeno before dicing.
TIA MUSSER, HUDSON, INDIANA

1	large red onion, chopped
1	medium sweet red pepper, chopped
1	jalapeno pepper, seeded and minced
2	tablespoons olive oil
3	garlic cloves, minced
3	cans (15 ounces each) black beans, rinsed and drained
3-1/2	cups vegetable broth
1	can (14-1/2 ounces) diced tomatoes with mild green chilies, undrained
1	can (4 ounces) chopped green chilies
1/3	cup sherry or additional vegetable broth
2	tablespoons minced fresh cilantro
1/2	cup fat-free sour cream
1/4	cup shredded cheddar cheese

1. In a Dutch oven, saute onion and peppers in oil until tender. Add garlic; cook 1 minute longer.

2. Stir in the beans, broth, tomatoes and chopped green chilies. Bring to a boil. Reduce heat; simmer, uncovered, for 25 minutes. Add sherry and cilantro; cook 5 minutes longer.

3. Remove from the heat; cool slightly. Place half of soup in a blender; cover and process until pureed. Return to the pan and heat through. Top each serving with 2 teaspoons sour cream and 1 teaspoon cheese.

Yield: 12 servings (3/4 cup each).

NEW ORLEANS-STYLE SUBS

A true southern favorite, this hearty muffuletta-style sandwich contains loads of deli meats and cheeses.
SHANNON LEE DENNEY, MILWAUKEE, WISCONSIN

1-1/3	cups giardiniera
2/3	cup chopped pitted green olives
2/3	cup pitted ripe olives
2	loaves (1 pound each) unsliced French bread
1/4	cup fat-free Italian salad dressing
1/2	pound thinly sliced deli ham
1/2	pound thinly sliced deli turkey
1/2	pound sliced reduced-fat provolone cheese
1/2	pound thinly sliced deli roast beef
1/2	pound sliced reduced-fat Colby-Monterey Jack cheese
2	medium tomatoes, sliced
2	cups shredded lettuce
1	large red onion, thinly sliced and separated into rings

1. Place giardiniera and olives in a food processor; cover and process until coarsely chopped. Set aside.

2. Cut bread in half lengthwise; carefully hollow out top and bottom of loaves, leaving 1/2-in. shells (discard removed bread or save for another use). Place on two large baking sheets. Broil 4-6 in. from

toffee mocha cupcakes, pg. 186

mint chocolate torte, pg. 170

Delightful Desserts

"How sweet your words taste to me;
they are sweeter than honey."
Psalm 119:103

MINT CHOCOLATE TORTE

I created this recipe to combine two different ones...the chocolate cake from my childhood and the filling from a pie I saw in a cookbook. The flavor is reminiscent of an after-dinner chocolate mint.

NADINE TAYLOR, DURHAM, NORTH CAROLINA

3/4	cup baking cocoa
1/2	cup hot water
2	cups sugar
1-3/4	cups all-purpose flour
1	teaspoon baking soda
1	teaspoon salt
1/4	teaspoon baking powder
1	cup milk
1/2	cup mayonnaise
2	eggs
2	teaspoons vanilla extract

FILLING:

2	cups miniature marshmallows
1/4	cup milk
Dash salt	
1/8	to 1/4 teaspoon peppermint extract
2	to 3 drops green food coloring, optional
1	cup heavy whipping cream, whipped

TOPPING:

1	cup (6 ounces) semisweet chocolate chips
1/3	cup heavy whipping cream

1. In a small bowl, combine cocoa and water until smooth; set aside. In a large bowl, combine the sugar, flour, baking soda, salt and baking powder. Add the milk, mayonnaise, eggs, vanilla and cocoa mixture; beat on medium speed for 2 minutes.

2. Pour into three greased and floured 9-in. round baking pans. Bake at 350° for 15-20 minutes or until a toothpick inserted near the center comes out clean. Cool for 10 minutes before removing from pans to wire racks to cool completely.

3. For filling, combine the marshmallows, milk and salt in a small saucepan; cook and stir over low heat until marshmallows are melted. Remove from the heat; stir in peppermint extract and food coloring if desired. Transfer to a bowl; refrigerate until chilled.

4. Fold in whipped cream. Place bottom cake layer on a serving plate; spread with a third of the filling. Repeat layers twice.

5. For topping, combine chocolate chips and cream in a small saucepan; cook and stir over low heat until chips are melted. Drizzle over top and down sides of cake. Store in the refrigerator.

Yield: 14 servings.

Leveled Layers

Stacking layers for a layered cake is easier when the layers are level. When the cake is cool, use a long serrated knife to slice the high spot from the bottom layer of the two-layer or the bottom and middle layers of a three-layer cake.

BUTTERSCOTCH PEANUT BARS

Loaded with peanuts and butterscotch flavor plus a rich, buttery crust, these no-fuss bars are too good not to make.
MARGERY RICHMOND, FORT COLLINS, COLORADO

1/2	cup butter, softened
3/4	cup packed brown sugar
1-1/2	cups all-purpose flour
1/2	teaspoon salt
3	cups salted peanuts

TOPPING:

1	package (10 to 11 ounces) butterscotch chips
1/2	cup light corn syrup
2	tablespoons butter
1	tablespoon water

1. Line a 15-in. x 10-in. x 1-in. baking pan with aluminum foil. Coat the foil with cooking spray; set aside.

2. In a small bowl, cream butter and brown sugar until light and fluffy. Combine flour and salt; gradually add to creamed mixture and mix well.

3. Press into prepared pan. Bake at 350° for 6 minutes. Sprinkle with peanuts.

4. In a large saucepan, combine topping ingredients. Cook and stir over medium heat until chips and butter are melted. Spread over hot crust. Bake for 12-15 minutes longer or until topping is bubbly. Cool on a wire rack. Cut into bars.

Yield: 4 dozen.

LEMON TEA CAKES

Whenever I serve these lovely bite-size glazed cakes, they get rave reviews...and I get requests for the recipe. Lemon and cream cheese make for a winning combination.
CHARLENE CRUMP, MONTGOMERY, ALABAMA

1-1/2	cups butter, softened
1	package (8 ounces) cream cheese, softened
2-1/4	cups sugar
6	eggs
3	tablespoons lemon juice
2	teaspoons lemon extract
1	teaspoon vanilla extract
1-1/2	teaspoons grated lemon peel
3	cups all-purpose flour

GLAZE:

5-1/4	cups confectioners' sugar
1/2	cup plus 3 tablespoons 2% milk
3-1/2	teaspoons lemon extract

1. In a large bowl, cream the butter, cream cheese and sugar until light and fluffy. Add eggs, one at a time, beating well after each addition. Beat in the lemon juice, extracts and lemon peel. Add flour; beat just until moistened.

2. Fill greased miniature muffin cups two-thirds full. Bake at 325° for 10-15 minutes or until a toothpick inserted near the center comes out clean. Cool for 5 minutes before removing from pans to wire racks to cool completely.

3. In a small bowl, combine glaze ingredients. Dip tops of cakes into glaze; place on waxed paper to dry.

Yield: 8-1/2 dozen.

CANDY COOKIE CUPS

These rich cookies make baking easy because they make the most out of convenience products.
SARAH VASQUES, MILFORD, NEW HAMPSHIRE

1/2	cup finely chopped macadamia nuts
1	package (16 ounces) individually portioned refrigerated white chip macadamia nut cookie dough
24	miniature peanut butter cups

1. Sprinkle macadamia nuts into 24 greased miniature muffin cups, 1 teaspoon in each. Cut each portion of cookie dough in half; place each half in a muffin cup.

2. Bake at 325° for 11-13 minutes or until golden brown. Immediately place a peanut butter cup in each cookie; press down gently. Cool completely before removing from pans to wire racks.

Yield: 2 dozen.

TRUFFLE CHOCOLATE CUPCAKES

(pictured at right)
I love food served with an unexpected twist, like these cupcakes with a creamy chocolate truffle center. My kids love to help me make them, but I have to be sure to have enough truffles saved to actually fill the cupcakes!
AMANDA NOLL, SPANAWAY, WASHINGTON

1-1/2	cups semisweet chocolate chips
1/2	cup plus 2 tablespoons sweetened condensed milk
1	teaspoon butter
2	teaspoons vanilla extract

CUPCAKES:

1	package (18-1/4 ounces) devil's food cake mix
4	eggs
1	cup (8 ounces) sour cream
3/4	cup canola oil
1/2	cup water
2	teaspoons vanilla extract
1	cup heavy whipping cream, whipped, optional

1. For truffles, in a small saucepan, melt the chocolate, milk and butter over low heat; stir until blended. Remove from the heat. Stir in the vanilla. Transfer to a small bowl; cover and refrigerate until firm, about 1 hour. Roll into twenty-four 1-in. balls; chill 1 hour longer.

2. For cupcakes, in a large bowl, combine the cake mix, eggs, sour cream, oil, water and vanilla; beat on low speed for 30 seconds. Beat on medium for 2 minutes.

3. Fill paper-lined muffin cups one-third full. Drop a truffle into the center of each cupcake. Top with remaining batter. Bake at 350° for 17-22 minutes or until a toothpick inserted near the center comes out clean.

4. Cool for 10 minutes before removing from pans to wire racks to cool completely. Top with whipped cream if desired.

Yield: 2 dozen.

COCONUT ALMOND CANDIES

I love Christmas candy, and these simple but special chocolates are among my favorites. They're easy to assemble in paper-lined muffin cups which make them perfect for a dessert tray or cookie swap.

DONALD BROWNELL, MT. CRAWFORD, VIRGINIA

2	cups flaked coconut, chopped
3	tablespoons sweetened condensed milk
3	tablespoons confectioners' sugar
2	teaspoons butter, softened
1	package (12 ounces) semisweet chocolate chips, divided
8	ounces white candy coating
1	tablespoon shortening
1	package (2-1/4 ounces) unblanched almonds

1. In a large bowl, beat the coconut, milk, confectioners' sugar and butter until blended (mixture will be sticky); set aside.

2. In a microwave-safe bowl, melt chocolate chips, candy coating and shortening; stir until smooth. Spoon about 1/2 teaspoon chocolate mixture into 42 paper-lined miniature muffin cups.

3. Shape 1/2 teaspoonfuls of coconut mixture into balls; gently press into chocolate. Top each with an almond. Spoon 1 teaspoon chocolate mixture over each. Let stand until set. Store in an airtight container.

Yield: 3-1/2 dozen.

WHITE CHOCOLATE CRANBERRY COOKIES

These sweet cookies feature white chocolate and cranberries for a delightful taste and a splash of color that adds a festive feel to any cookie tray.

DONNA BECK, SCOTTDALE, PENNSYLVANIA

1/3	cup butter, softened
1/2	cup packed brown sugar
1/3	cup sugar
1	egg
1	teaspoon vanilla extract
1-1/2	cups all-purpose flour
1/2	teaspoon each salt and baking soda
3/4	cup dried cranberries
1/2	cup white baking chips

1. In a large bowl, beat butter and sugars until crumbly, about 2 minutes. Beat in egg and vanilla. Combine the flour, salt and baking soda; gradually add to butter mixture and mix well. Stir in cranberries and chips.

2. Drop by heaping tablespoonfuls 2 in. apart onto baking sheets coated with cooking spray. Bake at 375° for 8-10 minutes or until lightly browned. Cool for 1 minute before removing to wire racks.

Yield: 2 dozen.

SURPRISE CUPCAKES

My mother taught me this simple way to fill cupcakes with fruit jelly. Take these tender treats to your next get-together and watch faces light up after just one bite.

EDITH HOLLIDAY, FLUSHING, MICHIGAN

1	cup shortening
2	cups sugar
2	eggs
2	teaspoons vanilla extract
3-1/2	cups all-purpose flour
5	teaspoons baking powder
1	teaspoon salt
1-1/2	cups 2% milk
3/4	cup strawberry or grape jelly
	Frosting of your choice
	Colored sprinkles, optional

1. In a large bowl, cream shortening and sugar until light and fluffy. Add eggs, one at a time, beating well after each addition. Beat in vanilla. Combine the flour, baking powder and salt; add to creamed mixture alternately with milk, beating well after each addition.

2. Fill 36 paper-lined muffin cups half full. Spoon 1 teaspoon jelly in the center of each.

3. Bake at 375° for 15-20 minutes or until a toothpick inserted 1 in. from the edge comes out clean. Cool for 5 minutes; remove from pans to wire racks to cool completely. Frost cupcakes; decorate with sprinkles if desired.

Yield: 3 dozen.

4. For icing, in a small bowl, combine butter and reserved strawberries. Gradually beat in confectioners' sugar until light and fluffy. Place one cake layer on a serving platter; top with half of the icing. Repeat layers.

Yield: 16 servings.

S'MORE DROPS

I first tried these gooey morsels in a sixth-grade home economics class. I still reminisce about these indoor s'mores served at sleepovers with tall glasses of cold milk.

LAST MINUTE!

DIANE ANGELL, ROCKFORD, ILLINOIS

4	cups Golden Grahams
1-1/2	cups miniature marshmallows
1	cup (6 ounces) semisweet chocolate chips
1/3	cup light corn syrup
1	tablespoon butter
1/2	teaspoon vanilla extract

1. In a large bowl, combine the cereal and marshmallows; set aside. Place the chocolate chips, corn syrup and butter in a 1-qt. microwave-safe dish.

2. Microwave, uncovered, on high for 1-2 minutes or until smooth, stirring every 30 seconds. Stir in vanilla. Pour over cereal mixture and mix well. Drop by tablespoonfuls onto waxed paper-lined baking sheets. Cool.

Yield: 2-1/2 dozen.

Editor's Note: This recipe was tested in a 1,100-watt microwave.

MAKEOVER STRAWBERRY CAKE

My family just loves this wonderful and easy cake that's as pretty as it is tasty!

GAIL LONG, PELHAM, ALABAMA

1	package (18-1/4 ounces) white cake mix
1	package (.3 ounce) sugar-free strawberry gelatin
4	egg whites
1/3	cup canola oil
1	cup frozen unsweetened strawberries, thawed
1/2	cup water

ICING:

1/3	cup butter, softened
2-1/3	cups confectioners' sugar

1. Line two 9-in. round baking pans with waxed paper. Coat pans with cooking spray and sprinkle with flour; set aside. In a large bowl, combine cake mix and gelatin. Add egg whites and oil; beat until well blended.

2. In a small bowl, mash strawberries in their juice. Set aside 3 tablespoons for icing. Add water and remaining berries to the batter; mix well.

3. Pour into prepared pans. Bake at 350° for 20-25 minutes or until a toothpick inserted near the center comes out clean. Cool for 10 minutes before removing from pans to wire racks to cool completely.

LEMON SHORTBREAD COOKIES

I received this recipe from my cousin who tried to duplicate cookies she loved from a restaurant. It was in a cookbook she made for the family for Christmas!

LORIE MINER, KAMAS, UTAH

1/2	cup butter, softened
1/3	cup sugar
4	teaspoons grated lemon peel
1	teaspoon vanilla extract
1	cup all-purpose flour
2	tablespoons plus 1-1/2 teaspoons cornstarch
1/4	teaspoon ground nutmeg
1/8	teaspoon salt

DRIZZLE:

1/2	cup confectioners' sugar
2	to 3 teaspoons lemon juice

1. In a small bowl, cream the butter and sugar until light and fluffy. Beat in lemon peel and vanilla. Combine the flour, cornstarch, nutmeg, and salt; gradually add to creamed mixture and mix well. (Dough will be crumbly.) Shape into a ball.

2. On a lightly floured surface, press dough to 1/2-in. thickness. Cut with a floured 1-in. fluted cookie cutter; place 1 in. apart on ungreased baking sheets. Prick cookies with a fork. Reroll scraps if desired.

3. Bake at 350° for 12-15 minutes or until firm. Cool for 2 minutes before carefully removing to wire racks to cool completely.

4. Combine confectioners' sugar and lemon juice; drizzle over cookies. Store in an airtight container.

Yield: 2 dozen.

Baking & Taking Cookies
When taking cookies to a potluck, store soft cookies and crisp cookies in separate airtight containers. If stored together, the moisture from the soft cookies will soften the crisp cookies, making them lose their crunch.

CHOCOLATE CHIP RASPBERRY BARS

Chocolate and raspberry are a perfect pairing in these bars featuring a buttery shortbread crust. They are a special treat and so easy to make.

BEV CUDRAK, COALDALE, ALBERTA

1-3/4	cups all-purpose flour
1	cup sugar
1	cup cold butter, cubed
1	egg
1/2	teaspoon almond extract
1	cup seedless raspberry jam
1/2	cup miniature semisweet chocolate chips

1. In a large bowl, combine flour and sugar. Cut in butter until mixture resembles coarse crumbs. Stir in egg and extract just until moistened. Set aside 1 cup crumb mixture for topping.

2. Press the remaining mixture into a greased 11-in. x 7-in. baking pan. Bake at 350° for 5 minutes. Spread with jam and sprinkle with reserved crumb mixture. Bake 35-40 minutes longer or until golden brown.

3. Sprinkle with semisweet chips. Return to the oven for 30 seconds or until chips are glossy. Cool completely on a wire rack. Cut into bars.

Yield: about 3 dozen.

Chocolate Chip Strawberry Bars: Substitute strawberry jam for the raspberry jam.

Chocolate Chip Blackberry Bars: Substitute blackberry jam for the raspberry jam.

LEMON BURST TARTLETS

*You'll love the taste of lemon and raspberry in these quick
and easy bites. They're perfect for a party or as a simple dessert.*
PAM JAVOR, NORTH HUNTINGDON, PENNSYLVANIA

2	packages (1.9 ounces each) frozen miniature phyllo tart shells
1	jar (10 ounces) lemon curd
1	carton (8 ounces) frozen whipped topping, thawed
5	to 6 drops yellow food coloring, optional
2/3	cup raspberry cake and pastry filling
30	fresh raspberries

1. Bake shells according to package directions; cool completely on a wire rack.

2. In a large bowl, combine the lemon curd, whipped topping and food coloring if desired until smooth. Spoon 1 teaspoon raspberry filling into each tart shell. Pipe or spoon lemon mixture over filling. Garnish each with a raspberry. Refrigerate leftovers.

Yield: 30 servings.

Editor's Note: This recipe was tested with Solo brand cake and pastry filling. Look for it in the baking aisle.

RIBBON CRISPIES

These dressed-up rice treats are a fabulous twist on a longtime favorite. They're perfect for buffet tables and meals eaten on the run. Kids of all ages love them, and they're always appreciated no matter where or when I share them.
NANCY BAKER, BOONVILLE, MISSOURI

1/2	cup butter, cubed
2	jars (7 ounces each) marshmallow creme
11	cups crisp rice cereal
1	to 1-1/2 cups peanut butter
1	to 1-1/2 cups hot fudge ice cream topping, warmed

1. In a large saucepan, melt butter over medium-low heat. Stir in the marshmallow creme until smooth. Remove from the heat; stir in cereal until blended.

2. Press half of the mixture into a greased 15-in. x 10-in. x 1-in. pan; spread with peanut butter. Carefully spread with hot fudge topping. Press the remaining cereal mixture over fudge layer (pan will be full). Cool for 10 minutes before cutting.

Yield: 3 dozen.

BUTTERSCOTCH BLISS LAYERED DESSERT

Four easy layers come together for a fantastic treat that's perfect for cooling down summer nights. Take a pan to a gathering, and we bet you'll bring it home empty.
JANICE VERNON, LAS CRUCES, NEW MEXICO

1-1/2	cups graham cracker crumbs
	Sugar substitute equivalent to 1/2 cup sugar, divided
6	tablespoons butter, melted
2	packages (8 ounces each) reduced-fat cream cheese
3	cups cold fat-free milk, divided
2	packages (1 ounce each) sugar-free instant butterscotch pudding mix
1	carton (8 ounces) frozen reduced-fat whipped topping, thawed
1/2	teaspoon rum extract

1. In a small bowl, combine the cracker crumbs, 1/4 cup sugar substitute and butter. Press into a 13-in. x 9-in. dish coated with cooking spray.

2. In a small bowl, beat the cream cheese, 1/4 cup milk and remaining sugar substitute until smooth. Spread over crust.

3. In another bowl, whisk remaining milk with the pudding mix for 2 minutes. Let stand for 2 minutes or until soft-set. Gently spread over cream cheese layer. Combine whipped topping and extract; spread over the top. Refrigerate for at least 4 hours.

Yield: 24 servings.

Editor's Note: This recipe was tested with Splenda no-calorie sweetener.

POTATO CHIP COOKIES

Give this cookie a try the next time you're looking for a sweet and salty treat! They quickly bake to a crispy, golden brown...and the irresistible flavor combination makes them disappear even faster!

MONNA LU BAUER, LEXINGTON, KENTUCKY

1	cup butter-flavored shortening
3/4	cup sugar
3/4	cup packed brown sugar
2	eggs
2	cups all-purpose flour
1	teaspoon baking soda
2	cups crushed potato chips
1	cup butterscotch chips

1. In a large bowl, cream shortening and sugars until light and fluffy. Beat in eggs. Combine flour and baking soda; gradually add to creamed mixture and mix well. Stir in potato chips and butterscotch chips.

2. Drop by tablespoonfuls 2 in. apart onto ungreased baking sheets. Bake at 375° for 10-12 minutes or until golden brown. Cool for 1 minute before removing to wire racks.
Yield: 4 dozen.

BERRY SURPRISE CUPCAKES

These cupcakes have a surprise inside them: Fruit Roll-Ups. They give cupcakes a sweet fruity flavor and they are sure to be a hit at any get-together.

SUSAN LUCAS, BRAMPTON, ONTARIO

1	package (18-1/4 ounces) white cake mix
1-1/3	cups water
3	egg whites
2	tablespoons canola oil
3	strawberry Fruit Roll-Ups, unrolled
1	can (16 ounces) vanilla frosting
6	pouches strawberry fruit snacks

1. In a large bowl, combine the cake mix, water, egg whites and canola oil. Beat on low speed for 30 seconds. Beat on medium for 2 minutes.

2. Fill paper-lined muffin cups half full. Cut each fruit roll into eight pieces; place one piece over batter in each cup. Fill two-thirds full with remaining batter.

3. Bake at 350° for 15-20 minutes or until a toothpick inserted near the center comes out clean. Cool for 10 minutes before removing from pans to wire racks to cool completely. Frost with vanilla frosting; decorate with fruit snacks.

Yield: 2 dozen.

Editor's Note: This recipe was tested with Betty Crocker Fruit Roll-Ups and Nabisco Fruit Snacks.

CARAMEL MARSHMALLOW TREATS

I created this candy by combining my husband's favorite cookie recipe and my mom's caramel dip. These sweets really appeal to kids. Plus, they can help make them.

TAMARA HOLSCHEN, ANCHOR POINT, ALASKA

5	cups crisp rice cereal, coarsely crushed
1	can (14 ounces) sweetened condensed milk
1	package (14 ounces) caramels
1	cup butter, cubed
1	teaspoon ground cinnamon
1/2	teaspoon vanilla extract
1	package (16 ounces) large marshmallows

1. Line two baking sheets with waxed paper; set aside. Place cereal in a shallow bowl.

2. In a large saucepan, cook and stir the milk, caramels and butter over low heat until melted and smooth. Remove from the heat; stir in the cinnamon and vanilla.

3. With a toothpick, dip each marshmallow into warm caramel mixture; turn to coat. Press marshmallow bottoms in cereal; place on prepared pans. Let stand until set.

Yield: 5 dozen.

LEMON PUDDING DESSERT

A piece of this fluffy dessert is pure heaven! We indulge in this yummy treat during the holidays because it's something you can make in advance and keep refrigerated until serving time.

JANICE HURD, CHURCH HILL, TENNESSEE

1	cup all-purpose flour
1/2	cup chopped pecans
1/2	cup butter, melted
1	tablespoon sugar

FILLING:

1	package (8 ounces) cream cheese, softened
1	cup confectioners' sugar
1	carton (12 ounces) frozen whipped topping, thawed, divided
4	cups cold 2% milk
3	packages (3.4 ounces each) instant lemon pudding mix

1. In a small bowl, combine the flour, pecans, butter and sugar. Press onto the bottom of a greased 13-in. x 9-in. baking dish. Bake at 350° for 12-15 minutes or until edges are lightly browned. Cool completely on a wire rack.

2. In a large bowl, beat cream cheese and confectioners' sugar until smooth. Fold in half of the whipped topping. Spread over crust.

3. In a large bowl, whisk milk and pudding mix for 2 minutes. Let stand for 2 minutes or until soft-set. Spread over cream cheese layer; top with remaining whipped topping. Refrigerate until chilled.

Yield: 20 servings.

CARAMEL PRALINE TART

For something that is easy enough to make every day but special enough to serve guests or take to a potluck, try this rich and nutty tart. It's sure to win over anyone who tries it.

KATHLEEN SPECHT, CLINTON, MONTANA

1	sheet refrigerated pie pastry
36	caramels
1	cup heavy whipping cream, divided
3-1/2	cups pecan halves
1/2	cup semisweet chocolate chips, melted

1. Unroll pastry on a lightly floured surface. Transfer to an 11-in. fluted tart pan with removable bottom; trim edges.

2. Line unpricked pastry shell with a double thickness of heavy-duty foil. Bake at 450° for 8 minutes. Remove foil; bake 5-6 minutes longer or until light golden brown. Cool on a wire rack.

3. In a large saucepan, combine caramels and 1/2 cup cream. Cook and stir over medium-low heat until caramels are melted. Stir in pecans. Spread filling evenly into crust. Drizzle with melted chocolate.

4. Refrigerate for 30 minutes or until set. Whip remaining cream; serve with tart.

Yield: 16 servings.

FROSTING:

1/2	cup butter, softened
1	package (3 ounces) cream cheese, softened
1/2	teaspoon coconut extract
1/2	teaspoon almond extract
1/4	cup pineapple preserves
1/4	cup apricot preserves
3-3/4	cups confectioners' sugar
1	cup flaked coconut
36	maraschino cherries with stems

1. In a large bowl, cream the butter, shortening and sugar until light and fluffy. Add the egg yolks, one at a time, beating well after each addition. Beat in the extract.

2. In another bowl, whisk the sour cream, apricot nectar and preserves. Combine the flour, baking powder, salt and baking soda; add to creamed mixture alternately with sour cream mixture. Beat just until blended. Stir in pecans. Beat egg whites until stiff peaks form; fold into batter.

3. Fill paper-lined muffin cups three-fourths full. Bake at 350° for 18-22 minutes or until a toothpick inserted near the center comes out clean. Cool for 10 minutes before removing from pans to wire racks to cool completely.

4. For frosting, in a large bowl, cream the butter, cream cheese and extracts until light and fluffy. Beat in preserves. Gradually beat in confectioners' sugar until blended.

5. Frost cupcakes; sprinkle with coconut. Garnish with cherries.

Yield: 3 dozen.

AMBROSIA CUPCAKES

These unbeatable cupcakes are just like the classic Southern salad, only sweeter! Pineapple, apricot, coconut...your taste buds will be dancing! The addition of butter, shortening and sour cream to the batter guarantees a moist, tender cake. Yum!
ZAN BROCK, JASPER, ALABAMA

1/2	cup butter, softened
1/2	cup butter-flavored shortening
2	cups sugar
5	eggs, separated
1	teaspoon rum extract
1/2	cup sour cream
1/2	cup apricot nectar
1/4	cup pineapple preserves
1/4	cup apricot preserves
2	cups cake flour
1	teaspoon baking powder
1/2	teaspoon salt
1/4	teaspoon baking soda
1	cup chopped pecans

Perfectly Portioned Cupcakes
To make cupcakes all equal size, use an ice cream scoop to measure the batter. It speeds up the process, and the tops of the cupcakes come out nice and round.

MAKEOVER PEACH BOWL PIZZA

Imagine a crispy, crumbly shortbread crust, covered in a layer of fluffy, sugary cream cheese and topped with juicy fresh peaches. That's exactly what you're getting in this fantastic dessert!

SARAH FILSON, GALVA, ILLINOIS

1-1/4	cups all-purpose flour
6	tablespoons sugar
1/4	teaspoon salt
9	tablespoons cold butter
1	package (8 ounces) reduced-fat cream cheese
1/2	cup confectioners' sugar
1/4	teaspoon almond extract
1	cup reduced-fat whipped topping
4	medium peaches, peeled and diced

1. In a large bowl, combine the flour, sugar and salt. Cut in butter until crumbly. Press onto an ungreased 12-in. pizza pan. Bake at 350° for 15-18 minutes or until lightly browned. Cool on a wire rack.

2. In a small bowl, beat the cream cheese, confectioners' sugar and extract until smooth; fold in whipped topping. Spread over crust. Arrange the peaches on top. Refrigerate leftovers.

Yield: 16 slices.

CHOCOLATE CHIP CREAM CHEESE BARS

Lower in fat and calories than you might ever guess, these sweet bars couldn't be easier to whip up, boast a great chocolaty flavor, and make a fun, quick dessert to bring to parties or serve to company!

JENNIFER RAFFERTY, MILFORD, OHIO

1	package (18-1/4 ounces) German chocolate cake mix
1/3	cup canola oil
1	egg

FILLING:

1	package (8 ounces) reduced-fat cream cheese
1/3	cup sugar
1	egg
1	cup miniature semisweet chocolate chips

1. In a large bowl, combine the cake mix, oil and egg. Set aside 1 cup for topping. Press remaining crumb mixture into a 13-in. x 9-in. baking pan coated with cooking spray. Bake at 350° for 10-12 minutes or until set.

2. For filling, in a large bowl, beat cream cheese and sugar until smooth. Add egg; beat well. Spread over crust. Sprinkle with chocolate chips and reserved crumb mixture.

3. Bake for 18-20 minutes or until set. Cool on a wire rack. Cut into bars. Store in the refrigerator.

Yield: 2 dozen.

stirring, at a moderate-steady rate for 4 minutes. Remove from the heat; stir in milk. Return to the heat. Reduce to medium-low; cook and stir until a candy thermometer reads 245° (firm-ball stage). Keep warm.

2. Pour 2 cups caramel mixture into a 2-cup glass measuring cup. Quickly dip each pretzel halfway into caramel. Allow excess to drip off. Place on well-buttered baking sheets; let stand until hardened.

3. In a microwave, melt white candy coating; stir until smooth. Dip half of the caramel-coated pretzels into coating. Melt milk chocolate coating; dip remaining pretzels. Drizzle white-coated pretzels with milk chocolate coating; drizzle milk chocolate-coated pretzels with white coating. Sprinkle with walnuts if desired. Store in an airtight container.

Yield: about 2-1/2 dozen.

Editor's Note: We recommend that you test your candy thermometer before each use by bringing water to a boil; the thermometer should read 212°. Adjust your recipe temperature up or down based on your test. Any remaining caramel mixture may be poured into a well-buttered 8-in x 4-in. x 2-in. loaf pan. Cool to room temperature before cutting into squares and wrapping in waxed paper.

CARAMEL PRETZEL STICKS

Homemade caramel, smooth almond bark and chopped nuts make these pretzel rods sinfully delicious. This treat is always a huge hit at holiday parties. I especially like that people think you spent all day in the kitchen!
MARY BOWN, EVANSTON, WYOMING

2	cups sugar
1	cup light corn syrup
1	cup butter, cubed
1	can (14 ounces) sweetened condensed milk
1	package (10 ounces) pretzel rods
6	to 12 ounces white candy coating
6	to 12 ounces milk chocolate candy coating
3/4	cup finely chopped walnuts, optional

1. In a large heavy saucepan, combine the sugar, corn syrup and butter. Bring just to a boil over medium heat, stirring constantly. Continue boiling, without

FRESH PEACH LEMONADE

Looking for a new twist on lemonade? Fresh peaches lend a fruity flavor to this summertime must-have.
JOAN HALLFORD, NORTH RICHLAND HILLS, TEXAS

4	cups water, divided
2	medium peaches, chopped
1	cup sugar
3/4	cup lemon juice
1	medium lemon, sliced
	Mint sprigs, optional

1. In a small saucepan, bring 2 cups water, peaches and sugar to a boil. Reduce heat; cover and simmer for 5-7 minutes or until peaches are tender. Remove from the heat. Cool. Strain, discarding peach skins.

2. In a large pitcher, combine the peach mixture, lemon juice and remaining water. Add lemon slices and mint if desired. Serve over ice.

Yield: 5 servings.

CHOCOLATE MINT WAFERS

I created these melt-in-your-mouth thin mints for a cookie exchange, and everyone raved about them. To switch up the flavor, try using different extracts instead of peppermint.
MICHELLE KESTER, CLEVELAND, OHIO

4	ounces dark chocolate candy coating
1/8	to 1/4 teaspoon peppermint extract
18	to 24 vanilla wafers

1. Place candy coating and the extract in a microwave-safe bowl. Microwave, uncovered, on high for 30-60 seconds or until smooth, stirring every 15 seconds.

2. Dip vanilla wafers in coating; allow excess to drip off. Place on waxed paper; let stand until set. Store in an airtight container.

Yield: about 1-1/2 dozen.

Editor's Note: This recipe was tested in a 1,100-watt microwave.

TOFFEE MOCHA CUPCAKES

(pictured at right)
Chocolate, toffee and espresso make a truly decadent combination in this recipe. The yummy sweets are perfect for any party or gathering. Make plenty, they'll go fast!
BRENDA MELANCON, GONZALES, LOUISIANA

2	tablespoons instant espresso granules
1	cup boiling water
1/2	cup butter-flavored shortening
1-1/4	cups sugar
2	eggs
1-3/4	cups all-purpose flour
1/4	cup baking cocoa
1-1/2	teaspoons baking powder
1/2	teaspoon baking soda
1/2	teaspoon salt
1	cup milk chocolate toffee bits

FROSTING:

1	can (16 ounces) vanilla frosting
2	teaspoons instant espresso granules
1/3	cup miniature semisweet chocolate chips
1/4	cup milk chocolate toffee bits

1. Dissolve espresso granules in boiling water; cool.

2. In a large bowl, cream shortening and sugar until light and fluffy. Add eggs, one at a time, beating well after each addition. Combine the flour, cocoa, baking powder, baking soda and salt; add to creamed mixture alternately with espresso mixture and mix well. Fold in toffee bits.

3. Fill paper-lined muffin cups three-fourths full. Bake at 350° for 20-22 minutes or until a toothpick inserted near the center comes out clean. Cool for 10 minutes before removing from pans to wire racks.

4. In a large bowl, combine frosting and espresso granules. Frost cupcakes; sprinkle with chocolate chips and toffee bits.

Yield: 16 cupcakes.

BLACK FOREST CAKE

Applesauce is used to keep this light version of Black Forest Cake healthy. Now, even people who are on watching their diets can enjoy a slice of rich chocolate cake!
NANCY ZIMMERMAN, CAPE MAY COURT HOUSE, NEW JERSEY

2	cups cherry juice blend
1-3/4	cups sugar
1/2	cup unsweetened applesauce
1/4	cup canola oil
2	eggs
2	tablespoons cider vinegar
3	teaspoons vanilla extract
3	cups all-purpose flour
1/3	cup baking cocoa
2	teaspoons baking soda
1	teaspoon salt
1-1/2	cups cold fat-free milk
1	package (1.4 ounces) sugar-free instant chocolate pudding mix
1	can (20 ounces) reduced-sugar cherry pie filling
1-1/2	cups frozen fat-free whipped topping, thawed

1. In a large bowl, beat the cherry juice, sugar, applesauce, oil, eggs, vinegar and vanilla until well blended.

2. In a large bowl, combine the flour, cocoa, baking soda and salt; gradually beat into cherry juice mixture until blended.

3. Pour into a 13-in. x 9-in. baking pan coated with cooking spray. Bake at 350° for 35-40 minutes or until a toothpick inserted near the center comes out clean. Cool completely on a wire rack.

4. In a small bowl, whisk milk and pudding mix for 2 minutes. Let stand for 2 minutes or until soft-set. Frost top of cake with pudding. Cover and refrigerate for 15 minutes. Top with pie filling. Chill until serving. Serve with whipped topping.

Yield: 24 servings.

PUMPKIN PIE DIP

I came up with this rich creamy dip when I had a small amount of canned pumpkin left in the fridge after my holiday baking.
LAURIE LACLAIR, NORTH RICHLAND HILLS, TEXAS

1	package (8 ounces) cream cheese, softened
2	cups confectioners' sugar
1	cup canned pumpkin
1/2	cup sour cream
1	teaspoon ground cinnamon
1	teaspoon pumpkin pie spice
1/2	teaspoon ground ginger
	Gingersnap cookies

1. In a bowl, beat cream cheese and confectioners' sugar until smooth. Beat in the pumpkin, sour cream, cinnamon, pumpkin pie spice and ginger until blended. Serve with gingersnaps. Refrigerate leftovers.

Yield: 4 cups.

1/2 cup semisweet chocolate chips
1 teaspoon shortening
24 maraschino cherries, well drained
3-1/4 cups confectioners' sugar
2 tablespoons coarse sugar

1. For ganache, place vanilla chips and butter in a large bowl. In a small saucepan, bring cream just to a boil. Pour over chip mixture; whisk until smooth. Stir in extract. Cover and refrigerate for at least 4 hours, stirring occasionally.

2. In a large bowl, beat the pie filling, buttermilk and eggs until well blended. Combine the flour, sugar, cocoa, baking soda, baking powder and salt; gradually beat into pie filling mixture until blended.

3. Fill paper-lined muffin cups one-third full. Cut candy bars in half; place half of a candy bar in center of each cupcake. Cover each with 2 tablespoonfuls batter.

4. Bake at 375° for 16-20 minutes or until a toothpick inserted near the center comes out clean. Cool for 10 minutes before removing from pans to wire racks to cool completely.

5. Meanwhile, in a microwave, melt chocolate chips and shortening; stir until smooth. Dip cherries in chocolate mixture; allow excess to drip off. Place on a waxed paper-lined baking sheet. Refrigerate until set.

6. Remove ganache from refrigerator; gradually beat in confectioners' sugar until frosting is light and fluffy. Pipe over cupcakes; sprinkle with coarse sugar. Garnish with chocolate-dipped cherries.

Yield: 2 dozen.

CHERRY CHOCOLATE COCONUT CUPCAKES

Chocolate-covered coconut candy is tucked inside each of these moist morsels. The cream cheese frosting is complemented by coarse sugar and chocolate-covered cherries.
SANDY PLOY, WHITEFISH BAY, WISCONSIN

1 package (10 to 12 ounces) vanilla or white chips
1/2 cup butter, cubed
1 cup heavy whipping cream
1 teaspoon coconut extract
1 can (21 ounces) cherry pie filling
1 cup buttermilk
2 eggs
2 cups all-purpose flour
2 cups sugar
3/4 cup baking cocoa
2 teaspoons baking soda
1 teaspoon baking powder
1/2 teaspoon salt
6 packages (1.9 ounces each) chocolate-covered coconut candy bars

Frosting in a Flash
Don't have time to make homemade frosting? Mix a can of store-bought frosting (any flavor) with an 8-ounce container of whipped topping. The result is so soft, creamy and easy to spread that everyone will think you made it from scratch.

BAKLAVA TARTLETS

Want a quick treat that's delicious and easy to do? These tartlets will do the trick. You can serve them right away, but they're better after chilling for about an hour in the refrigerator. A little sprig of mint adds just a touch of color.

ASHLEY EAGON, KETTERING, OHIO

2	cups finely chopped walnuts
3/4	cup honey
1/2	cup butter, melted
1	teaspoon ground cinnamon
1	teaspoon lemon juice
1/4	teaspoon ground cloves
3	packages (1.9 ounces each) frozen miniature phyllo tart shells

1. In a small bowl, combine the first six ingredients; spoon 2 teaspoonfuls into each tart shell. Refrigerate tartlets until serving.

Yield: 45 tartlets.

BLOND BUTTERSCOTCH BROWNIES

Toffee and chocolate dot the golden brown batter of these fudge-like brownies. I do a lot of cooking for the people I work with, and they always line up for these delicious bars. One never seems to be enough!
JENNIFER ANN SOPKO, BATTLE CREEK, MICHIGAN

2	cups all-purpose flour
2	cups packed brown sugar
2	teaspoons baking powder
1/4	teaspoon salt
1/2	cup butter, melted and cooled
2	eggs
1	teaspoon vanilla extract
1	cup semisweet chocolate chunks
4	Heath candy bars (1.4 ounces each), coarsely chopped

1. In a large bowl, combine the flour, brown sugar, baking powder and salt. In another bowl, beat the butter, eggs and vanilla until smooth. Stir into dry ingredients just until combined (batter will be thick).

2. Spread into a 13-in. x 9-in. baking pan coated with cooking spray. Sprinkle with chocolate chunks and chopped candy bars; press gently into batter.

3. Bake at 350° for 20-25 minutes or until a toothpick inserted near the center comes out clean. Cool on a wire rack. Cut into bars.
Yield: 2 dozen.

PINEAPPLE ORANGE CAKE

If I had to choose my favorite cake, this one would have to be it. It's moist and light yet so satisfying. I've been adapting it for years and now it's almost guilt-free.
PAM SJOLUND, COLUMBIA, SOUTH CAROLINA

1	package (18-1/4 ounces) yellow cake mix
1	can (11 ounces) mandarin oranges, undrained
4	egg whites
1/2	cup unsweetened applesauce

TOPPING:

1	can (20 ounces) crushed pineapple, undrained
1	package (1 ounce) sugar-free instant vanilla pudding mix
1	carton (8 ounces) reduced-fat whipped topping

1. In a large bowl, beat the cake mix, oranges, egg whites and applesauce on low speed for 2 minutes. Pour into a 13-in. x 9-in. baking dish coated with cooking spray.

2. Bake at 350° for 25-30 minutes or until a toothpick inserted near the center comes out clean. Cool on a wire rack.

3. In a bowl, combine the pineapple and pudding mix. Fold in whipped topping just until blended. Spread over cake. Refrigerate for at least 1 hour before serving.
Yield: 15 servings.

4. Beat the chocolate mixture until soft peaks form. Pipe or spoon into the tart shells. Garnish with whipped cream, raspberries and confectioners' sugar if desired.

Yield: 2 dozen.

CHOCOLATE MACAROON BARS

Here's a nice chocolaty treat that takes very little effort. The classic combination of chocolate and coconut is timeless.
LORAINE MEYER, BEND, OREGON

2	cups chocolate wafer crumbs
6	tablespoons confectioners' sugar
1/2	cup butter, melted
1	can (14 ounces) sweetened condensed milk
3-3/4	cups flaked coconut
1	cup sliced almonds, toasted
1-1/2	cups semisweet chocolate chips
1/3	cup heavy whipping cream

1. In a small bowl, combine the wafer crumbs, confectioners' sugar and butter; press into a greased 13-in. x 9-in. baking pan. In a large bowl, combine the milk, coconut and almonds. Drop by spoonfuls over crust; spread evenly.

2. Bake at 350° for 20-25 minutes or until edges begin to brown. Cool completely on a wire rack. In a microwave-safe bowl, melt chips and cream; stir until smooth. Drizzle over top. Refrigerate until firm. Cut into bars.

Yield: 4 dozen.

CHOCOLATE GANACHE TARTS

Decadent, chocolate mousse-like filling and a flaky, tender crust make this very special. Be sure to coat hands well with flour when putting the dough into pastry cups.
LORRAINE CALAND, THUNDER BAY, ONTARIO

1/2	cup butter, softened
1	package (3 ounces) cream cheese, softened
1	cup all-purpose flour
1/2	cup semisweet chocolate chips
1/2	cup milk chocolate chips
2/3	cup heavy whipping cream
	Whipped cream, fresh raspberries and confectioners' sugar, optional

1. In a small bowl, beat butter and cream cheese until smooth; beat in flour. Drop dough by scant tablespoonfuls into greased miniature muffin cups; with well-floured hands, press dough onto bottoms and up sides of cups.

2. Bake at 325° for 20-25 minutes or until golden brown. Cool for 5 minutes before removing from pans to wire racks to cool completely.

3. Place chocolate chips in a small bowl. In a small saucepan, bring cream just to a boil. Pour over chocolate; whisk until smooth. Transfer to a small bowl; cover and refrigerate until firm.

Bakery-Style Brownies
For picture-perfect brownies and bars, bake them in a foil-lined pan. Use the foil to lift them out after they're cooled. Trim the bars' edges and use a ruler to score the lines to cut. Use a serrated knife and cut downward (not a sawing motion).

PECAN BUTTERSCOTCH COOKIES

These are the quickest, tastiest cookies I've ever made. They can be varied endlessly with your choice of pudding mix and nuts, but I come back to this version time after time.
TRISHA KRUSE, EAGLE, IDAHO

LAST MINUTE!

1	cup complete buttermilk pancake mix
1	package (3.4 ounces) instant butterscotch pudding mix
1/3	cup butter, melted
1	egg
1/2	cup chopped pecans, toasted

1. In a large bowl, beat the pancake mix, dry pudding mix, butter and egg until blended. Stir in pecans.

2. Roll into 1-1/2-in. balls. Place 2 in. apart on greased baking sheets. Flatten with the bottom of a glass. Bake at 350° for 8-10 minutes or until edges begin to brown. Remove to wire racks to cool.

Yield: about 1-1/2 dozen.

Editor's Note: You may substitute regular biscuit/baking mix for the buttermilk pancake mix.

CREAM CHEESE POUND CAKE

Fresh fruit and a dollop of whipped cream dress up this moist and tender pound cake. It's a favorite!
RICHARD HOGG, ANDERSON, SOUTH CAROLINA

1-1/2	cups butter, softened
1	package (8 ounces) cream cheese, softened
3	cups sugar
6	eggs
2	teaspoons vanilla extract
1	teaspoon lemon extract
3	cups all-purpose flour
1/2	teaspoon baking powder
1/4	teaspoon salt

Confectioners' sugar, sliced fresh strawberries and whipped cream, optional

1. In a large bowl, cream the butter, cream cheese and sugar until light and fluffy. Add eggs, one at a time, beating well after each addition. Beat in extracts. Combine the flour, baking powder and salt; beat into creamed mixture until blended.

2. Pour into a greased and floured 10-in. fluted tube pan. Bake at 325° for 1-1/4 to 1-1/2 hours or until a toothpick inserted near the center comes out clean.

3. Cool for 10 minutes before removing from pan to a wire rack to cool completely. Garnish with confectioners' sugar, strawberries and whipped cream if desired.

Yield: 16 servings.

Cranberry-Pecan Pound Cake: Omit lemon extract. Add 3/4 teaspoon grated orange peel with vanilla. Fold in 3/4 cup each dried cranberries and chopped pecans.

HEAVENLY FILLED STRAWBERRIES

Nothing says strawberry season like these luscious bites. The stuffed berries are a great bite-size dessert for any party.

STEPHEN MUNRO, BEAVER BANK, NOVA SCOTIA

1	pound fresh strawberries
2	packages (one 8 ounces, one 3 ounces) cream cheese, softened
1/2	cup confectioners' sugar
1/4	teaspoon almond extract
	Grated chocolate

1. Remove stems from strawberries; cut a deep "X" in the tip of each berry. Gently spread berries open.

2. In a small bowl, beat the cream cheese, confectioners' sugar and extract until light and fluffy. Pipe or spoon about 2 teaspoons into each berry; sprinkle with chocolate. Chill until serving.

Yield: about 3 dozen.

COCONUT-PECAN BROWNIES

(pictured at left)

These moist, bakery-style brownies are made even better with a cream cheese frosting featuring coconut and pecans.

LESLEY PEW, LYNN, MASSACHUSETTS

1	cup butter, cubed
4	ounces bittersweet chocolate, chopped
4	eggs
2-1/2	cups sugar
2	teaspoons vanilla extract
2	cups all-purpose flour
1/2	teaspoon salt
2	cups chopped pecans

FROSTING:

3/4	cup white baking chips
2	packages (3 ounces each) cream cheese, softened
1/2	cup butter, softened
1-1/2	cups confectioners' sugar
3	tablespoons brown sugar
3/4	teaspoon vanilla extract
1/8	teaspoon salt
3/4	cup each flaked coconut and chopped pecans

1. In a microwave, melt butter and chocolate; stir until smooth. Cool slightly. In a large bowl, beat the eggs, sugar and vanilla. Stir in chocolate mixture. Combine flour and salt; gradually add to chocolate mixture. Fold in pecans.

2. Transfer to a greased 13-in. x 9-in. baking pan. Bake at 350° for 35-40 minutes or until a toothpick inserted near the center comes out clean. Cool on a wire rack.

3. For frosting, in a microwave, melt baking chips; stir until smooth. Cool slightly. In a large bowl, beat cream cheese and butter until fluffy. Add the melted chips, sugars, vanilla and salt; beat until smooth. Stir in coconut and pecans. Spread over brownies. Store in the refrigerator.

Yield: 2 dozen.

mini spider bites, pg. 218

holiday pork roast, pg. 207

Seasonal Fare

"For everything there is a season,
a time for every activity under heaven."
Ecclesiastes 3:1

CHRISTMAS EVE CONFETTI PASTA

This fabulously easy pasta has become a holiday tradition. All the prep is done before we attend Christmas Eve service. On returning, I just boil water and saute. It's so colorful and goes great with a tossed salad and garlic bread.

ELLEN FIORE, RIDGEWOOD, NEW JERSEY

1	package (16 ounces) linguine
1	cup each chopped sweet red pepper and chopped green pepper
1/3	cup chopped onion
3	garlic cloves, peeled and thinly sliced
1/4	teaspoon each salt and dried oregano
1/8	teaspoon crushed red pepper flakes and pepper
1/4	cup olive oil
2	pounds cooked small shrimp, peeled and deveined
1/2	cup shredded Parmesan cheese

1. Cook linguine according to package directions. Meanwhile, in a Dutch oven, saute the peppers, onion, garlic and seasonings in oil until vegetables are tender.

2. Add the shrimp; cook and stir 2-3 minutes longer or until heated through. Drain linguine; toss with shrimp mixture. Sprinkle with cheese.

Yield: 8 servings.

TASTES LIKE EGGNOG CAKE

My holiday eggnog cake uses a convenient boxed mix and comes out perfect every time. It always gets compliments, and most people think that I spend hours in the kitchen working on it!
LISA BARRETT, DURANGO, COLORADO

1	package (18-1/4 ounces) yellow cake mix
1	teaspoon ground nutmeg
1/4	teaspoon ground ginger

FROSTING:

1-1/2	cups heavy whipping cream
3	tablespoons confectioners' sugar
1	teaspoon rum extract

1. Prepare cake batter according to package directions, adding nutmeg and ginger to dry ingredients. Pour into a greased 13-in. x 9-in. baking pan.

2. Bake at 350° for 25-30 minutes or until a toothpick inserted near the center comes out clean. Cool on a wire rack.

3. For frosting, in a small bowl, beat cream and confectioners' sugar until stiff peaks form. Fold in extract. Spread over cake. Store in the refrigerator.

Yield: 12-15 servings.

SPICY BARBECUED CHICKEN

My grown children still beg for my chicken. They like the savory barbecue sauce so much, they've been known to hover over me, trying to snitch a spoonful.
PATRICIA PARKER, CONNELLY SPRINGS, NORTH CAROLINA

1-1/2	cups sugar
1-1/2	cups ketchup
1/2	cup water
1/4	cup lemon juice
1/4	cup cider vinegar
1/4	cup Worcestershire sauce
2	tablespoons plus 2 teaspoons chili powder
2	tablespoons plus 2 teaspoons prepared mustard
1	teaspoon salt
1/2	teaspoon crushed red pepper flakes
2	broiler/fryer chickens (3-1/2 to 4 pounds each), cut up

1. In a large saucepan, combine the first 10 ingredients; bring to a boil. Reduce heat; simmer, uncovered, for 15 minutes.

2. Grill chicken, covered, over medium heat for 40 minutes, turning several times. Set half of the barbecue sauce aside. Baste chicken with remaining sauce; grill 5-10 minutes longer or until juices run clear. Serve with reserved sauce.

Yield: 8 servings.

1. Place egg whites in a large bowl; let stand at room temperature for 30 minutes. Sift confectioners' sugar and flour together twice; set aside.

2. Add the cream of tartar, vanilla and salt to egg whites; beat on medium speed until soft peaks form. Gradually add sugar, about 2 tablespoons at a time, beating on high until stiff glossy peaks form and sugar is dissolved. Gradually fold in flour mixture, about 1/2 cup at a time.

3. Gently spoon into an ungreased 10-in. tube pan. Cut through the batter with a knife to remove air pockets. Bake on the lowest oven rack at 325° for 50-60 minutes or until lightly browned and entire top appears dry. Immediately invert pan; cool completely, about 1 hour.

4. Run a knife around side and center tube of pan. Remove cake to a serving plate. Brush top and sides of cake with vodka. Combine cornstarch and water; set aside.

For sauce: In a small saucepan, combine 1-1/2 cups raspberries, 1 cup blueberries, pineapple juice and liqueur. Bring to a boil. Stir cornstarch mixture and add to the pan. Bring to a boil; cook and stir for 2 minutes or until thickened.

Remove from the heat; stir in the strawberries, blackberries and remaining raspberries and blueberries. Serve sauce with cake.

Yield: 16 servings (6 cups sauce).

ANGEL FOOD CAKE WITH BERRY SAUCE

Top this airy angel food cake with the accompanying berry sauce, and you'll have a heavenly dessert. It's the perfect light finale to a heavy meal.

TASTE OF HOME TEST KITCHEN

12	egg whites
1	cup confectioners' sugar
1	cup cake flour
1	teaspoon cream of tartar
1	teaspoon vanilla extract
1/4	teaspoon salt
1-1/4	cups sugar
1/3	cup blueberry vodka
1	tablespoon cornstarch
1	tablespoon water

SAUCE:

2-1/2	cups fresh raspberries, divided
2	cups fresh blueberries, divided
1/3	cup unsweetened pineapple juice
3	tablespoons raspberry liqueur
2	cups halved fresh strawberries
1	cup fresh blackberries

Heavenly Results
When baking an angel food cake, use an oven thermometer to make sure your oven is not baking at a higher temperature. Also, place the pan on the lowest rack to give the light and airy cake plenty of room to expand.

HOLIDAY GLAZED HAM

I like to serve this juicy, mouthwatering ham with mashed potatoes and colorful vegetables. The apricot glaze is delicious, and the pineapple and cloves assure a truly lovely presentation.

DIANE FREEMAN, FALKLAND, BRITISH COLUMBIA

1	boneless fully cooked ham (about 6 pounds)
1	tablespoon whole cloves
1	can (20 ounces) sliced pineapple
1	cup apricot preserves
1	teaspoon ground mustard
1/2	teaspoon ground allspice

Maraschino cherries

1. Place ham on a rack in a shallow roasting pan. Score the surface of the ham, making diamond shapes 1/2 in. deep; insert a clove in each diamond. Bake, uncovered, at 325° for 1 hour.

2. Drain pineapple, reserving juice. In a small saucepan, combine the pineapple juice, preserves, mustard and allspice. Bring to a boil; cook and stir for 10 minutes or until slightly thickened.

3. Spoon half of the glaze over ham. Secure pineapple slices and cherries on top and sides of ham with toothpicks.

4. Bake 40-45 minutes longer or until a thermometer reads 140°, basting twice with remaining glaze.

Yield: 16 servings.

PEANUT BUTTER EASTER EGGS

You won't be able to eat just one of these peanut buttery treats. You can even get the kids involved with this wonderful recipe—it'll be worth the sticky fingers!

MARY JOYCE JOHNSON, UPPER DARBY, PENNSYLVANIA

1/2	cup butter, softened
2-1/3	cups confectioners' sugar
1	cup graham cracker crumbs
1/2	cup creamy peanut butter
1/2	teaspoon vanilla extract
1-1/2	cups dark chocolate chips
2	tablespoons shortening

Pastel sprinkles

1. In a large bowl, cream butter; gradually add the confectioners' sugar, cracker crumbs, peanut butter and vanilla. Shape into 16 eggs; place on waxed paper-lined baking sheets. Refrigerate for 30 minutes or until firm.

2. In a microwave, melt chocolate chips and shortening; stir until smooth. Dip eggs in chocolate; allow excess to drip off. Decorate with sprinkles; return eggs to waxed paper. Chill until set. Store in an airtight container in the refrigerator.

Yield: 16 eggs.

MANGO CRANBERRY SAUCE

I got this recipe from a friend. It's definitely worth the effort if you want to wow your gang at Thanksgiving. The leftovers are great with chicken or ham.

REBECCA LITTLEJOHN, MEADOW VISTA, CALIFORNIA

1-1/2	cups whole-berry cranberry sauce
3	tangerines, peeled, seeded and chopped
1	medium mango, peeled and diced
1	cup diced fresh pineapple
1/4	cup finely chopped red onion
1/4	cup minced fresh cilantro
1	jalapeno pepper, seeded and finely chopped

1. In a large bowl, combine all the ingredients. Cover and refrigerate until serving.

Yield: 4-1/2 cups.

Editor's Note: Wear disposable gloves when cutting hot peppers; the oils can burn skin. Avoid touching your face.

GRILLED BURGERS

(pictured at right)

No way did I want to give up juicy, delicious hamburgers when I learned that I needed to eat gluten-free. I made a few adjustments to my recipe to meet the requirements.

PEGGY GWILLIM, STRASBOURG, SASKATCHEWAN

1	egg, lightly beaten
1/2	cup 4% cottage cheese
1	cup cooked long grain rice
1	small onion, finely chopped
1/2	cup shredded cheddar cheese
2	tablespoons plus 1-1/2 teaspoons gluten-free onion soup mix
2	tablespoons gluten-free all-purpose flour
2	tablespoons grated Parmesan cheese
1-1/2	teaspoons gluten-free Worcestershire sauce
3	garlic cloves, minced
1/2	teaspoon salt
1/4	teaspoon pepper
1-1/2	pounds ground beef

Sliced tomatoes, lettuce leaves and sliced onions, optional

1. In a large bowl, combine the first 12 ingredients. Crumble beef over mixture and mix well. Shape into 10 patties.

2. Grill, uncovered, over medium-hot heat for 5-6 minutes on each side or until a meat thermometer reads 160° and juices run clear. Serve with the tomatoes, lettuce and onions if desired.

Yield: 10 servings.

Editor's Note: Read all ingredient labels for possible gluten content prior to use. Ingredient formulas can change, and production facilities vary among brands. If you're concerned that your brand may contain gluten, contact the company.

The Perfect Burger

To keep grilled burgers from drying out, be careful not to overhandle the meat before cooking. If you add seasonings to the ground beef, gently mix them in just until combined.

CHIPOTLE-RUBBED BEEF TENDERLOIN

Go ahead, rub it in! Coating traditional tenderloin with lively peppery flavors gives it a south-of-the-border twist. Here is a roast that's guaranteed to impress.

TASTE OF HOME TEST KITCHEN

1	beef tenderloin roast (2 pounds)
2	teaspoons canola oil
3	teaspoons coarsely ground pepper
3	garlic cloves, minced
2-1/2	teaspoons brown sugar
1	teaspoon salt
1	teaspoon ground coriander
1/2	teaspoon ground chipotle pepper
1/4	teaspoon cayenne pepper

1. Brush beef with oil. Combine the remaining ingredients; rub over meat. Cover and refrigerate for 2 hours.

2. Place on a rack coated with cooking spray in a shallow roasting pan. Bake, uncovered, at 400° for 45-55 minutes or until meat reaches desired doneness (for medium-rare, a thermometer should read 145°; medium, 160°; well-done, 170°). Let stand for 10 minutes before slicing.

Yield: 8 servings.

VEGGIE HAM CRESCENT WREATH

Impress your guests with the look and flavor of this pretty crescent roll appetizer. The pineapple cream cheese adds a special touch.

DIXIE LUNDQUIST, CHANDLER, ARIZONA

2	tubes (8 ounces each) refrigerated crescent rolls
1/2	cup spreadable pineapple cream cheese
1/3	cup diced fully cooked ham
1/4	cup finely chopped sweet yellow pepper
1/4	cup finely chopped green pepper
1/2	cup chopped fresh broccoli florets
6	grape tomatoes, quartered
1	tablespoon chopped red onion

1. Remove crescent dough from tubes (do not unroll). Cut each roll into eight slices. Arrange in an 11-in. circle on an ungreased 14-in. pizza pan.

2. Bake at 375° for 15-20 minutes or until golden brown. Cool for 5 minutes before carefully removing to a serving platter; cool completely.

3. Spread cream cheese over wreath; top with ham, peppers, broccoli, tomatoes and onion. Store in the refrigerator.

Yield: 16 appetizers.

FROSTED PUMPKIN BARS

Classic pumpkin bars are a staple for fall events. When topped with a luscious cream cheese frosting they disappear fast!
SANDY MCKENZIE, BRAHAM, MINNESOTA

2	cups all-purpose flour
1-1/2	cups sugar
2	teaspoons baking powder
2	teaspoons ground cinnamon
1	teaspoon baking soda
1/4	teaspoon salt
1/4	teaspoon ground cloves
4	eggs
1	can (15 ounces) solid-pack pumpkin
1	cup canola oil

CREAM CHEESE FROSTING:

1/2	cup butter, softened
2	packages (3 ounces each) cream cheese, softened
2	teaspoons vanilla extract
4	cups confectioners' sugar
30	pumpkin-shaped candies

1. In a large bowl, combine the first seven ingredients. In another bowl, combine the eggs, pumpkin and oil; stir into dry ingredients. Spread into a greased 15-in. x 10-in. x 1-in. baking pan. Bake at 350° for 18-22 minutes or until a toothpick inserted near the center comes out clean. Cool on a wire rack.

2. For frosting, in a large bowl, beat the butter, cream cheese and vanilla until smooth. Gradually add the confectioners' sugar; mix well. Spread over top. Cut into 30 bars; top each bar with a pumpkin candy.

Yield: 2-1/2 dozen.

TRICK-OR-TREAT TURNOVERS

I carved these clever pumpkin pastries to feed my hungry bunch at Halloween. The ground beef filling has a hint of onion and mustard.
MARGE FREE, BRANDON, MISSISSIPPI

1/2	pound ground beef
1	tablespoon finely chopped onion
4	ounces cubed part-skim mozzarella cheese
1/4	cup prepared mustard
2	tubes (16.3 ounces each) large refrigerated flaky biscuits
1	egg, lightly beaten

1. In a large skillet, cook beef and onion over medium heat until meat is no longer pink; drain. Add cheese and mustard; cook and stir until cheese is melted. Cool slightly.

2. Flatten each biscuit into a 4-in. circle; place four biscuits in each of two greased 15-in. x 10-in. x 1-in. baking pans. Spoon 2 heaping tablespoons of meat mixture onto each.

3. Using a sharp knife or cookie cutters, cut out jack-o'-lantern faces from remaining biscuit circles; place over meat mixture and pinch edges to seal tightly. Reroll scraps if desired and cut out stems for pumpkins.

4. Brush with egg. Bake at 350° for 10-15 minutes or until golden brown.

Yield: 8 servings.

CHAMPAGNE BAKED HAM

Champagne, brown sugar and honey combine to make a beautiful glaze for ham that turns out tender and juicy every time.
LINDA FOREMAN, LOCUST GROVE, OKLAHOMA

1	boneless fully cooked ham (9 pounds)
1-1/2	cups Champagne
3/4	cup packed brown sugar
4-1/2	teaspoons honey
3/4	teaspoon each ground ginger and ground mustard

1. Place ham on a rack in a shallow roasting pan. Score the surface of the ham, making diamond shapes 1/2 in. deep. Bake, uncovered, at 325° for 2-1/2 hours.

2. Meanwhile, in a small saucepan, combine the remaining ingredients. Bring to a boil; cook until glaze is reduced by half. Remove from the heat.

3. Baste ham with glaze; bake 30 minutes longer or until a thermometer reads 140°, basting twice with glaze. Serve with remaining glaze.

Yield: 18 servings.

HOLIDAY PORK ROAST

(pictured at left)
This special dish is perfect for Christmas or New Year's Eve. A mouthwatering ginger gravy and tender vegetables complement the tender herbed roast.
MARY ANN DELL, PHOENIXVILLE, PENNSYLVANIA

1	boneless whole pork loin roast (5 pounds)
1	tablespoon minced fresh gingerroot
2	garlic cloves, minced
1	teaspoon rubbed sage
1/4	teaspoon salt
1/3	cup apple jelly
1/2	teaspoon hot pepper sauce
2	medium carrots, sliced
2	medium onions, sliced
1-1/2	cups water, divided
1	teaspoon browning sauce, optional

1. Place pork roast on a rack in a shallow roasting pan. Combine the ginger, garlic, sage and salt; rub over meat. Bake, uncovered, at 350° for 1 hour.

2. Combine jelly and pepper sauce; brush over the roast. Arrange carrots and onions around roast. Pour 1/2 cup water into pan. Bake 40-50 minutes longer or until a thermometer reads 145°. Remove roast to a serving platter; let stand for 10 minutes before slicing.

3. Skim fat from pan drippings. Transfer drippings and vegetables to a food processor; cover and process until smooth. Pour into a small saucepan. Add browning sauce if desired and remaining water; heat through. Slice roast; serve with gravy.

Yield: 16 servings.

Browning Sauce Basics
Browning sauce is a blend of caramel color, vegetable concentrates and seasonings. Available since the early 1900s, the sauce is used to add a rich dark color to foods.

LEMON RICOTTA CAKE

This recipe is a family gem that was passed down from my grandmother and mother. Garnished with shaved lemon peel, the moist four-layer cake is the perfect dessert when you want to impress.

NAN SLAUGHTER, SAMMAMISH, WASHINGTON

3	eggs
2	egg yolks
2/3	cup sugar
1/3	cup lemon juice
1/3	cup butter, cubed

CAKE BATTER:

1	cup butter, softened
2	cups sugar
3	eggs
1	cup ricotta cheese
1	cup buttermilk
1	tablespoon grated lemon peel
1-1/2	teaspoons vanilla extract
1	teaspoon lemon juice
3	cups all-purpose flour
1/2	teaspoon baking powder
1/2	teaspoon baking soda
1/2	teaspoon salt

SUGARED LEMON PEEL:

6	medium lemons
1/4	cup sugar

FROSTING:

2/3	cup butter, softened
5-1/2	cups confectioners' sugar
1/3	cup milk
1-1/2	teaspoons grated lemon peel
1-1/2	teaspoons vanilla extract
1/8	teaspoon salt

1. For lemon curd, in a small bowl, combine eggs and egg yolks. In a heavy saucepan, cook and stir the sugar, lemon juice and butter over medium heat until smooth. Stir a small amount of hot mixture into eggs; return all to the pan, stirring constantly. Bring to a gentle boil, cook and stir for 2 minutes. Cool slightly. Cover and chill for 1-1/2 hours or until thickened.

2. In a large bowl, cream butter and sugar until light and fluffy. Add eggs, one at a time, beating well after each addition. Combine the ricotta cheese, buttermilk, lemon peel, vanilla and lemon juice. Combine the flour, baking powder, baking soda and salt; add to the creamed mixture alternately with the buttermilk mixture, beating well after each addition.

3. Pour into two greased and floured 9-in. round baking pans. Bake at 350° for 30-35 minutes or until a toothpick inserted near the center comes out clean. Cool for 10 minutes before removing from pans to wire racks to cool completely.

4. Using a citrus zester, remove peel from lemons in long narrow strips; toss with sugar. Let stand for 30 minutes. (Save fruit for another use.) Meanwhile, in a large bowl, cream butter until light and fluffy. Add the confectioners' sugar, milk, lemon peel, vanilla and salt; beat until smooth.

5. Cut each cake in half horizontally. Place one cake layer on a serving plate. Pipe a circle of frosting around the edge of the cake. Spread a third of the lemon curd inside the frosting. Repeat layers twice. Top with remaining cake layer. Frost top and sides of cake. Garnish the top with sugared lemon peel. Store in the refrigerator.

Yield: 12-16 servings.

PUFF PASTRY HOLLY LEAVES

These elegant appetizers look like you've worked for hours in the kitchen, but they can be assembled in a jiffy. They always earn raves at my office holiday party.

ANGELA KING, WALNUT COVE, NORTH CAROLINA

1	package (17.3 ounces) frozen puff pastry, thawed
1	egg
1	tablespoon water
4	ounces cream cheese, softened
1	cup (4 ounces) crumbled feta cheese
1/2	cup minced fresh parsley
1/2	cup prepared pesto
24	pimiento pieces

1. Unfold pastry sheets onto a lightly floured surface. From each sheet, cut out 12 leaves with a floured 3-1/2-in. leaf-shaped cookie cutter. Place on ungreased baking sheets. With a toothpick, score veins in leaves. In a small bowl, beat egg and water; brush over pastry.

2. Bake at 400° for 12-14 minutes or until golden brown. Remove to wire racks to cool.

3. In a large bowl, combine the cheeses, parsley and pesto. Split pastry leaves in half. Spread 1 tablespoon cheese mixture over bottom halves; replace tops. Add a pimiento piece on each for a holly berry. Refrigerate leftovers.

Yield: 2 dozen.

FESTIVE BROCCOLI-CAULIFLOWER SALAD

I came up with this recipe when unexpected company arrived and I didn't have enough lettuce and tomatoes on hand to make a traditional salad. Everyone enjoyed it so much that it became a regular at our table.

AVANELL HEWITT, NORTH RICHLAND HILLS, TEXAS

1	bunch broccoli, cut into florets
3	cups fresh cauliflowerets
1	medium green pepper, julienned
2	medium carrots, thinly sliced
1/2	cup thinly sliced red onion
1/2	cup small pitted ripe olives, halved
1/2	cup cubed sharp cheddar cheese

DRESSING:

1	cup mayonnaise
1/2	cup ranch salad dressing
1	teaspoon Italian seasoning
1/2	teaspoon garlic powder
1/2	teaspoon dill weed
1/2	cup sunflower kernels

1. In a large bowl, combine the first seven ingredients.

2. In a small bowl, whisk the mayonnaise, salad dressing, Italian seasoning, garlic powder and dill. Pour over salad; toss to coat. Cover and refrigerate for at least 1 hour.

3. Just before serving, sprinkle with sunflower kernels.

Yield: 14 servings (2/3 cup each).

GINGERBREAD CUPCAKES

With the heartwarming flavors of molasses, allspice and cinnamon, these cupcakes taste like the holidays! Garnish each with a dollop of whipped cream or whipped topping for a presentation that's sure to draw compliments.

BUGZBUNNY, TASTE OF HOME ONLINE COMMUNITY

2/3	cup sugar
1/2	cup canola oil
2	egg whites
1	egg
1	cup unsweetened applesauce
1	cup molasses
1-1/2	cups all-purpose flour
1	cup whole wheat flour
2-1/2	teaspoons baking soda
1	teaspoon each ground ginger, ground cinnamon and ground allspice
1/2	teaspoon salt
1-1/3	cups reduced-fat whipped topping

1. In a large bowl, beat the sugar, oil, egg whites and egg until well blended. Add applesauce and molasses; mix well. In a small bowl, combine the flours, baking soda, ginger, cinnamon, allspice and salt; gradually beat into applesauce mixture until blended.

2. Fill paper-lined muffin cups two-thirds full. Bake at 350° for 18-22 minutes or until a toothpick inserted near the center comes out clean. Cool for 10 minutes before removing from pans to wire racks to cool completely. Just before serving, top each cupcake with 1 tablespoon whipped topping.

Yield: 21 cupcakes.

TURKEY WITH CRANBERRY SAUCE

This is a very tasty and easy way to cook a turkey breast in the slow cooker. Ideal for holiday potlucks, the sweet cranberry sauce complements the turkey nicely.

MARIE RAMSDEN, FAIRGROVE, MICHIGAN

2	boneless skinless turkey breast halves (3 pounds each)
1	can (14 ounces) jellied cranberry sauce
1/2	cup plus 2 tablespoons water, divided
1	envelope onion soup mix
2	tablespoons cornstarch

1. Place turkey breasts in a 5-qt. slow cooker. In a large bowl, combine the cranberry sauce, 1/2 cup water and soup mix. Pour over turkey. Cover and cook on low for 4-6 hours or until meat is tender. Remove turkey and keep warm.

2. Transfer cooking juices to a large saucepan. Combine the cornstarch and remaining water until smooth. Bring cranberry mixture to a boil; gradually stir in cornstarch mixture until smooth. Cook and stir for 2 minutes or until thickened. Slice turkey; serve with cranberry sauce. May be frozen for up to 3 months.

Yield: 15 servings.

CRISP LEMON COOKIES

These light citrus cookies are a nice change of pace from typical sugar cookies. Melted vanilla chips drizzled over the top is a fantastic finishing touch.

DARLENE DIXON, HANOVER, MINNESOTA

1-1/3	cups butter, softened
2	cups confectioners' sugar
2	tablespoons lemon juice
2	teaspoons grated lemon peel
1/2	teaspoon vanilla extract
3	cups all-purpose flour
1/4	cup sugar
3/4	cup vanilla or white chips, melted

1. In a large bowl, cream butter and confectioners' sugar until light and fluffy. Beat in the lemon juice, peel and vanilla. Gradually add flour and mix well.

2. Shape dough into 1-in. balls. Place 2 in. apart on ungreased baking sheets. Coat the bottom of a glass with cooking spray; dip in sugar. Flatten cookies with glass, redipping in sugar as needed.

3. Bake at 325° for 11-13 minutes or until edges are lightly browned. Remove to wire racks to cool. Drizzle with melted vanilla chips.

Yield: about 4-1/2 dozen.

PECAN CANDY CLUSTERS

Grandchildren and kids love helping me make (and eat) these yummy four-ingredient treats! They're tasty and simple gifts.
FLO BURTNETT, GAGE, OKLAHOMA

LAST MINUTE!

2	cups milk chocolate chips, divided
64	pecan halves (about 1-1/2 cups)
28	caramels
2	tablespoons heavy whipping cream

1. Line a baking sheet with waxed paper; set aside. In a microwave, melt 1 cup chocolate chips; stir until smooth. Drop chocolate by tablespoonfuls onto prepared baking sheet. Immediately place four pecans on top of each chocolate drop.

2. Place the caramels in a 1-qt. microwave-safe dish; add cream. Microwave, uncovered, on high for 2 minutes, stirring once. Spoon onto the middle of each cluster.

3. Melt the remaining chocolate chips; stir until smooth. Spread over caramel. Let stand until set.

Yield: 16 candies.

Editor's Note: This recipe was tested in a 1,100-watt microwave.

PUMPKIN TIRAMISU

(pictured at right)
Tiramisu is a classic dessert that everyone enjoys. To add a more seasonal fall flavor, try this beautiful version that's reminiscent of pumpkin pie.
HOLLY BILLINGS, BATTLEFIELD, MISSOURI

1-1/2	cups heavy whipping cream
2	packages (8 ounces each) cream cheese, softened
1	can (15 ounces) solid-pack pumpkin
3/4	cup milk
1/2	cup packed brown sugar
4	teaspoons pumpkin pie spice, divided
2	teaspoons vanilla extract, divided
1	cup strong brewed coffee, room temperature
2	packages (3 ounces each) ladyfingers, split
1	carton (8 ounces) frozen whipped topping, thawed

Additional pumpkin pie spice

1. In a large bowl, beat cream until stiff peaks form; set aside. In another bowl, beat the cream cheese, pumpkin, milk, brown sugar, 1 teaspoon pie spice and 1 teaspoon vanilla until blended. Fold in whipped cream.

2. In a small bowl, combine coffee and remaining pie spice and vanilla; brush over ladyfingers. In a 3-qt. trifle dish, layer a fourth of the ladyfingers, pumpkin mixture and whipped topping. Repeat layers two times. Sprinkle with additional pie spice.

3. Cover and refrigerate for 4 hours or until chilled.

Yield: 16 servings.

Easy Whipped Cream
Before whipping cream, refrigerate the bowl and beaters for about 30 minutes. Pour cream into a deep, chilled bowl. Whip on high until soft peaks form if using as a garnish or until stiff peaks form if frosting a cake.

ARTICHOKE SPINACH LASAGNA

We were served this meatless entree while visiting friends in Maryland. We took the recipe with us when we left and have since added a few more ingredients that make it even better.
CAROLE RAGO, ALTOONA, PENNSYLVANIA

1/2	cup chopped onion
1	tablespoon olive oil
4	garlic cloves, minced
1	can (14-1/2 ounces) vegetable or chicken broth
1	teaspoon dried rosemary, crushed
1/4	teaspoon ground nutmeg and pepper
1	can (14 ounces) water-packed artichoke hearts, rinsed, drained and quartered
1	package (10 ounces) frozen chopped spinach, thawed and squeezed dry
1/2	cup sliced fresh mushrooms
1	jar (16 ounces) roasted garlic Alfredo or Parmesan and mozzarella pasta sauce
12	no-cook lasagna noodles
3	cups (12 ounces) shredded part-skim mozzarella cheese, divided
1	cup crumbled tomato and basil feta cheese or feta cheese
1/8	teaspoon garlic powder
1/8	teaspoon each dried oregano, parsley flakes and basil

1. In a large saucepan, saute onion in oil for 2-3 minutes or until tender. Add garlic; cook 1 minute longer. Stir in the broth, rosemary, nutmeg and pepper. Bring to a boil. Add the artichokes, spinach and mushrooms. Reduce heat; cover and simmer for 5 minutes. Stir in pasta sauce.

2. Spread 1 cup sauce mixture into a greased 13-in. x 9-in. baking dish. Top with three noodles and 3/4 cup mozzarella cheese. Repeat layers three times. Top with remaining sauce mixture and mozzarella cheese. Sprinkle with feta cheese, garlic powder, oregano, parsley and basil.

3. Cover and bake at 350° for 40 minutes. Uncover; bake 15 minutes longer or until heated through. Let stand for 10 minutes before cutting.

Yield: 12 servings.

TURKEY AND STUFFING PIE

For a fast and flavorful way to use up Thanksgiving leftovers, try this main-dish pie. Because it uses ready-made ingredients and one dish, it's such a handy recipe during the holidays.
DEBBI BAKER, GREEN SPRINGS, OHIO

3	cups prepared stuffing
2	cups cubed cooked turkey
1	cup (4 ounces) shredded Swiss cheese
3	eggs
1/2	cup milk

1. Press stuffing onto the bottom and up the sides of a well-greased 9-in. pie plate. Top with turkey and cheese. Beat eggs and milk; pour over cheese.

2. Bake at 350° for 35-40 minutes or until a knife inserted near the center comes out clean. Let stand 5-10 minutes before serving.

Yield: 8 servings.

APPLE DUMPLINGS

Luscious dumplings are a popular fundraiser for our Church Women's Association. We up our fresh apple order by a bushel each year to prepare for these treats.

COLLEGE HILL PRESBYTERIAN CHURCH WOMEN'S ASSOCIATION, BEAVER FALLS, PENNSYLVANIA

8	cups all-purpose flour
3	tablespoons baking powder
4-1/2	teaspoons salt
1-1/2	pounds butter-flavored shortening
2	cups 2% milk
24	medium tart apples, peeled and cored
1-1/2	cups sugar
1	teaspoon ground cinnamon
1/2	cup butter, divided

SYRUP:

2-1/2	cups packed brown sugar
1-1/2	cups water
1	cup butter, cubed
1	teaspoon ground cinnamon

1. In a large bowl, combine the flour, baking powder and salt; cut in shortening until crumbly. Gradually add milk, tossing with a fork until dough forms a ball. Divide into 24 portions. Cover and refrigerate for at least 1 hour or until easy to handle.

2. On a well-floured surface, roll each portion of dough into a 7-in. square. Place an apple on each square. Combine sugar and cinnamon; place 1 tablespoonful into the core of each apple. Dot each with 1 teaspoon butter.

3. Gently bring up corners of pastry to center; pinch edges to seal. Place in four greased 13-in. x 9-in. baking dishes. Bake at 350° for 15 minutes.

4. Meanwhile, in a large saucepan, combine the syrup ingredients. Bring to a boil; cook and stir until smooth and blended. Pour over apples.

5. Bake 35-40 minutes longer or until apples are tender and pastry is golden brown. Serve warm.

Yield: 24 servings.

ROASTED FALL VEGETABLES

I love serving this tender veggie side dish as part of a comforting dinner on a chilly night. The cayenne pepper lends zippy flavor that's not overpowering.

JULI MEYERS, HINESVILLE, GEORGIA

1	large acorn squash, peeled and cut into 1-1/2-inch cubes
1	large rutabaga, peeled and cut into 1-inch cubes
1	medium pie pumpkin or butternut squash, peeled and cut into 1-inch cubes
3	large carrots, peeled and cut into 1-1/2-inch pieces
1	medium parsnip, peeled and cut into 1-inch cubes
1/4	cup grated Parmesan cheese
1/4	cup canola oil
3	tablespoons minced fresh parsley
2	tablespoons paprika
2	teaspoons salt
1	teaspoon garlic powder
1/2	teaspoon cayenne pepper

1. In a large bowl, combine the first five ingredients. In a small bowl, combine the remaining ingredients. Pour over vegetables; toss to coat.

2. Transfer to two greased 15-in. x 10-in. x 1-in. baking pans. Bake, uncovered, at 425° for 40-50 minutes or until tender, stirring occasionally.

Yield: 14 servings.

PILGRIM HAT COOKIES

We dreamed up this combination for a yummy treat to take to school before our Thanksgiving break. Everyone loved them!

MEGAN AND MITCHELL VOGEL, JEFFERSON, WISCONSIN

1	cup vanilla frosting
7	drops yellow food coloring
32	miniature peanut butter cups
1	package (11-1/2 ounces) fudge-striped cookies
32	pieces orange mini Chiclets gum

1. In a small shallow bowl, combine the frosting and food coloring. Remove paper liners from peanut butter cups.

2. Holding the bottom of a peanut butter cup, dip top of cup in yellow frosting. Position over center hole on the bottom of cookie, forming the hatband and crown. Add a buckle of Chiclets gum. Repeat with remaining cups and cookies.

Yield: 32 cookies.

CRANBERRY TURKEY CROSTINI

(pictured at left)

Here's a holiday appetizer that's bursting with a variety of flavors and textures.. Jalapenos balance out the other ingredients perfectly. If you don't have shaved turkey, shaved chicken works just as well.

BRIDGETTA EALY, PONTIAC, MICHIGAN

1	package (12 ounces) fresh or frozen cranberries
1	medium tangerine, peeled and seeded
1/2	cup red wine vinegar
1/4	cup chopped shallots
1/2	cup sugar
1/4	cup chopped seeded jalapeno peppers
1/4	teaspoon pepper
30	slices French bread (1/4 inch thick)
Cooking spray	
1	package (8 ounces) reduced-fat cream cheese
1/2	pound shaved deli smoked turkey

1. Place cranberries and tangerine in a food processor; cover and process until coarsely chopped. Set aside.

2. In a small saucepan, bring vinegar and shallots to a boil. Reduce heat; simmer, uncovered, for 5 minutes or until mixture is reduced to 1/3 cup, stirring occasionally.

3. Stir in the sugar, jalapenos, pepper and reserved cranberry mixture. Cook for 5 minutes over medium heat, stirring frequently. Transfer to a small bowl; refrigerate until chilled.

4. Place bread on ungreased baking sheets; lightly spray bread on both sides with cooking spray. Broil 3-4 in. from the heat for 1-2 minutes on each side or until lightly browned. Spread each slice with 1-1/2 teaspoons cream cheese; top with turkey and 1 tablespoon cranberry mixture.

Yield: 2-1/2 dozen.

Editor's Note: Wear disposable gloves when cutting hot peppers; the oils can burn skin. Avoid touching your face.

MAPLE PUMPKIN CHEESECAKE

For our first Thanksgiving with my husband's family, I wanted to bring a special dish and decided I couldn't go wrong with a dessert that combines cheesecake and pumpkin pie. It was a huge success!

JODI GOBRECHT, BUCYRUS, OHIO

- 1-1/4 cups graham cracker crumbs
- 1/4 cup sugar
- 1/4 cup butter, melted
- 3 packages (8 ounces each) cream cheese, softened
- 1 can (14 ounces) sweetened condensed milk
- 1 can (15 ounces) solid-pack pumpkin
- 1/4 cup maple syrup
- 1-1/2 teaspoons ground cinnamon
- 1 teaspoon ground nutmeg
- 1/2 teaspoon salt
- 3 eggs, lightly beaten

TOPPING:
- 2 cups (16 ounces) sour cream
- 1/3 cup sugar
- 1 teaspoon vanilla extract

1. In a small bowl, combine the cracker crumbs, sugar and butter. Press onto the bottom of a greased 9-in. springform pan. Place on a baking sheet. Bake at 325° for 12 minutes. Cool on a wire rack.

2. In a large bowl, beat cream cheese and milk until smooth. Beat in the pumpkin, syrup, cinnamon, nutmeg and salt. Add eggs; beat on low speed just until combined.

3. Pour into crust. Place pan on baking sheet. Bake at 325° for 70-75 minutes or until center is almost set. Combine the topping ingredients; spread over cheesecake. Bake 5 minutes longer.

4. Cool on a wire rack for 10 minutes. Carefully run a knife around edge of pan to loosen; cool 1 hour longer. Refrigerate overnight. Remove sides of pan. Refrigerate leftovers.

Yield: 12-14 servings.

MINI SPIDER BITES

These little cupcakes are almost too sweet to eat! Best of all, they're a great way to get your little goblins involved in some fall baking fun.

SARA MARTIN, BROOKFIELD, WISCONSIN

LAST MINUTE!

- Miniature cupcakes of your choice
- 1 can (16 ounces) chocolate frosting
- M&M's miniature baking bits
- Chocolate sprinkles
- Pastry tip #151; round tip #7
- 1 can (16 ounces) vanilla frosting
- Shoestring black licorice

1. Generously frost cupcakes with chocolate frosting; add M&M's for noses. Top with chocolate sprinkles.

2. Insert tip #7 into a pastry bag; fill with vanilla frosting and pipe spider's eyes. Add M&M's for pupils. Cut black licorice into 2-in. pieces; attach eight legs to each cupcake.

Yield: varies.

MAGNIFICENT CARROT CAKE

If you're looking for something traditional, nothing says Easter like a homemade carrot cake covered in rich cream cheese frosting. A touch of rum extract lends wonderful flavor to every bite of this baked-from-scratch indulgence.

MELANIE MADEIRA, DALLAS, PENNSYLVANIA

2	cups sugar
3/4	cup buttermilk
3/4	cup canola oil
3	eggs
3	teaspoons rum extract
2	cups all-purpose flour
2	teaspoons baking soda
2	teaspoons ground cinnamon
1/2	teaspoon salt
1/2	teaspoon ground allspice
2	cups shredded carrots
1	can (8 ounces) crushed pineapple, drained
3/4	cup chopped walnuts
3/4	cup dried currants

GLAZE:

1/2	cup sugar
1/4	cup buttermilk
1/4	cup butter, cubed
1/2	teaspoon corn syrup
1/4	teaspoon baking soda
1/2	teaspoon vanilla extract

FROSTING:

2	packages (8 ounces each) cream cheese, softened
2/3	cup butter, softened
4	cups confectioners' sugar
4	teaspoons rum extract

1. In a large bowl, beat the sugar, buttermilk, oil, eggs and extract until well blended. In another bowl, combine the flour, baking soda, cinnamon, salt and allspice; gradually beat into sugar mixture until blended. Stir in the carrots, pineapple, walnuts and currants.

2. Transfer to two greased and floured 9-in. round baking pans. Bake at 350° for 30-35 minutes or until a toothpick inserted near the center comes out clean.

3. Meanwhile, for glaze, combine the sugar, buttermilk, butter, corn syrup and baking soda in a small saucepan. Bring to a boil; cook and stir for 4 minutes. Remove from the heat; stir in vanilla.

4. Pour glaze over hot cakes; cool for 10 minutes before removing from pans to wire racks to cool completely.

5. For frosting, in a large bowl, beat cream cheese and butter until fluffy. Add confectioners' sugar and extract; beat until smooth.

6. Place one cake layer on a serving plate; spread with 1 cup frosting. Top with remaining cake layer. Frost top and sides of cake. Store in the refrigerator.

Yield: 16 servings.

HAM AND SWISS CASSEROLE

Here's a rich, creamy all-in-one meal. We just love the easy-to-make sauce, and it's a great way to use up leftover ham. For a comforting side dish, simply eliminate the ham.

JULIE JACKMAN, BOUNTIFUL, UTAH

- 8 ounces uncooked penne pasta
- 2 envelopes country gravy mix
- 1 package (10 ounces) frozen chopped spinach, thawed and squeezed dry
- 2 cups (8 ounces) shredded Swiss cheese
- 2 cups cubed fully cooked ham
- 4-1/2 teaspoons ground mustard

1. Cook pasta according to package directions. Meanwhile, in a large saucepan, cook gravy mix according to package directions. Stir in the spinach, cheese, ham and mustard. Drain pasta; stir into ham mixture.

2. Transfer to a greased 13-in. x 9-in. baking dish. Cover and bake at 350° for 20 minutes. Uncover; bake 10-15 minutes longer or until heated through.

Yield: 8 servings.

PETER PUMPKIN CHEESE PUFFS

(pictured at right)

You, too, can be "Peter the Pumpkin Eater" from the classic nursery rhyme when you prepare a batch of these fluffy and tender cheese puffs that look like mini pumpkins. Romano cheese gives them a nice tang and their cream cheese stems complete the seasonal look.

TASTE OF HOME TEST KITCHEN

- 2 tablespoons cream cheese, softened
- 1/2 teaspoon balsamic vinegar
- 1/2 cup water
- 1/4 cup butter, cubed
- 1/4 teaspoon salt
- 1/2 cup all-purpose flour
- 4 drops yellow paste food coloring
- 1 drop red paste food coloring
- 1/2 cup grated Romano cheese
- 2 eggs
- Fresh parsley leaves

1. In a small bowl, combine cream cheese and vinegar. Cover and refrigerate. In a large saucepan, bring the water, butter and salt to a boil. Add flour all at once and stir until a smooth ball forms. Remove from the heat; let stand for 5 minutes.

2. In a small bowl, combine the yellow and red food coloring; stir Romano cheese and food coloring into dough. Add eggs, one at a time; beating well after each addition. Continue beating until mixture is smooth and shiny.

3. Drop by level tablespoonfuls 3 in. apart onto a greased baking sheet. Bake at 400° for 15-20 minutes or until lightly browned. Remove to a wire rack to cool.

4. Using a star tip and reserved cream cheese mixture, pipe stems onto puffs. Garnish with parsley. Refrigerate leftovers.

Yield: about 1-1/2 dozen.

PARSNIP-ASPARAGUS AU GRATIN

We pair parsnips with fresh asparagus to create a terrific spring side dish. The cheesy and buttery crumb topping will entice everyone to eat their veggies!
TASTE OF HOME TEST KITCHEN

10	medium parsnips, peeled and cut into 1-inch slices
1/2	teaspoon salt
1/8	teaspoon pepper
1/2	cup butter, divided
2	pounds fresh asparagus, trimmed and cut into 2-inch pieces
2	medium onions, chopped
4	garlic cloves, minced
2	cups soft bread crumbs
1/2	cup grated Parmesan cheese

1. In a large bowl, combine the parsnips, salt and pepper. In a microwave, melt 2 tablespoons butter. Drizzle over parsnips; toss to coat. Transfer to a greased 15-in. x 10-in. x 1-in. baking pan. Bake at 400° for 20 minutes.

2. Meanwhile, in a microwave, melt 2 tablespoons butter. Combine asparagus and melted butter; add to parsnips. Bake 20-25 minutes longer or until vegetables are tender.

3. In a large saucepan, saute the onions in remaining butter until tender. Add the garlic; saute 1 minute longer. Add bread crumbs; cook and stir until lightly toasted. Stir in cheese. Transfer parsnip mixture to a serving platter; sprinkle with crumb mixture.

Yield: 16 servings.

SQUASH CORN BREAD

Enjoy the fresh flavor of summer squash with this moist and hearty cornbread. This is good enough to eat by itself!
MARLENE HUFFSTETLER, CHAPIN, SOUTH CAROLINA

5	medium yellow summer squash (about 2 pounds), chopped
2	packages (8-1/2 ounces each) corn bread/muffin mix
4	eggs, lightly beaten
2/3	cup 4% cottage cheese
1/2	cup shredded cheddar cheese
1/2	cup chopped onion
1/4	teaspoon each salt and pepper

1. Place squash in a steamer basket; place in a large saucepan over 1 in. of water. Bring to a boil; cover and steam for 3-5 minutes or until tender. Drain and squeeze dry.

2. In a large bowl, combine corn bread mixes and eggs. Fold in the squash, cheeses, onion, salt and pepper.

3. Pour into two 8-in. square baking pans coated with cooking spray. Bake at 400° for 20-25 minutes or until a toothpick inserted near the center comes out clean.

4. Serve warm or cool for 10 minutes before removing from pans to wire racks to cool completely. Wrap in foil and freeze for up to 3 months.

To use frozen bread: Thaw at room temperature. Serve warm.

Yield: 2 dozen.

GOBBLER COBBLER

I often save some turkey from the holidays and freeze it so I can make this hot turkey salad pie on New Year's Day. Pineapple adds a bit of crunch and sweetness.
DARLENE BRENDEN, SALEM, OREGON

1-1/2	cups all-purpose flour
1/2	teaspoon salt
1/2	cup shortening
1/2	cup shredded cheddar cheese
1/4	cup milk

FILLING:

2	cups cubed cooked turkey
1	cup pineapple tidbits, drained
1	cup chopped walnuts
1/4	cup chopped onion
1/4	cup chopped celery
1	cup (8 ounces) sour cream
2/3	cup mayonnaise
1/4	cup shredded cheddar cheese
1/4	cup sliced ripe olives, optional

1. In a bowl, combine the flour and salt; cut in shortening until crumbly. Fold in cheese. Gradually add milk, tossing with a fork until dough forms a ball. Roll out pastry to fit a 9-in. pie plate.

2. Transfer pastry to pie plate. Trim to 1/2 in. beyond edge of plate; flute edges. Line unpricked pastry shell with a double thickness of heavy-duty foil. Bake at 450° for 8 minutes. Remove the foil; bake 5 minutes longer. Cool on a wire rack. Reduce the heat to 350°.

3. In a bowl, combine the turkey, pineapple, walnuts, onion and celery. Combine sour cream and mayonnaise; fold into turkey mixture. Spoon into crust. Sprinkle with cheese and olives if desired. Bake, uncovered, for 25-30 minutes or until heated through.

Yield: 6-8 servings.

SANTA CUPCAKES

My children decorate these cupcakes every year for Christmas. We use chocolate chips for Santa's eyes and a red-hot for his nose, but you can use any kind of candy you like.
SHARON SKILDUM, MAPLE GROVE, MINNESOTA

1	package (18-1/4 ounces) white cake mix
1	can (16 ounces) or 2 cups vanilla frosting, divided

Red gel or paste food coloring

Miniature marshmallows, chocolate chips, red-hot candies and flaked coconut

1. Prepare and bake cake mix according to package directions for cupcakes. Cool for 10 minutes; remove from pans to wire racks to cool completely.

2. Place 2/3 cup frosting in a small bowl; tint with red food coloring. Set aside 3 tablespoons white frosting for decorating. Cover two-thirds of the top of each cupcake with remaining white frosting. Frost the rest of cupcake top with red frosting for hat. Place reserved white frosting in a small heavy-duty resealable plastic bag; cut a 1/4-in. hole in one corner.

3. On each cupcake, pipe a line of frosting to create fur band of hat. Press a marshmallow on one side of hat for pom-pom. Under hat, place two chocolate chips for eyes and one red-hot for nose. Gently press coconut onto face for beard.

Yield: about 1-1/2 dozen.

party meatballs, pg. 230

creamy buffalo chicken dip, pg. 238

Feeding a Crowd

"Then he broke the loaves and gave them to the disciples, and the disciples gave them to the crowds. And they all ate and were satisfied." Matt. 14:19-20

WARM SAVORY CHEESE SPREAD

Served in a bread bowl, this colorful cheese blend gets added flavor from bacon and veggies. It is perfect for parties any time of the year but especially nice around the holidays because of the red and green peppers.

MARILU HYNES, MCLEOD HILL, NEW BRUNSWICK

2	cups mayonnaise
2	cups (8 ounces) shredded cheddar cheese
1	large onion, finely chopped
8	bacon strips, cooked and crumbled
1/2	cup finely chopped sweet red pepper
1/2	cup finely chopped green pepper
1	teaspoon dried oregano
1/2	teaspoon garlic powder
1	round loaf (1 pound) sourdough bread
	Assorted crackers

1. In a large bowl, combine the first eight ingredients. Cut the top fourth off the loaf of bread; carefully hollow out bottom, leaving a 1-in. shell (save removed bread for another use).

2. Spoon cheese mixture into bread shell. Wrap in a piece of heavy-duty foil (about 24 in. x 18 in.). Bake at 350° for 1 hour or until heated through. Serve with crackers.

Yield: 4 cups.

AU GRATIN PARTY POTATOES

When putting on a party for their American Legion Post, my father and uncle prepared this yummy potato dish. I've used the recipe for smaller groups by making a half or quarter of it. It's simple to divide and turns out just as delicious.
CRYSTAL KOLADY, HENRIETTA, NEW YORK

20	pounds potatoes, peeled, cubed and cooked
4	cans (12 ounces each) evaporated milk
3	packages (16 ounces each) process cheese (Velveeta), cubed
1	cup butter, cubed
2	tablespoons salt
2	teaspoons pepper
	Paprika, optional

1. In several large bowls, combine potatoes, milk, cheese, butter, salt and pepper. Transfer to four greased 13-in. x 9-in. baking dishes.

2. Bake, uncovered, at 350° for 45-50 minutes or until bubbly. Sprinkle with paprika if desired.

Yield: about 60 (3/4-cup) servings.

BUTTERSCOTCH PEANUT BUTTER FUDGE

You don't have to be experienced at making candy to try your hand at this no-fail fudge. The simply delicious confection makes a great gift everyone appreciates.
MARINA CASTLE, LA CRESCENTA, CALIFORNIA

1	teaspoon plus 1/2 cup butter, divided
1	package (11 ounces) butterscotch chips
1	cup creamy peanut butter
2	cups miniature marshmallows
1/2	cup chopped unsalted peanuts

1. Line an 11-in. x 7-in. pan with foil and grease the foil with 1 teaspoon butter; set aside.

2. In a large saucepan, combine the butterscotch chips, peanut butter and remaining butter. Cook and stir over medium heat until melted. Remove from the heat; stir in marshmallows until smooth. Spread into prepared pan; sprinkle with peanuts. Chill until firm.

3. Using foil, lift the fudge out of pan. Discard the foil; cut the fudge into 1-in. squares. Store in an airtight container.

Yield: about 2 pounds.

3. Meanwhile, in a skillet, cook bacon over medium heat until crisp. Remove to paper towels; drain, reserving 1 tablespoon drippings. Set bacon aside. Cook onion in drippings until tender; set aside.

4. Punch dough down. Turn onto a lightly floured surface; divide into fourths. Roll each portion into a 15-in. x 10-in. rectangle. Sprinkle each with a fourth of the cheese, about 1/3 cup bacon and about 2 tablespoons onion.

5. Roll up jelly-roll style, starting with a long side; pinch seam to seal. Cut each into 12 slices. Place cut side down 2 in. apart on ungreased baking sheets. Cover and let rise until doubled, about 30 minutes.

6. Bake at 350° for 25-30 minutes or until golden brown. Remove from pans to wire racks. Store in the refrigerator.

Yield: 4 dozen.

BACON-CHEESE PINWHEEL ROLLS

It's no wonder my husband adores these pinwheels. I got the original recipe from his mother. They taste great warm or cold and freeze well in plastic bags.
WENDY MALLARD, STONY PLAIN, ALBERTA

2	packages (1/4 ounce each) active dry yeast
2	teaspoons plus 1/2 cup sugar, divided
2	cups warm water (110° to 115°), divided
1	cup warm milk (110° to 115°)
2/3	cup butter, melted
2	eggs, lightly beaten
2	teaspoons salt
8-3/4 to 9-1/4	cups all-purpose flour
1	pound sliced bacon, diced
1/2	cup finely chopped onion
4	cups (16 ounces) shredded cheddar cheese

1. In a large bowl, dissolve yeast and 2 teaspoons sugar in 1 cup warm water; let stand for 5 minutes. Add the milk, butter, eggs, salt, 7 cups flour and remaining water and sugar. Beat until smooth. Stir in enough remaining flour to form a soft dough.

2. Turn onto a floured surface; knead until smooth and elastic, about 6-8 minutes. Place in a greased bowl, turning once to grease top. Cover and let rise in a warm place until doubled, about 1 hour.

ROUNDUP-DAY BEANS

The hearty noon meal at our spring cattle roundup always features these sweet, smoky beans fit for any occasion. Neighbors gather to help for a day of work and socialization.
JENNY HUGHSON, MITCHELL, NEBRASKA

2	pounds ground beef
1	cup chopped onion
1-1/2	cups chopped green pepper
3	cans (53 ounces each) pork and beans
1	cup ketchup
6	tablespoons brown sugar
1/4	cup molasses
2	tablespoons Liquid Smoke, optional
1-1/2	teaspoons salt
1	teaspoon pepper

1. In large Dutch ovens, cook beef, onion and green pepper over medium heat until meat is no longer pink and vegetables are tender. Drain. Add the remaining ingredients; bring to a boil. Reduce the heat; cover and simmer for 30 minutes.

Yield: 45-50 servings.

BOW TIE SEAFOOD SALAD

I served this satisfying pasta salad to a group of hospital volunteers who were quick with compliments. It is brimming with shrimp and imitation crab and accented with dill.

LILY JULOW, GAINESVILLE, FLORIDA

3	pounds uncooked bow tie pasta
1-1/2	pounds imitation crabmeat, chopped
1	pound frozen cooked salad shrimp, thawed
4	celery ribs, chopped
1	cup finely chopped green onions
1	medium green pepper, diced
4	cups mayonnaise
1/4	cup dill pickle relish
1/4	cup Dijon mustard
1	tablespoon salt
1	tablespoon dill weed
3/4	teaspoon pepper

1. Cook pasta according to package directions; drain and rinse in cold water. Place in a large bowl; add the crab, shrimp, celery, onions and green pepper.

2. In another bowl, whisk the mayonnaise, pickle relish, mustard, salt, dill and pepper. Pour over pasta mixture and toss to coat. Cover and refrigerate for at least 2 hours before serving.

Yield: 32 (1-cup) servings.

TOFFEE MALTED COOKIES

As much as I delight in sharing these goodies, my family considers them "keepers." It's a wonder I ever get them out the door to take to meetings! With their luscious melt-in-your-mouth texture, they're always popular.

SHARON TIMPE, JACKSON, WISCONSIN

1	cup butter, softened
1/2	cup sugar
1/2	cup packed brown sugar
2	eggs
1	package (3.4 ounces) instant vanilla pudding mix
1	teaspoon vanilla extract
2-1/4	cups all-purpose flour
1	cup quick-cooking oats
1	teaspoon baking soda
1/2	teaspoon salt
1	cup malted milk balls, chopped
3/4	cup English toffee bits or almond brickle chips

1. In a large bowl, cream butter and sugars until light and fluffy. Add eggs, one at a time, beating well after each addition. Add pudding mix and vanilla. Combine the flour, oats, baking soda and salt; add to creamed mixture and mix well. Fold in malted milk balls and toffee bits (dough will be stiff).

2. Drop by rounded teaspoonfuls 2 in. apart onto ungreased baking sheets. Bake at 350° for 12-15 minutes or until golden brown. Cool for 2 minutes before removing to wire racks.

Yield: 7 dozen.

PARTY MEATBALLS

Meatballs are always great for parties. This is an easy twist on the usual recipe, and it's very fast to make.

DEBBIE PAULSEN, APOLLO BEACH, FLORIDA

- 1   package (32 ounces) frozen fully cooked homestyle meatballs, thawed
- 1   bottle (14 ounces) ketchup
- 1/4   cup A.1. steak sauce
- 1   tablespoon minced garlic
- 1   teaspoon Dijon mustard

1. Place the meatballs in a 3-qt. slow cooker. In a small bowl, combine the ketchup, steak sauce, garlic and mustard. Pour over meatballs. Cover and cook on low for 3-4 hours or until meatballs are heated through.

Yield: about 6 dozen.

COCONUT-ALMOND FUDGE CUPS

(pictured at right)

With a coconut filling, the flavor of these fudgy bites is reminiscent of a favorite candy bar. The recipe makes a big batch so you'll have plenty to share with others.

LAST MINUTE!

MAYBRIE, TASTE OF HOME ONLINE COMMUNITY

- 1   package (18-1/4 ounces) chocolate fudge cake mix
- 1/2   cup butter, melted
- 1   egg

FILLING:

- 1/4   cup sugar
- 1/4   cup evaporated milk
- 7   large marshmallows
- 1   cup flaked coconut

TOPPING:

- 3/4   cup semisweet chocolate chips
- 1/4   cup evaporated milk
- 2   tablespoons butter
- 1/2   cup sliced almonds

1. In a large bowl, beat the cake mix, butter and egg until well blended. Shape into 1-in. balls; place in foil-lined miniature muffin cups. Bake at 350° for 8 minutes.

2. Using the end of a wooden spoon handle, make a 1/2-in.-deep indentation in the center of each cup. Bake 2-3 minutes longer or until cake springs back when lightly touched. Remove from pans to wire racks to cool.

3. For filling, in a microwave-safe bowl, heat sugar and milk on high for 2 minutes, stirring frequently. Add marshmallows; stir until melted. Stir in coconut. Spoon into cooled cups.

4. For topping, in another microwave-safe bowl, combine the chocolate chips, milk and butter. Microwave in 10- to 20-second intervals until melted; stir until smooth. Stir in almonds. Spread over filling. Store in the refrigerator.

Yield: 4 dozen.

Editor's Note: This recipe was tested in a 1,100-watt microwave.

BLUE CHEESE DATE WRAPS

My friends and I used to make the traditional bacon-wrapped jalapenos at cookouts. I decided to sweeten them up a bit with dates and apricots, which are also more kid-friendly.
SUSAN HINTON, APEX, NORTH CAROLINA

LAST MINUTE!

12	bacon strips
36	pitted dates
2/3	cup crumbled blue cheese

1. Cut each bacon strip into thirds. In a large skillet, cook bacon in batches over medium heat until partially cooked but not crisp. Remove to paper towels to drain; keep warm.

2. Carefully cut a slit in the center of each date; fill with blue cheese. Wrap a bacon piece around each stuffed date; secure with wooden toothpicks.

3. Place on ungreased baking sheets. Bake at 375° for 10-12 minutes or until bacon is crisp.

Yield: 3 dozen.

THREE-MEAT STROMBOLI

This hearty and spicy appetizer is a real crowd-pleaser. No one believes me when I tell them it's a simple recipe.
JUDE MULVEY, EAST SCHODACK, NEW YORK

4	loaves (1 pound each) frozen bread dough, thawed
1/2	pound thinly sliced deli salami
1/2	pound thinly sliced deli ham
1/2	pound thinly sliced pepperoni
1/2	pound thinly sliced provolone cheese
2	cups (8 ounces) shredded part-skim mozzarella cheese
1/2	cup grated Romano or Parmesan cheese
1	tablespoon each garlic powder and dried oregano
1	teaspoon each dried parsley flakes and pepper
1	egg yolk, lightly beaten

1. Let dough rise until doubled, according to the package directions. Punch down. Roll each loaf into a 15-in. x 12-in. rectangle. Arrange a fourth of the salami, ham, pepperoni and provolone cheese over each rectangle. Sprinkle each with a fourth of the mozzarella cheese, Romano cheese, garlic powder, oregano, parsley and pepper.

2. Roll up each rectangle jelly-roll style, beginning with a long side. Seal seams and ends. Place seam side down on two greased baking sheets. Brush with egg yolk.

3. Bake at 375° for 25-30 minutes or until golden brown. Let stand for 5 minutes before slicing. Serve warm. Refrigerate leftovers.

Yield: 4 loaves (8 slices each).

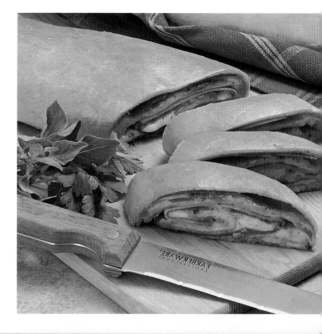

FAMILY GATHERING POTATOES

This delicious Amish side dish always wins raves. Almost everyone comes back for second helping.
JOLYNN HILL, ROOSEVELT, UTAH

4	cans (10-3/4 ounces each) condensed cream of celery soup, undiluted
4	cans (10-3/4 ounces each) condensed cream of chicken soup, undiluted
2	pounds process American cheese (Velveeta), cubed
4	cups (32 ounces) sour cream
1-1/3	cups butter, divided
4	teaspoons seasoned salt
2	teaspoons garlic powder
2	teaspoons pepper
20	pounds potatoes, peeled, cubed and cooked
2	cups crushed Club crackers (about 40)

1. In four Dutch ovens, combine soups, cheese, sour cream, 1 cup butter, seasoned salt, garlic power and pepper. Cook and stir until cheese is melted and mixture is smooth. Add potatoes; mix well. Transfer to four greased 13-in. x 9-in. baking dishes (dishes will be full).

2. Bake, uncovered, at 350° for 45-60 minutes or until bubbly. Melt remaining butter; toss with cracker crumbs. Sprinkle over potatoes. Bake 10-15 minutes longer or until topping is lightly browned. Let stand for 5 minutes before serving.
Yield: 60-65 servings.

Eliminate Any Guesswork
When you bring a dish to pass, write the name of the recipe on a small piece of paper (like that which resembles a toy boat sail), attach the label to a wooden skewer and stand the skewer in the dish.

COOKIE DOUGH TRUFFLES

The flavorful filling at the center of these yummy candies tastes like genuine chocolate chip cookie dough; without the worry of raw eggs. That's what makes them so appealing. Plus, they're easy to make.
LANITA DEDON, SLAUGHTER, LOUISIANA

1/2	cup butter, softened
3/4	cup packed brown sugar
1	teaspoon vanilla extract
2	cups all-purpose flour
1	can (14 ounces) sweetened condensed milk
1/2	cup miniature semisweet chocolate chips
1/2	cup chopped walnuts
1-1/2	pounds dark chocolate candy coating, coarsely chopped

1. In a large bowl, cream the butter and brown sugar until light and fluffy. Beat in vanilla. Gradually add flour, alternately with milk, beating well after each addition. Stir in chocolate chips and walnuts.

2. Shape into 1-in. balls; place on waxed paper-lined baking sheets. Loosely cover and refrigerate for 1-2 hours or until firm.

3. In a microwave, melt candy coating; stir until smooth. Dip balls in coating; allow excess to drip off. Place on waxed paper-lined baking sheets. Refrigerate until firm, about 15 minutes. If desired, remelt remaining candy coating and drizzle over candies. Store in the refrigerator.
Yield: 5-1/2 dozen.

NO-BAKE COOKIE BALLS

These quick bites are great when you're short on time or don't want to turn on the oven. I make them a day or two ahead to let the flavors blend.
CARMELETTA DAILEY, WINFIELD, TEXAS

1	cup (6 ounces) semisweet chocolate chips
3	cups confectioners' sugar
1-3/4	cups crushed vanilla wafers (about 55 wafers)
1	cup chopped walnuts, toasted
1/3	cup orange juice
3	tablespoons light corn syrup
Additional confectioners' sugar	

1. In a large microwave-safe bowl, melt chocolate chips; stir until smooth. Stir in the confectioners' sugar, vanilla wafers, walnuts, orange juice and corn syrup.

2. Roll into 1-in. balls; roll in additional confectioners' sugar. Store in an airtight container.

Yield: 5 dozen.

ASPARAGUS CHEESE TRIANGLES

(pictured at left)
I came up with this take-off on Greek spanakopita (spinach pie) when I had an overabundance of asparagus and a package of phyllo dough. Sometimes I add leftover chopped chicken and cut into larger triangles for meals.
COLETTE GEROW, RAYTOWN, MISSOURI

2	quarts water
2	pounds fresh asparagus, trimmed and chopped
2	cups (8 ounces) shredded part-skim mozzarella cheese
1	cup (8 ounces) ricotta cheese
1	small onion, chopped
1/2	teaspoon garlic powder
1/4	teaspoon salt
1/8	teaspoon pepper
9	tablespoons butter, melted
30	sheets phyllo dough (14 inches x 9 inches)

1. In a large saucepan, bring water to a boil; add asparagus. Cover and cook for 4-6 minutes or until crisp-tender. Drain and immediately rinse with cold water; drain and pat dry. In a large bowl, combine the asparagus, cheeses, onion, garlic powder, salt and pepper.

2. Brush a 15-in. x 10-in. x 1-in. baking pan with some of the butter. Unroll phyllo sheets; trim short side to fit pan. Cover dough with plastic wrap and a damp cloth while assembling. Place two sheets of phyllo in pan; brush with butter. Repeat eight times. Spread with asparagus mixture. Layer with remaining phyllo sheets, brushing each with butter.

3. Bake at 350° for 40-45 minutes or until golden brown. Cool on a wire rack for 5 minutes. Cut into 24 pieces; cut each piece in half diagonally. Serve warm. Refrigerate leftovers.

Yield: 4 dozen.

SPINACH ARTICHOKE-STUFFED MUSHROOMS

Guests will think you fussed over these rich, creamy stuffed mushrooms, but they go together so easily! The flavorful artichoke filling makes this party appetizer something special.
AMY GAISFORD, SALT LAKE CITY, UTAH

1	package (3 ounces) cream cheese, softened
1/2	cup mayonnaise
1/2	cup sour cream
1	can (14 ounces) water-packed artichoke hearts, rinsed, drained and chopped
1	package (10 ounces) frozen chopped spinach, thawed and squeezed dry
1/3	cup shredded part-skim mozzarella cheese
4	tablespoons shredded Parmesan cheese, divided
3/4	teaspoon garlic salt
30	to 35 large fresh mushrooms

1. In a small bowl, beat the cream cheese, mayonnaise and sour cream. Stir in the artichokes, spinach, mozzarella cheese, 3 tablespoons Parmesan cheese and garlic salt.

2. Remove stems from mushrooms (discard stems or save for another use). Fill each mushroom cap with about 1 tablespoon of filling. Sprinkle with remaining Parmesan cheese.

3. Place on foil-lined baking sheets. Bake at 400° for 16-20 minutes or until mushrooms are tender.
Yield: 30-35 appetizers.

ANTIPASTO SALAD

This colorful salad is a tasty crowd-pleaser. Guests love the homemade, from-scratch dressing, which is a nice change from the bottled Italian variety.
LINDA HARRINGTON, WINDHAM, NEW HAMPSHIRE

2	packages (1 pound each) spiral pasta
4	cups chopped green peppers
4	cups chopped seeded tomatoes
3	cups chopped onions
2	cans (15 ounces each) garbanzo beans or chickpeas, rinsed and drained
1	pound thinly sliced Genoa salami, julienned
1	pound sliced pepperoni, julienned
1/2	pound provolone cheese, cubed
1	cup pitted ripe olives, halved
1-1/2	cups olive oil
1	cup red wine vinegar
1/2	cup sugar
2	tablespoons dried oregano
2	teaspoons salt
1	teaspoon pepper

1. Cook pasta according to package directions. Drain and rinse in cold water. In several large bowls, combine the pasta, green peppers, tomatoes, onions, beans, salami, pepperoni, cheese and olives.

2. In a large bowl, whisk the oil, vinegar, sugar, oregano, salt and pepper. Pour over pasta salad; toss to coat. Cover and refrigerate for 4 hours or overnight.
Yield: 50 (3/4-cup) servings.

CAJUN MEAT LOAF

A jambalaya of flavors greets guests who sample my zippy meat loaf. I received the recipe years ago from a friend who lived in Jamaica.
ANNA FREE, CLEVELAND, OHIO

40	bay leaves
1/2	cup salt
1/4	cup each pepper, white pepper, cayenne pepper, ground cumin and nutmeg
40	green onions, thinly sliced
15	medium onions, chopped
10	medium green peppers, chopped
40	garlic cloves, minced
4	cups butter
1	cup Worcestershire sauce
2/3	cup hot pepper sauce
6	cans (12 ounces each) evaporated milk
1	bottle (64 ounces) ketchup
8	packages (8 ounces each) dry bread crumbs (20 cups)
36	eggs, beaten
30	pounds lean ground beef (90% lean)
10	pounds ground pork

1. Combine the seasonings; set aside. In Dutch ovens, saute onions, green peppers and garlic in butter until tender. Add Worcestershire sauce, hot pepper sauce and reserved seasonings. Cook and stir for 8-10 minutes. Discard bay leaves. Remove from the heat; stir in milk and ketchup. Cool.

2. Add bread crumbs and eggs; mix well. In several large bowls, combine beef, pork and vegetable mixture; mix well. Pat into 11 greased 13-in. x 9-in. baking pans.

3. Bake at 350° for 65-75 minutes or until no pink remains and a thermometer reads 160°; drain.

Yield: 175-200 servings.

CHOCOLATE PUDDING SANDWICHES

These frozen cookie sandwiches are a favorite dessert and after-school snack for my kids...and even my diabetic husband enjoys one now and then.
JAN THOMAS, RICHMOND, VIRGINIA

1-1/2	cups cold fat-free milk
1	package (1.4 ounces) sugar-free instant chocolate pudding mix
1	carton (8 ounces) frozen reduced-fat whipped topping, thawed
1	cup miniature marshmallows
2	packages (9 ounces each) chocolate wafers

1. In a large bowl, whisk the milk and pudding mix for 2 minutes; let stand for 2 minutes or until slightly thickened. Fold in the whipped topping, then marshmallows.

2. For each sandwich, spread about 2 tablespoons of pudding mixture on the bottom of a chocolate wafer; top with another wafer. Stack sandwiches in an airtight container.

3. Freeze until firm, about 3 hours. Remove from the freezer 5 minutes before serving.

Yield: 43 sandwiches.

CREAMY BUFFALO CHICKEN DIP

This slightly spicy dip cleverly captures the flavor of buffalo chicken wings. Using canned chicken adds to the convenience.
ALLYSON DILASCIO, SALTSBURG, PENNSYLVANIA

1	package (8 ounces) cream cheese, softened
1	cup Louisiana-style hot sauce
1	cup ranch salad dressing
3	cans (4-1/2 ounces each) chunk white chicken, drained and shredded
1	cup (4 ounces) shredded cheddar cheese

Thinly sliced green onions, optional
Corn or tortilla chips

1. In a small bowl, combine the cream cheese, hot pepper sauce and salad dressing. Stir in chicken.

2. Spread into an ungreased 11-in. x 7-in. baking dish. Sprinkle with cheddar cheese. Bake, uncovered, at 350° for 20-22 minutes or until heated through. Sprinkle with green onions if desired. Serve with chips.

Yield: 5 cups.

SWEET PEA SALAD

This lovely salad is perfect for a spring luncheon. Serve it with a fruit salad and fresh roll and your lunch menu is complete!

BETTY OTTEN, TEA, SOUTH DAKOTA

5	pounds uncooked bow tie pasta
1	pound carrots, shredded
1	package (16 ounces) frozen peas, thawed
10	celery ribs, diced
1	small onion, finely chopped
5	cups mayonnaise
4	cups sweetened condensed milk
2-1/2	cups sugar
3/4	cup cider vinegar
3/4	cup buttermilk
2	teaspoons salt
1	teaspoon pepper

1. Cook pasta according to package the directions; drain. In three large bowls, combine the pasta, carrots, peas, celery and onion.

2. In another large bowl, combine the remaining ingredients. Stir a third of the dressing into each bowl of the pasta mixture. Cover and refrigerate until chilled.

Yield: 58 servings.

REUBEN ROLLS

I wanted the flavor of a classic Reuben in a fun-to-eat appetizer. The empty plate at my party signaled these rolls were a hit!

DARLENE ABNEY, MUENSTER, TEXAS

1	package (8 ounces) cream cheese, softened
3	tablespoons spicy brown mustard
1/4	teaspoon prepared horseradish
5	flour tortillas (10 inches), room temperature
7	packages (2 ounces each) thinly sliced deli corned beef
15	thin slices Swiss cheese
1	can (14 ounces) sauerkraut, rinsed and well drained

1. In a small bowl, beat the cream cheese, mustard and horseradish until blended. Spread a heaping tablespoonful of cream cheese mixture over each tortilla.

2. Layer each tortilla with eight slices of corned beef, three slices of cheese, another heaping tablespoonful of cream cheese mixture and 1/2 cup sauerkraut. Roll up tightly. Chill for 1 hour. Cut each roll-up into 1/2-in. slices.

Yield: about 8 dozen.

4. Drop by tablespoonfuls 2 in. apart onto greased baking sheets. Bake at 350° for 12-14 minutes or until set. Remove to wire racks to cool completely.

5. In a large bowl, beat the butter, confectioners' sugar and salt until blended. Add enough milk to achieve desired consistency. Crumble eight cookies and set aside.

6. Frost remaining cookies; sprinkle with cookie crumbs. Store in an airtight container or freeze for up to 1 month.

Yield: 7-1/2 dozen.

RED VELVET COOKIES

My mother made these unique cookies when I was little, and now I often bake a batch for my own family.
MINDY YOUNG, HANOVER, PENNSYLVANIA

1	cup shortening
1	cup sugar
3/4	cup packed brown sugar
3	eggs, separated
2	teaspoons red food coloring
4	cups all-purpose flour
3	tablespoons baking cocoa
3	teaspoons baking powder
1	teaspoon salt
1	cup buttermilk
2	cups (12 ounces) semisweet chocolate chips

FROSTING:

1-1/2	cups butter, softened
3-3/4	cups confectioners' sugar
1/8	teaspoon salt
3	to 4 tablespoons 2% milk

1. In a large bowl, cream the shortening and sugars until light and fluffy. Beat in the egg yolks and the food coloring.

2. Combine the flour, cocoa, baking powder and salt. Add to the creamed mixture alternately with buttermilk, beating well after each addition.

3. In another bowl with clean beaters, beat egg whites until stiff peaks form; fold into batter. Fold in chocolate chips.

WILD RICE BREAD

Wild rice gives this tender bread a tasty nutty flavor. This recipe makes five loaves, which are great for sharing. We enjoy slices warmed for dinner and toasted for breakfast.
SUSAN SCHOCK, HIBBING, MINNESOTA

2	packages (1/4 ounce each) active dry yeast
4-1/2	cups warm water (110° to 115°), divided
8	tablespoons sugar, divided
1/2	cup each molasses and canola oil
2	tablespoons salt
1-1/2	cups cooked wild rice
14	to 15 cups all-purpose flour

1. In a bowl, dissolve yeast in 1 cup warm water. Add 1 tablespoon sugar; let stand for 5 minutes. Add the molasses, oil, salt and remaining water and sugar; mix well. Add wild rice. Stir in enough flour to form a soft dough. Turn onto a floured surface; knead until smooth and elastic, about 6-8 minutes. Place in a greased bowl, turning once to grease top. Cover and let rise in a warm place until doubled, about 1-1/2 hours.

2. Punch dough down. Cover and let rise until doubled, about 1 hour. Punch dough down. Turn onto a lightly floured surface; divide into five portions. Shape each into a loaf. Place in five greased 9-in. x 5-in. loaf pans. Cover and let rise until doubled, about 1 hour.

3. Bake at 375° for 25-35 minutes or golden brown. Remove from pans to wire racks to cool.

Yield: 5 loaves.

CHEESY MUSHROOM MORSELS

There's plenty of happy munching all around the table when I dish up these luscious morsels. Ideal for a large crowd, they taste like quiche without the crust or the fuss.
MARIAN PLATT, SEQUIM, WASHINGTON

1	pound fresh mushrooms, sliced
1	large onion, chopped
1/2	cup butter
1	large green pepper, chopped
2	garlic cloves, minced
10	eggs, lightly beaten
4	cups (16 ounces) shredded Monterey Jack cheese
2	cups (16 ounces) small-curd cottage cheese
1/2	cup all-purpose flour
1	teaspoon baking powder
3/4	teaspoon each salt, dried basil and ground nutmeg

1. In a large skillet, saute mushrooms and onion in butter until tender. Add green pepper and garlic; saute 1 minute longer. Remove from the heat; drain.

2. In a large bowl, combine the eggs, cheeses, flour, baking powder, salt, basil and nutmeg. Add the mushroom mixture. Pour into a greased 15-in. x 10-in. x 1-in. baking pan.

3. Bake, uncovered, at 350° for 30-35 minutes or until edges are golden and a knife inserted near the center comes out clean. Let stand for 15 minutes. Cut into squares.
Yield: about 12 dozen.

ENCHILADA MEATBALLS

Before I retired, these tasty little treats were popular during snack time at work. They are a delicious and creative way to use up leftover corn bread.
MEARL HARRIS, WEST PLAINS, MISSOURI

2	cups crumbled corn bread
1	can (10 ounces) enchilada sauce, divided
1/2	teaspoon salt
1-1/2	pounds ground beef
1	can (8 ounces) tomato sauce
1/2	cup shredded Mexican cheese blend

1. In a large bowl, combine the corn bread, 1/2 cup enchilada sauce and salt. Crumble beef over mixture; mix well. Shape into 1-in. balls.

2. Place meatballs on a greased rack in a shallow baking pan. Bake, uncovered, at 350° for 18-22 minutes or until meat is no longer pink; drain.

3. Meanwhile, in a small saucepan, heat tomato sauce and remaining enchilada sauce. Drain meatballs; place in a serving dish. Top with sauce and sprinkle with cheese. Serve with toothpicks.
Yield: about 4-1/2 dozen.

CRAN-ORANGE RELISH

With its festive color and refreshing citrus-cranberry flavor, this lovely relish works well at large holiday gatherings. It's also convenient because you can make it in advance.

CLARA HONEYAGER, NORTH PRAIRIE, WISCONSIN

8	packages (12 ounces each) fresh cranberries
6	large unpeeled navel oranges, cut into wedges
4	cups sugar

1. In a food processor, process the cranberries and oranges in batches until finely chopped. Place in a large container; stir in sugar. Cover and refrigerate until serving.

Yield: 4-1/2 quarts.

BIG-BATCH MARINARA SAUCE

(pictured at right)

I typically freeze part of this marinara sauce to have on hand for guests or when I am craving a comforting pasta dish. It adds a fresh, herby layer of flavor.

CYNDY GERKEN, NAPLES, FLORIDA

4	large onions, chopped
2	tablespoons olive oil
10	garlic cloves, minced
4	cans (28 ounces each) crushed tomatoes
7	cans (15 ounces each) tomato sauce
2	cans (6 ounces each) tomato paste
1	cup grated Parmesan cheese
1	cup minced fresh parsley
3/4	cup minced fresh basil or 1/4 cup dried basil
2	tablespoons minced fresh oregano or 2 teaspoons dried oregano
2	tablespoons herbes de Provence or Italian seasoning
	Hot cooked spaghetti

1. In a stockpot, saute onions in oil until tender. Add garlic; cook 2 minutes longer. Add the crushed tomatoes, tomato sauce, tomato paste, cheese and herbs. Bring to a boil. Reduce heat; simmer, uncovered, for 2-3 hours or until desired consistency, stirring occasionally.

2. Serve desired amount over spaghetti. Cool remaining sauce; transfer to freezer containers. Freeze for up to 3 months.

To use frozen sauce: Thaw in the refrigerator overnight. Place in a saucepan and heat through.

Yield: 6 quarts.

Editor's Note: Look for herbes de Provence in the spice aisle.

Pasta Pointers

To cook pasta more evenly, prevent it from sticking together and avoid boil-overs, always cook it in a large kettle or Dutch oven. Don't cook more than 2 pounds of pasta at a time.

MOM'S MEATBALLS

This recipe bakes a large batch of moist meatballs that are both tender and flavorful. Serve some for dinner and freeze the extras for other meals throughout the month when you are too busy to cook.

DOROTHY SMITH, EL DORADO, ARKANSAS

1-1/2	cups chopped onion
1/3	cup ketchup
3	tablespoons lemon juice
1	tablespoon Worcestershire sauce
3/4	cup crushed saltines (about 24 crackers)
3	pounds ground beef

1. In a large bowl, combine the onion, ketchup, lemon juice, Worcestershire sauce and crackers. Crumble beef over mixture and mix well. Shape into 1-in. balls.

2. Place meatballs on a greased rack in a shallow baking pan. Bake, uncovered, at 400° for 10 minutes or until meat is no longer pink; drain. Serve meatballs immediately, or refrigerate or freeze for use in other recipes.

Yield: 7 dozen.

MARSHMALLOW FUDGE

It's nearly impossible to resist this rich chocolate delight. Chock-full of marshmallows and graham crackers, no one will believe that this tantalizing treat is low in fat.
HOLLY MANN, TEMPLE, NEW HAMPSHIRE

- 1-1/3   cups semisweet chocolate chips
- 2/3   cup fat-free sweetened condensed milk
- 1   teaspoon vanilla extract
- 1-1/3   cups miniature marshmallows
- 2   whole reduced-fat graham crackers, broken into bite-size pieces

1. Line an 8-in. square pan with foil and coat with cooking spray; set aside. In a small heavy saucepan over low heat, melt chocolate chips with milk; stir until smooth. Remove from the heat; cool for 2 minutes. Stir in vanilla. Fold in marshmallows and graham crackers.

2. Pour into prepared pan. Refrigerate for 1 hour or until firm. Using foil, lift fudge out of pan. Discard foil; cut into 48 pieces.

Yield: 4 dozen.

CHEESY CHILI DIP

I would often make this delicious dip as an after-school snack for my children. They're grown now but still enjoy this easy-to-make treat.
VERDI WILSON, VISALIA, CALIFORNIA

- 1   package (8 ounces) cream cheese, softened
- 1   can (15 ounces) chili without beans
- 1/4   cup finely chopped green onions
- 4   to 8 garlic cloves, minced
- 1   can (4 ounces) chopped green chilies
- 1   can (16 ounces) refried beans
- 1   cup (4 ounces) shredded Mexican cheese blend
   Breadsticks

1. In a small bowl, beat cream cheese until smooth. Spread into a greased microwave-safe 1-1/2-qt. dish. Layer with chili, onions, garlic, green chilies and refried beans. Sprinkle with cheese.

2. Microwave, uncovered, on high for 6-8 minutes until cheese is melted and edges are bubbly. Serve warm with breadsticks.

Yield: 5 cups.

Editor's Note: This recipe was tested in a 1,100-watt microwave.

POTATOES FOR A CROWD

When I need a side dish sure to please a large group, I always turn to this hearty, cheesy casserole. It's so simple to assemble, and everyone likes the flavor.
MERRILL POWERS, SPEARVILLE, KANSAS

5	cans (12 ounces each) evaporated milk
7-1/2	cups milk
5	cans (10-3/4 ounces each) condensed cream of chicken soup, undiluted
5	cans (10-3/4 ounces each) condensed cheddar cheese soup, undiluted
1	pound butter, melted
1	package (12 ounces) cornflakes, crushed
3	medium onions, finely chopped
10	packages (2 pounds each) frozen cubed hash brown potatoes, thawed

1. In several large bowls, combine all ingredients. Transfer to 10 greased 11-in. x 7-in. baking dishes. Bake, uncovered, at 350° for 45-55 minutes or until potatoes are tender.

Yield: 10 casseroles (about 10 servings each).

BERRY 'N' SMOKED TURKEY TWIRLS

Here's a new twist on a traditional appetizer that's just bursting with low-fat flavor. You won't even miss the extra fat! Make ahead for added convenience on hectic party days.
PATRICIA HARMON, BADEN, PENNSYLVANIA

1	package (8 ounces) reduced-fat cream cheese
1	cup shredded reduced-fat Mexican cheese blend
1/4	pound thinly sliced deli smoked turkey, finely chopped
2	tablespoons chopped dried cranberries
2	tablespoons chopped pimiento-stuffed olives
2	tablespoons salsa
3/4	teaspoon chili powder
4	flour tortillas (10 inches), room temperature

1. In a small bowl, beat cream cheese until smooth. Stir in the cheese blend, turkey, cranberries, olives, salsa and chili powder. Spread 1/2 cup mixture over each tortilla; roll up tightly. Wrap in plastic wrap and refrigerate for 2 hours or until firm.

2. Unwrap and cut into scant 1-in. slices. Serve chilled or place 1 in. apart on a baking sheet coated with cooking spray. Bake at 400° for 5-7 minutes or until heated through.

Yield: 40 appetizers.

2. Combine sugar and cinnamon; sprinkle over filling. Bake, uncovered, at 350° for 30-35 minutes or until golden brown and set. Remove to wire racks. Serve warm. Refrigerate leftovers.

Yield: 10 coffee cakes (8 servings each).

Editor's Note: If using frozen rhubarb, measure rhubarb while still frozen, then thaw completely. Drain in a colander, but do not press liquid out.

COCONUT ROCKY ROAD TREATS

My sister gave me the recipe for these chocolaty morsels. She has baked them for many Christmas celebrations.
DAWN SUPINA, EDMONTON, ALBERTA

1	cup butterscotch chips
1	cup semisweet chocolate chips
1	package (8 ounces) cream cheese, cubed
2	cups miniature marshmallows
1/2	cup chopped walnuts
2	cups flaked coconut

1. Line a baking sheet with waxed paper; set aside. In a saucepan, combine the butterscotch chips, chocolate chips and cream cheese. Cook and stir over low heat until smooth. Remove from the heat; stir in marshmallows and nuts. Cool slightly.

2. Shape into 1-in. balls and roll in coconut. Place on prepared baking sheet. Refrigerate for 1 hour or until firm. Store in an airtight container in the refrigerator.

Yield: about 4-1/2 dozen.

RHUBARB BISCUIT COFFEE CAKES

Enjoy the mouthwatering aroma of rhubarb and cinnamon from these luscious coffeecakes. Preparation is a snap.
CARLA HODENFIELD, RAY, NORTH DAKOTA

10	tubes (12 ounces each) refrigerated buttermilk biscuits
20	cups sliced fresh or frozen rhubarb (about 6 pounds)
2-1/2	cups sugar
5	teaspoons cornstarch
10	eggs, lightly beaten
5	cartons (16 ounces each) sour cream
1	pint heavy whipping cream
2-1/2	teaspoons vanilla extract

TOPPING:

3	tablespoons sugar
1-3/4	teaspoons ground cinnamon

1. Divide the biscuits among 10 ungreased 9-in. pie plates; top each with 2 cups rhubarb. In a large bowl, combine the sugar, cornstarch, eggs, sour cream, cream and vanilla. Beat on high for 2 minutes; pour over rhubarb.

3. Position a wonton wrapper with one point toward you. (Keep remaining wrappers covered with a damp paper towel until ready to use.) Place 2 heaping teaspoons of filling in the center of wrapper. Fold bottom corner over filling; fold sides toward center over filling. Roll toward the remaining point. Moisten top corner with water; press to seal. Repeat with remaining wrappers and filling.

4. In an electric skillet or deep-fat fryer, heat oil to 375°. Fry spring rolls, a few at a time, for 1-2 minutes on each side or until golden brown. Drain on paper towels. Serve warm with sweet-and-sour sauce.

Yield: about 5 dozen.

PORK 'N' SHRIMP SPRING ROLLS

Give your appetizer table an Asian accent with these crisp spring rolls. The recipe makes a big batch, so guests can enjoy seconds!
DEBBIE TERENZINI-WILKERSON, LUSBY, MARYLAND

1	pound ground pork
1	can (14 ounces) bean sprouts, drained
1	can (8 ounces) bamboo shoots, drained and chopped
1/2	pound cooked medium shrimp, peeled, deveined and finely chopped
1	can (4 ounces) mushroom stems and pieces, drained and chopped
4	green onions, chopped
1	tablespoon cornstarch
3	tablespoons soy sauce
1	tablespoon water
1	teaspoon garlic powder
1	teaspoon canola oil
2	packages (12 ounces each) wonton wrappers

Oil for frying
Sweet-and-sour sauce

1. In a large skillet, cook pork over medium heat until no longer pink; drain. Stir in the bean sprouts, bamboo shoots, shrimp, mushrooms and onions.

2. In a small bowl, whisk the cornstarch, soy sauce, water, garlic powder and oil until smooth; stir into skillet. Bring to a boil; cook and stir for 1 minute or until thickened. Remove from the heat.

MEXICAN ROLL-UPS

These tasty appetizers are perfect for parties and other fun gatherings. Kids love to eat them since the rolls are so little!
LEIGH THOMAS, HAHIRA, GEORGIA

1	package (8 ounces) cream cheese, softened
1	cup (8 ounces) sour cream
1	cup (4 ounces) shredded cheddar cheese
1	can (4 ounces) chopped green chilies, drained
4	green onions, chopped
1	can (4-1/4 ounces) chopped ripe olives, drained
1	teaspoon garlic powder
5	flour tortillas (10 inches), room temperature

Salsa, optional

1. In a small bowl, combine the first seven ingredients. Spread over tortillas. Roll up tightly and wrap in plastic wrap. Refrigerate for 1 hour or until firm.

2. Unwrap and cut into scant 1-in. slices. Serve with salsa if desired.

Yield: about 4 dozen.

CHERRY OATMEAL COOKIES

I like to make these old-fashioned treats with raspberry chips, but cherry-flavored work well in a pinch to add color and sweetness. These cookies stack nicely for packing.
BETTY HUDDLESTON, LIBERTY, INDIANA

1	cup butter, softened
1	cup packed brown sugar
1/2	cup sugar
2	eggs
1	teaspoon vanilla extract
3	cups old-fashioned oats
1-1/2	cups all-purpose flour
1	teaspoon baking soda
1	teaspoon ground cinnamon
1/2	teaspoon salt
1	package (10 ounces) cherry chips
1/2	cup chopped walnuts

1. In a large bowl, cream butter and sugars until light and fluffy. Beat in eggs and vanilla. Combine the oats, flour, baking soda, cinnamon and salt; gradually add to creamed mixture and mix well. Stir in chips and walnuts.

2. Drop by tablespoonfuls 3 in. apart onto ungreased baking sheets. Bake at 350° for 11-13 minutes or until lightly browned. Cool for 2 minutes before removing to wire racks.

Yield: about 4 dozen.

PIZZA ENGLISH MUFFINS

My mother fixed these fun mini pizzas for me from the time I started elementary school until I went to college. The meaty muffins please people of all ages and freeze well, too.
LEA DELUCA, ST. PAUL, MINNESOTA

1	pound ground beef
3/4	pound bulk pork sausage
1	small onion, chopped
1/2	cup tomato paste
1/2	teaspoon each garlic salt and dried oregano
1/4	teaspoon cayenne pepper
3	packages (12 ounces each) English muffins, split
1-1/2	cups (6 ounces) shredded part-skim mozzarella cheese
1	cup (4 ounces) shredded cheddar cheese
1	cup (4 ounces) shredded Swiss cheese

1. In a Dutch oven, cook the beef, sausage and onion over medium heat until meat is no longer pink; drain. Stir in the tomato paste, garlic salt, oregano and cayenne. Spread over the cut side of each English muffin. Place on baking sheets. Combine the cheeses; sprinkle over meat mixture.

2. Freeze for up to 3 months or bake at 350° for 15-20 minutes or until heated through.

Yield: 3 dozen.

Editor's Note: To use frozen Pizza English Muffins: Bake at 350° for 30 minutes.

GENERAL RECIPE INDEX

APPETIZERS & SNACKS
Cold Appetizers
Antipasto Salad, 236
Apricot-Ricotta Stuffed Celery, 13
Berry 'n' Smoked Turkey Twirls, 246
Cheddar-Veggie Appetizer Torte, 18
Chicken Salad Croissants, 160
Cucumber-Stuffed Cherry Tomatoes, 13
Cucumber Tea Sandwiches, 165
Guacamole Appetizer Squares, 24
Homemade Guacamole, 21
Jalapenos with Olive-Cream Filling, 19
Lemon Burst Tartlets, 178
Lime Cucumber Salsa, 8
Mexican Roll-Ups, 248
Nacho Party Cheesecake, 27
Peter Pumpkin Cheese Puffs, 220
Pineapple-Pecan Cheese Spread, 29
Pretty Stuffed Spring Peas, 22
Puff Pastry Holly Leaves, 209
Reuben Rolls, 239
Veggie Ham Crescent Wreath, 204
Veggie Tortilla Pinwheels, 14
Walnut-Cream Cheese Finger Sandwiches, 146

Dips & Spreads
Cheesy Chili Dip, 245
Chili Cheese Dip, 60
Cranberry Jalapeno Cheese Spread, 17
Creamy Artichoke Dip, 62
Creamy Buffalo Chicken Dip, 238
Fresh Summer Salsa, 26
Fruit Salsa, 24
Fruit Salsa with Cinnamon Chips, 29
Green Olive Dip, 56
Homemade Guacamole, 21
Hot Wing Dip, 10
Nacho Rice Dip, 22
Pepperoni Pizza Dip, 70
Pineapple-Pecan Cheese Spread, 29
Pumpkin Pie Dip, 188
Slow Cooker Mexican Dip, 64
Spinach Artichoke Dip, 68
Warm Savory Cheese Spread, 226

Hot Appetizers
Asparagus Cheese Triangles, 235
Berry 'n' Smoked Turkey Twirls, 246
BLT Bruschetta, 15
Blue Cheese Date Wraps, 232
Buffet Meatballs, 9
Cheddar-Veggie Appetizer Torte, 18
Cheesy Mushroom Morsels, 241
Chicken Artichoke Pizzas, 28
Chicken Little Sliders, 156
Cheesy Chili Dip, 245
Crab Salad Tarts, 23
Crab-Stuffed Mushrooms, 15
Creamy Artichoke Dip, 62
Creamy Buffalo Chicken Dip, 238
Crispy Chicken Wontons, 10
Enchilada Meatballs, 241
Glazed Kielbasa, 123
Green Olive Dip, 56
Guacamole Appetizer Squares, 24
Hot Wing Dip, 10
Mandarin Chicken Bites, 23
Mediterranean Tomato Bites, 21
Mini Burgers with the Works, 159
Mini Chicken Empanadas, 19
Mini-Burger Potato Bites, 28
Mini Phyllo Tacos, 14

Mom's Meatballs, 244
Party Meatballs, 230
Pepperoni Pizza Dip, 70
Pierogi Pasta Shells, 134
Pizza English Muffins, 249
Pork 'n' Shrimp Spring Rolls, 248
Savory Mushroom Tartlets, 8
Simmered Smoked Links, 71
Slow Cooker Mexican Dip, 64
Smoky Potato Rounds, 17
Spicy Maple Chicken Wings, 12
Spinach Artichoke Dip, 68
Spinach Artichoke-Stuffed Mushrooms, 236
Stuffed Baby Red Potatoes, 26
Sweet 'n' Sour Appetizer Meatballs, 20
Sweet & Sour Chicken Wings, 18
Sweet-and-Sour Chicken Wings, 64
Three-Meat Stromboli, 232
Warm Savory Cheese Spread, 226

Snacks
Corny Chocolate Crunch, 27
Crispy Snack Mix, 55
Nutty Caramel Corn, 9

APPLES
Apple Dumplings, 215
Apple Pork Roast, 143
Blue Cheese Waldorf Salad, 112
Picnic Sweet Potato Salad, 114
Rustic Autumn Soup, 166
Turkey, Gouda & Apple Tea Sandwiches, 155

ARTICHOKES
Artichoke Chicken Lasagna, 46
Artichoke Spinach Lasagna, 214
Chicken Artichoke Pizzas, 28
Creamy Artichoke Dip, 62
Spinach Artichoke Dip, 68
Spinach Artichoke-Stuffed Mushrooms, 236

BACON
Bacon-Cheese Pinwheel Rolls, 228
Bacon Cheeseburger Buns, 153
Bacon Spinach Strata, 91
Biscuit Egg Bake, 87
Brunch Pizza, 94
Lazy Pierogi Bake, 42
Picnic Sweet Potato Salad, 114
Stuffed Baby Red Potatoes, 26

BARS & BROWNIES
Bars
Butterscotch Peanut Bars, 171
Chocolate Chip Cream Cheese Bars, 184
Chocolate Chip Raspberry Bars, 177
Chocolate Macaroon Bars, 192
Frosted Pumpkin Bars, 205
Granola-To-Go Bars, 83
Lemon Pudding Dessert, 182
Ribbon Crispies, 179

Brownies
Blond Butterscotch Brownies, 191
Coconut-Almond Fudge Cups, 230
Coconut-Pecan Brownies, 195

BEANS
Brisket 'n' Bean Burritos, 128
Cherry Baked Beans, 119
Chicken Bean Soup, 161
Chicken Potpies, 123
Chili Cheese Dip, 60
Five-Bean Salad, 113

Hearty Baked Beans, 103
Hearty Chili Mac, 152
Hearty Minestrone, 160
Hearty Split Pea Soup, 148
Hearty Taco Chili, 66
Lasagna Corn Carne, 32
Roasted Vegetable Chili, 146
Roundup-Day Beans, 228
Slow-Cooked Vegetable Soup, 70
Southwest Bean Soup, 158
Spicy Black Bean Soup, 167
Taco Bean Soup, 150
Taco Casseroles, 41
Thick & Chunky Beef Chili, 164
Yellow Rice & Black Bean Salad, 108

BEEF (also see Ground Beef)
Main Dishes
Baked Barbecued Brisket, 143
Beef Barbecue, 156
Chipotle-Rubbed Beef Tenderloin, 204
Mushroom Pot Roast, 140
Pot Roast with Gravy, 142

Sandwiches
BBQ Beef Sandwiches, 65
Beef Barbecue, 156
Brisket 'n' Bean Burritos, 128
Chicago-Style Beef Sandwiches, 52
Deli Beef Heros, 157
Green Chili Beef Burritos, 61
New Orleans-Style Subs, 167
Shredded Steak Sandwiches, 71
Texas Beef Barbecue, 63

Soups, Stews & Chilis
Thick & Chunky Beef Chili, 164

BEVERAGES
Apricot-Apple Cider, 52
Fresh Peach Lemonade, 185
Hot Cranberry Punch, 51
Warm Pomegranate Punch, 60

BLUEBERRIES
Angel Food Cake with Berry Sauce, 200
Fruity Baked Oatmeal, 79
Streusel-Topped Blueberry Muffins, 84
Vanilla-Lime Fruit Salad, 103

BREADS & COFFEE CAKES
Bacon-Cheese Pinwheel Rolls, 228
Bacon Cheeseburger Buns, 153
Biscuit Egg Bake, 87
Cherry Coffee Cake, 80
Cinnamon Swirl Bread, 83
Lemon Crumb Muffins, 78
Lemon Raspberry Jumbo Muffins, 85
Meat 'n' Cheese Stromboli, 166
Orange-Cheesecake Breakfast Rolls, 77
Peaches 'n' Cream Muffins, 78
Pecan-Raisin Cinnamon Rolls, 87
Pull-Apart Sticky Bun Ring, 77
Rhubarb Biscuit Coffee Cakes, 247
Squash Corn Bread, 222
Streusel-Topped Blueberry Muffins, 84
Veggie Ham Crescent Wreath, 204
Wild Rice Bread, 240

BROCCOLI & CAULIFLOWER
Beef & Tater Bake, 32
Broccoli-Cauliflower Cheese Bake, 100
Broccoli Cheddar Brunch Bake, 91
Broccoli Chicken Supreme, 47
Broccoli Supreme, 105

Cauliflower Au Gratin, 116
Chicken Potpie with Cheddar Biscuit Topping, 46
Festive Broccoli-Cauliflower Salad, 209
Layered Salad with Curry Dressing, 118
Veggie Ham Crescent Wreath, 204
Veggie Potluck Salad, 104
Very Veggie Lasagna, 43

CABBAGE & SAUERKRAUT
Celery Root and Pear Slaw, 112
Layered Tortellini-Spinach Salad, 113
Lazy Pierogi Bake, 42
Pork and Cabbage Dinner, 132
Slow-Cooked Reuben Brats, 69

CAKES, CUPCAKES & TORTES
Ambrosia Cupcakes, 183
Angel Food Cake with Berry Sauce, 200
Berry Surprise Cupcakes, 181
Black Forest Cake, 188
Cherry Chocolate Coconut Cupcakes, 189
Cherry Coffee Cake, 80
Cream Cheese Pound Cake, 193
Gingerbread Cupcakes, 210
Lemon Ricotta Cake, 208
Lemon Tea Cakes, 171
Magnificent Carrot Cake, 219
Makeover Strawberry Cake, 176
Mini Spider Bites, 218
Mint Chocolate Torte, 170
Pineapple Orange Cake, 191
Santa Cupcakes, 223
Surprise Cupcakes, 175
Tastes Like Eggnog Cake, 199
Toffee Mocha Cupcakes, 186
Truffle Chocolate Cupcakes, 172

CANDIES
Butterscotch Peanut Butter Fudge, 227
Caramel Marshmallow Treats, 181
Caramel Pretzel Sticks, 185
Coconut Almond Candies, 174
Coconut Rocky Road Treats, 247
Cookie Dough Truffles, 233
Crunchy Candy Clusters, 51
Marshmallow Fudge, 245
Peanut Butter Easter Eggs, 201
Pecan Candy Clusters, 212
S'more Drops, 176

CASSEROLES (also see Meat Pies; Lasagna; Slow Cooker Recipes)
Artichoke Chicken Lasagna, 46
Au Gratin Party Potatoes, 227
Beef & Tater Bake, 32
Broccoli Chicken Supreme, 47
Broccoli Supreme, 105
Cheesy Carrot Casserole, 98
Chicken & Sausage Manicotti, 41
Chicken Potpie with Cheddar Biscuit Topping, 46
Chicken Tater Bake, 37
Creamy Chicken Casserole, 39
Creamy Chicken-Rice Casserole, 43
Double-Cheese Macaroni, 36
Fruity Baked Oatmeal, 79
Ham & Cheese Potato Casserole, 37
Ham and Swiss Casserole, 220
Hearty Baked Beans, 103
Hot Chicken Salad, 38
Lasagna Corn Carne, 32
Lazy Pierogi Bake, 42
Pepperoni Pizza Casserole, 42
Pesto Chicken Mostaccioli, 44
Potatoes for a Crowd, 246
Sausage Fettuccine Bake, 33
Scalloped Potatoes with Ham & Cheese, 34

Southwest Turkey Casserole, 34
Southwestern Shepherd's Pie, 38
Spaghetti Ham Bake, 44
Swiss-Onion Potato Bake, 109
Taco Casseroles, 41
Very Veggie Lasagna, 43
Zucchini Enchiladas, 136

CHEESE & CREAM CHEESE
Appetizers & Snacks
Apricot-Ricotta Stuffed Celery, 13
Asparagus Cheese Triangles, 235
Bacon-Cheese Pinwheel Rolls, 228
Blue Cheese Date Wraps, 232
Cheddar-Veggie Appetizer Torte, 18
Cheese Enchiladas, 138
Cheesy Chili Dip, 245
Cheesy Mushroom Morsels, 241
Cranberry Jalapeno Cheese Spread, 17
Creamy Artichoke Dip, 62
Green Olive Dip, 56
Hot Wing Dip, 10
Jalapenos with Olive-Cream Filling, 19
Mini Chicken Empanadas, 19
Moist Meat Loaves, 127
Nacho Party Cheesecake, 27
Nacho Rice Dip, 22
Pepperoni Pizza Dip, 70
Pesto Chicken Mostaccioli, 44
Peter Pumpkin Cheese Puffs, 220
Pierogi Pasta Shells, 134
Pineapple-Pecan Cheese Spread, 29
Pretty Stuffed Spring Peas, 22
Puff Pastry Holly Leaves, 209
Pumpkin Pie Dip, 188
Slow Cooker Mexican Dip, 64
Veggie Tortilla Pinwheels, 14
Very Veggie Lasagna, 43
Warm Savory Cheese Spread, 226

Breakfast & Brunch
Bacon Spinach Strata, 91
Biscuit Egg Bake, 87
Broccoli Cheddar Brunch Bake, 91
Brunch Pizza, 94
Crepe Quiche Cups, 88
Deluxe Breakfast Bake, 90
Feta Breakfast Bake, 94
Ham 'n' Cheese Squares, 82
Hash Brown Egg Breakfast, 59
Omelet Casserole for 60, 80
Vegetarian Egg Strata, 89

Desserts
Cream Cheese Pound Cake, 193
Lemon Ricotta Cake, 208
Maple Pumpkin Cheesecake, 218
Pumpkin Tiramisu, 212

Main Dishes
Artichoke Spinach Lasagna, 214
Asparagus Cheese Triangles, 235
Cheese Enchiladas, 138
Chicken & Sausage Manicotti, 41
Chicken Artichoke Pizzas, 28
Chicken Potpie with Cheddar Biscuit Topping, 46
Chicken Tater Bake, 37
Creamy Macaroni and Cheese, 59
Double-Cheese Macaroni, 36
Ham & Cheese Potato Casserole, 37
Ham and Swiss Casserole, 220
Kid-Pleasing Taco Pizza, 132
Lasagna Corn Carne, 32
Makeover Cheese-Stuffed Shells, 122
Mom's Scalloped Potatoes and Ham, 73
Pepperoni Pizza Casserole, 42

Scalloped Potatoes with Ham & Cheese, 34
Southwest Turkey Casserole, 34
Southwestern Shepherd's Pie, 38
Spaghetti Ham Bake, 44
Taco Casseroles, 41
Turkey and Stuffing Pie, 214

Sandwiches
Bacon Cheeseburger Buns, 153
Cucumber Tea Sandwiches, 165
Meat 'n' Cheese Stromboli, 166
New Orleans-Style Subs, 167
Pizzawiches, 164
Slow-Cooked Turkey Sandwiches, 159
Turkey, Gouda & Apple Tea Sandwiches, 155
Walnut-Cream Cheese Finger
 Sandwiches, 146

CHICKEN
Appetizers & Snacks
Chicken Artichoke Pizzas, 28
Creamy Buffalo Chicken Dip, 238
Crispy Chicken Wontons, 10
Hot Wing Dip, 10
Mandarin Chicken Bites, 23
Mini Chicken Empanadas, 19
Nacho Party Cheesecake, 27
Spicy Maple Chicken Wings, 12
Sweet & Sour Chicken Wings, 18

Main Dishes
Artichoke Chicken Lasagna, 46
Broccoli Chicken Supreme, 47
Chicken & Sausage Manicotti, 41
Chicken Little Sliders, 156
Chicken Potpie, 137
Chicken Potpie with Cheddar Biscuit Topping, 46
Chicken Potpies, 123
Chicken Salad with a Twist, 111
Chicken Tater Bake, 37
Chicken Tetrazzini, 129
Colorful Chicken Stew, 57
Cornmeal-Coated Chicken, 127
Creamy Chicken Casserole, 39
Creamy Chicken-Rice Casserole, 43
Fried Chicken Nuggets, 140
Hot Chicken Salad, 38
Lime Chicken Tacos, 54
Pesto Chicken Mostaccioli, 44
Presto Chicken Tacos, 124
Slow-Cooked Chicken Noodle Soup, 165
Spicy Barbecued Chicken, 199
Sweet & Spicy Chicken Drummies, 131
Sweet-and-Sour Chicken Wings, 64
Tropical BBQ Chicken, 69

Salad
Hot Chicken Salad, 38

Sandwiches
Chicken Little Sliders, 156
Chicken Salad Croissants, 160

Soups & Stews
Cajun Chicken & Rice Soup, 147
Chicken Bean Soup, 161
Colorful Chicken Stew, 57
Slow-Cooked Chicken Noodle Soup, 165

CHOCOLATE
Bars & Brownies
Blond Butterscotch Brownies, 191
Chocolate Chip Cream Cheese Bars, 184
Chocolate Chip Raspberry Bars, 177
Chocolate Macaroon Bars, 192
Coconut-Pecan Brownies, 195

Cakes & Cupcakes
Cherry Chocolate Coconut Cupcakes, 189
Toffee Mocha Cupcakes, 186
Truffle Chocolate Cupcakes, 172

Cookies & Candy
Caramel Pretzel Sticks, 185
Cherry Oatmeal Cookies, 249
Chocolate Mint Wafers, 186
Coconut-Almond Fudge Cups, 230
Coconut Rocky Road Treats, 247
Coconut Almond Candies, 174
Cookie Dough Truffles, 233
Corny Chocolate Crunch, 27
Marshmallow Fudge, 245
No-Bake Cookie Balls, 235
Peanut Butter Easter Eggs, 201
Pecan Candy Clusters, 212
Red Velvet Cookies, 240
S'more Drops, 176

Desserts
Chocolate Ganache Tarts, 192
Mint Chocolate Torte, 170

COCONUT
Coconut Almond Candies, 174
Coconut-Almond Fudge Cups, 230
Coconut Rocky Road Treats, 247
Coconut-Pecan Brownies, 195

COOKIES (also see Bars & Brownies)
Candy Cookie Cups, 172
Cherry Oatmeal Cookies, 249
Chocolate Mint Wafers, 186
Chocolate Pudding Sandwiches, 237
Coconut Almond Candies, 174
Coconut-Almond Fudge Cups, 230
Crisp Lemon Cookies, 211
Lemon Shortbread Cookies, 177
No-Bake Cookie Balls, 235
Pecan Butterscotch Cookies, 193
Pilgrim Hat Cookies, 217
Potato Chip Cookies, 180
Red Velvet Cookies, 240
Toffee Malted Cookies, 229
White Chocolate Cranberry Cookies, 175

DESSERTS (also see specific kinds)
Apple Dumplings, 215
Butterscotch Bliss Layered Dessert, 179
Caramel Pear Pudding, 63
Chocolate Pudding Sandwiches, 237
Coconut-Almond Fudge Cups, 230
Corny Chocolate Crunch, 27
Crunchy Candy Clusters, 51
Heavenly Filled Strawberries, 195
Lemon Pudding Dessert, 182
Lemon Tea Cakes, 171
Makeover Peach Bowl Pizza, 184
Maple Pumpkin Cheesecake, 218
Marshmallow Fudge, 245
Pumpkin Pie Dip, 188
Pumpkin Tiramisu, 212

EGGS
Bacon Spinach Strata, 91
Biscuit Egg Bake, 87
Broccoli Cheddar Brunch Bake, 91
Brunch Pizza, 94
Cheddar-Veggie Appetizer Torte, 18
Crepe Quiche Cups, 88
Deluxe Breakfast Bake, 90
Feta Breakfast Bake, 94
Ham 'n' Cheese Squares, 82

Hash Brown Egg Breakfast, 59
Omelet Casserole for 60, 80
Vegetarian Egg Strata, 89
Veggie Potato Salad, 111

FISH & SEAFOOD
Bow Tie Seafood Salad, 229
Caribbean Crabmeat Salad, 109
Confetti Pasta, 198
Crab Salad Tarts, 23
Crab-Stuffed Mushrooms, 15
Fiesta Tuna Salad Sandwiches, 151
Pork 'n' Shrimp Spring Rolls, 248

FRUIT (also see specific kinds)
Anise Fruit Bowl, 89
Blue Cheese Date Wraps, 232
Blue Cheese Waldorf Salad, 112
Caramel Pear Pudding, 63
Celery Root and Pear Slaw, 112
Chicken Salad Croissants, 160
Crunchy Pomegranate Salad, 100
Fabulous Fruit Salad, 98
Mango Cranberry Sauce, 202
Orzo Cheesecake Fruit Salad, 118
Vanilla-Lime Fruit Salad, 103
Warm Pomegranate Punch, 60
Watermelon and Tomato Salad, 105

GROUND BEEF
Appetizers & Snacks
Chili Cheese Dip, 60
Green Olive Dip, 56
Mini-Burger Potato Bites, 28
Mini Phyllo Tacos, 14
Nacho Rice Dip, 22
Slow Cooker Mexican Dip, 64
Sweet 'n' Sour Appetizer Meatballs, 20

Main Dishes
Bacon Cheeseburger Buns, 153
Beef & Tater Bake, 32
Cajun Meat Loaf, 237
Hearty Chili Mac, 152
Hearty Spaghetti, 129
Hearty Taco Chili, 66
Lasagna Corn Carne, 32
Makeover Cheese-Stuffed Shells, 122
Moist Meat Loaves, 127
Mom's Meatballs, 244
Potato-Bar Chili, 138
Southwestern Shepherd's Pie, 38
Taco Casseroles, 41

Sandwiches
Grilled Burgers, 202
Mini Burgers with the Works, 159
Pizzawiches, 164
Slow Cooker Sloppy Joes, 61
Trick-or-Treat Turnovers, 205

Side Dishes
Cherry Baked Beans, 119
Hearty Baked Beans, 103

Soups
Taco Bean Soup, 150

HAM
Appetizers
Veggie Ham Crescent Wreath, 204

Breakfast & Brunch
Deluxe Breakfast Bake, 90
Feta Breakfast Bake, 94

Ham 'n' Cheese Squares, 82
Hash Brown Egg Breakfast, 59
Omelet Casserole for 60, 80

Main Dishes
Champagne Baked Ham, 207
Cranberry-Glazed Ham, 124
Ham & Cheese Potato Casserole, 37
Ham and Spinach Crepes, 93
Ham and Swiss Casserole, 220
Holiday Glazed Ham, 201
Marmalade Baked Ham, 141
Mini Barbecued Ham Sandwiches, 162
Mom's Scalloped Potatoes and Ham, 73
New Orleans-Style Subs, 167
Raspberry-Chipotle Glazed Ham, 136
Scalloped Potatoes with Ham & Cheese, 34
Spaghetti Ham Bake, 44
Sweet 'n' Moist Ham, 122

Sandwiches
Meat 'n' Cheese Stromboli, 166
Mini Barbecued Ham Sandwiches, 162
New Orleans-Style Subs, 167

Soups
Hearty Split Pea Soup, 148

LEMON & LIME
Crisp Lemon Cookies, 211
Fresh Peach Lemonade, 185
Lemon Burst Tartlets, 178
Lemon Crumb Muffins, 78
Lemon-Poppy Seed Doughnut Holes, 93
Lemon Raspberry Jumbo Muffins, 85
Lemon Ricotta Cake, 208
Lemon Shortbread Cookies, 177
Lemon Tea Cakes, 171
Lime Chicken Tacos, 54
Lime Cucumber Salsa, 8
Mango Cranberry Sauce, 202
Vanilla-Lime Fruit Salad, 103

MUSHROOMS
Brunch Pizza, 94
Cheesy Mushroom Morsels, 241
Chicken Potpies, 123
Crab-Stuffed Mushrooms, 15
Mushroom Pot Roast, 140
Savory Mushroom Tartlets, 8
Spinach Artichoke-Stuffed Mushrooms, 236
Vegetarian Egg Strata, 89

MEAT LOAVES & MEATBALLS
Buffet Meatballs, 9
Cajun Meat Loaf, 237
Moist Meat Loaves, 127
Mom's Meatballs, 244
Party Meatballs, 230

MEAT PIES
Chicken Potpie, 137
Chicken Potpie with Cheddar Biscuit Topping, 46
Chicken Potpies, 123
Gobbler Cobbler, 223
Turkey and Stuffing Pie, 214

PASTA & NOODLES
(also see Lasagna; Spaghetti)
Main Dishes
Artichoke Chicken Lasagna, 46
Artichoke Spinach Lasagna, 214

Big-Batch Marinara Sauce, 242
Chicken & Sausage Manicotti, 41
Chicken Tetrazzini, 129
Confetti Pasta, 198
Creamy Chicken Casserole, 39
Creamy Macaroni and Cheese, 59
Double-Cheese Macaroni, 36
Ham and Swiss Casserole, 220
Hearty Chili Mac, 152
Hearty Pasta Tomato Soup, 65
Lasagna Corn Carne, 32
Lazy Pierogi Bake, 42
Makeover Cheese-Stuffed Shells, 122
Pepperoni Pizza Casserole, 42
Pesto Chicken Mostaccioli, 44
Pesto Pasta Medley, 105
Pierogi Pasta Shells, 134
Sausage Fettuccine Bake, 33
Slow-Cooked Chicken Noodle Soup, 165
Spaghetti Ham Bake, 44
Very Veggie Lasagna, 43

Salads
Antipasto Salad, 236
Bow Tie Seafood Salad, 229
Caribbean Crabmeat Salad, 109
Chicken Salad with a Twist, 111
Italian Orzo Salad, 117
Layered Tortellini-Spinach Salad, 113
Macaroni Coleslaw, 119
Orzo Cheesecake Fruit Salad, 118
Pearl Pasta Salad, 117
Pesto Pasta Medley, 105

Side Dishes
Savory Mediterranean Orzo, 110

PEAS
Creamed Garden Potatoes and Peas, 99
Layered Salad with Curry Dressing, 118
Pretty Stuffed Spring Peas, 22
Sweet Pea Salad, 239
Veggie Potato Salad, 111

PINEAPPLE
Anise Fruit Bowl, 89
Caribbean Crabmeat Salad, 109
Gobbler Cobbler, 223
Hawaiian Kielbasa Sandwiches, 55
Magnificent Carrot Cake, 219
Mango Cranberry Sauce, 202
Orzo Cheesecake Fruit Salad, 118
Pineapple Orange Cake, 191
Pineapple-Pecan Cheese Spread, 29
Sweet & Sour Chicken Wings, 18

PORK (also see Bacon; Ham; Sausage)
Apple Pork Roast, 143
Baja Pork Tacos, 131
Barbecue Country Ribs, 56
Cajun Meat Loaf, 237
Country Ribs with Ginger Sauce, 140
Glazed Pork Chops, 133
Hearty Minestrone, 160
Holiday Pork Roast, 207
Italian Pulled Pork Sandwiches, 151
Pork and Cabbage Dinner, 132
Pork 'n' Shrimp Spring Rolls, 248
Pork Sandwiches with Root Beer Barbecue
    Sauce, 155
Saucy Pork Chops, 137
Spicy Black Bean Soup, 167
Sweet Barbecued Pork Chops, 126

POTATOES & SWEET POTATOES
Main Dishes
Beef & Tater Bake, 32
Chicken Potpie, 137
Chicken Potpies, 123
Chicken Tater Bake, 37
Deluxe Breakfast Bake, 90
Ham & Cheese Potato Casserole, 37
Hash Brown Egg Breakfast, 59
Mom's Scalloped Potatoes and Ham, 73
Pierogi Pasta Shells, 134
Potato-Bar Chili, 138
Scalloped Potatoes with Ham & Cheese, 34
Spicy Sausage Hash Browns, 50

Salads
Grilled Three-Potato Salad, 102
Picnic Sweet Potato Salad, 114
Veggie Potato Salad, 111

Side Dishes
Au Gratin Party Potatoes, 227
Creamed Garden Potatoes and Peas, 99
Family Gathering Potatoes, 233
Mini-Burger Potato Bites, 28
Potatoes for a Crowd, 246
Smoky Potato Rounds, 17
Stuffed Baby Red Potatoes, 26
Swiss-Onion Potato Bake, 109
Tangy Mashed Potatoes, 113

Soup
Colorful Chicken Stew, 57
Hearty Split Pea Soup, 148
Rustic Autumn Soup, 166
Smoked Sausage Soup, 147
Veggie Potato Soup, 57
Veggie-Sausage Cheese Soup, 50

PUMPKIN
Frosted Pumpkin Bars, 205
Maple Pumpkin Cheesecake, 218
Pumpkin Pie Dip, 188
Pumpkin Tiramisu, 212

RASPBERRIES
Angel Food Cake with Berry Sauce, 200
Chocolate Chip Raspberry Bars, 177
Lemon Burst Tartlets, 178
Lemon Raspberry Jumbo Muffins, 85
Raspberry-Chipotle Glazed Ham, 136

RICE, WILD RICE & BARLEY
Cajun Chicken & Rice Soup, 147
Creamy Chicken-Rice Casserole, 43
Grilled Burgers, 202
Nacho Rice Dip, 22
Slow Cooker Mexican Dip, 64
Wild Rice Bread, 240
Yellow Rice & Black Bean Salad, 108

SALADS
Bean Salads
Five-Bean Salad, 113
Southwest Corn Bread Salad, 107

Fruit & Gelatin Salads
Anise Fruit Bowl, 89
Blue Cheese Waldorf Salad, 112
Crunchy Pomegranate Salad, 100
Fabulous Fruit Salad, 98
Orzo Cheesecake Fruit Salad, 118
Strawberry & Glazed Walnut Salad, 114
Vanilla-Lime Fruit Salad, 103
Watermelon and Tomato Salad, 105

Green Salads
Layered Salad with Curry Dressing, 118
Layered Tortellini-Spinach Salad, 113
Pistachio Lettuce Salad, 107
Strawberry & Glazed Walnut Salad, 114

Main-Dish Salads
Antipasto Salad, 236
Bow Tie Seafood Salad, 229
Chicken Salad with a Twist, 111
Hot Chicken Salad, 38

Pasta & Rice Salads
Antipasto Salad, 236
Bow Tie Seafood Salad, 229
Caribbean Crabmeat Salad, 109
Chicken Salad with a Twist, 111
Italian Orzo Salad, 117
Layered Tortellini-Spinach Salad, 113
Macaroni Coleslaw, 119
Pearl Pasta Salad, 117
Pesto Pasta Medley, 105
Sweet Pea Salad, 239
Yellow Rice & Black Bean Salad, 108

Potato Salads
Grilled Three-Potato Salad, 102
Picnic Sweet Potato Salad, 114
Veggie Potato Salad, 111

Vegetable Salads
Balsamic Green Bean Salad, 99
Festive Broccoli-Cauliflower Salad, 209
Southwest Corn Bread Salad, 107
Summer-Fresh Quinoa Salad, 108
Sweet Pea Salad, 239
Veggie Potluck Salad, 104
Watermelon and Tomato Salad, 105
Yellow Rice & Black Bean Salad, 108

SANDWICHES
Cold Sandwiches
Chicken Salad Croissants, 160
Cucumber Tea Sandwiches, 165
Deli Beef Heros, 157
Fiesta Tuna Salad Sandwiches, 151
Grilled Vegetable Sandwiches, 148
Turkey, Gouda & Apple Tea Sandwiches, 155
Walnut-Cream Cheese Finger
    Sandwiches, 146

Hot Sandwiches
Bacon Cheeseburger Buns, 153
BBQ Beef Sandwiches, 65
Chicago-Style Beef Sandwiches, 52
Chicken Little Sliders, 156
Cranberry BBQ Turkey Sandwiches, 152
Eggplant Muffuletta, 161
Grilled Burgers, 202
Hawaiian Kielbasa Sandwiches, 55
Italian Pulled Pork Sandwiches, 151
Meat 'n' Cheese Stromboli, 166
Mini Barbecued Ham Sandwiches, 162
Mini Burgers with the Works, 159
New Orleans-Style Subs, 167
Pizzawiches, 164
Pork Sandwiches with Root Beer Barbecue
    Sauce, 155
Shredded Steak Sandwiches, 71
Slow Cooker Sloppy Joes, 61
Slow-Cooked Reuben Brats, 69
Slow-Cooked Turkey Sandwiches, 159
Texas Beef Barbecue, 63
Trick-or-Treat Turnovers, 205

SAUSAGE

Antipasto Salad, 236
Brunch Pizza, 94
Chicken & Sausage Manicotti, 41
Crepe Quiche Cups, 88
Glazed Kielbasa, 123
Hawaiian Kielbasa Sandwiches, 55
Hearty Pasta Tomato Soup, 65
Makeover Cheese-Stuffed Shells, 122
Meat 'n' Cheese Stromboli, 166
Pepperoni Pizza Casserole, 42
Pepperoni Pizza Dip, 70
Pizza English Muffins, 249
Sausage Fettuccine Bake, 33
Simmered Smoked Links, 71
Slow-Cooked Reuben Brats, 69
Slow Cooker Mexican Dip, 64
Smoked Sausage Soup, 147
Spicy Sausage Hash Browns, 50
Taco Bean Soup, 150
Veggie-Sausage Cheese Soup, 50

SEAFOOD (see Fish & Seafood)

SIDE DISHES
Noodles & Pasta
Creamy Macaroni and Cheese, 59
Pierogi Pasta Shells, 134
Savory Mediterranean Orzo, 110
Sweet Pea Salad, 239

Potatoes
Au Gratin Party Potatoes, 227
Creamed Garden Potatoes and Peas, 99
Family Gathering Potatoes, 233
Picnic Sweet Potato Salad, 114
Pierogi Pasta Shells, 134
Potatoes for a Crowd, 246
Scalloped Potatoes with Ham & Cheese, 34
Swiss-Onion Potato Bake, 109
Tangy Mashed Potatoes, 113

Rice, Beans & Grains
Cherry Baked Beans, 119
Hearty Baked Beans, 103
Roundup-Day Beans, 228
Summer-Fresh Quinoa Salad, 108

Vegetables
Broccoli-Cauliflower Cheese Bake, 100
Broccoli Supreme, 105
Cauliflower Au Gratin, 116
Cheesy Carrot Casserole, 98
Grilled Vegetable Medley, 104
Parsnip-Asparagus Au Gratin, 222
Roasted Fall Vegetables, 215

SLOW COOKER RECIPES
Appetizers & Snacks
Buffet Meatballs, 9
Chili Cheese Dip, 60
Creamy Artichoke Dip, 62
Crispy Snack Mix, 55
Crunchy Candy Clusters, 51
Green Olive Dip, 56
Hot Wing Dip, 10
Nacho Rice Dip, 22
Party Meatballs, 230
Pepperoni Pizza Dip, 70
Simmered Smoked Links, 71
Slow Cooker Mexican Dip, 64
Spinach Artichoke Dip, 68
Sweet-and-Sour Chicken Wings, 64

Beverages
Apricot-Apple Cider, 52
Hot Cranberry Punch, 51
Warm Pomegranate Punch, 60

Desserts
Caramel Pear Pudding, 63

Main Dishes
Baja Pork Tacos, 131
Barbecue Country Ribs, 56
Butter & Herb Turkey, 134
Creamy Macaroni and Cheese, 59
Glazed Kielbasa, 123
Hash Brown Egg Breakfast, 59
Moist & Tender Turkey Breast, 66
Mom's Scalloped Potatoes and Ham, 73
Pork and Cabbage Dinner, 132
Pot Roast with Gravy, 142
Saucy Pork Chops, 137
Slow-Cooked Herbed Turkey, 73
Texas Beef Barbecue, 63
Tropical BBQ Chicken, 69
Turkey with Cranberry Sauce, 211

Sandwiches
BBQ Beef Sandwiches, 65
Beef Barbecue, 156
Brisket 'n' Bean Burritos, 128
Chicago-Style Beef Sandwiches, 52
Green Chili Beef Burritos, 61
Hawaiian Kielbasa Sandwiches, 55
Italian Pulled Pork Sandwiches, 151
Lime Chicken Tacos, 54
Pork Sandwiches with Root Beer Barbecue
  Sauce, 156
Shredded Steak Sandwiches, 71
Slow-Cooked Reuben Brats, 69
Slow-Cooked Turkey Sandwiches, 159
Slow Cooker Sloppy Joes, 61

Side Dishes
Spicy Sausage Hash Browns, 50
Stuffing from the Slow Cooker, 68

Soups & Stews
Chicken Bean Soup, 161
Colorful Chicken Stew, 57
Hearty Pasta Tomato Soup, 65
Hearty Taco Chili, 66
Slow-Cooked Chicken Noodle Soup, 165
Slow-Cooked Vegetable Soup, 70
Veggie Potato Soup, 57
Veggie-Sausage Cheese Soup, 50

SPINACH
Artichoke Spinach Lasagna, 214
Bacon Spinach Strata, 91
Ham and Spinach Crepes, 93
Layered Tortellini-Spinach Salad, 113
Makeover Cheese-Stuffed Shells, 122
Savory Mediterranean Orzo, 110
Southwest Turkey Casserole, 34
Spinach Artichoke Dip, 68
Spinach Artichoke-Stuffed Mushrooms, 236
Turkey, Gouda & Apple Tea Sandwiches, 155

SQUASH & ZUCCHINI
Eggplant Muffuletta, 161
Grilled Vegetable Sandwiches, 148
Hearty Minestrone, 160
Roasted Fall Vegetables, 215
Roasted Vegetable Chili, 146
Savory Mediterranean Orzo, 110
Squash Corn Bread, 222

Vegetarian Egg Strata, 89
Very Veggie Lasagna, 43
Zucchini Enchiladas, 136

STRAWBERRIES
Angel Food Cake with Berry Sauce, 200
Heavenly Filled Strawberries, 195
Makeover Strawberry Cake, 176
Strawberry & Glazed Walnut Salad, 114
Surprise Cupcakes, 175

TOMATOES
Big-Batch Marinara Sauce, 242
Cucumber-Stuffed Cherry Tomatoes, 13
Hearty Pasta Tomato Soup, 65
Mediterranean Tomato Bites, 21
Tomato Garlic Soup, 162
Watermelon and Tomato Salad, 105

TURKEY
Berry 'n' Smoked Turkey Twirls, 246
Butter & Herb Turkey, 134
Cranberry BBQ Turkey Sandwiches, 152
Cranberry Turkey Crostini, 217
Gobbler Cobbler, 223
Herb 'n' Spice Turkey Breast, 142
Honey-Apple Turkey Breast, 128
Kid-Pleasing Taco Pizza, 132
Makeover Cheese-Stuffed Shells, 122
Moist & Tender Turkey Breast, 66
New Orleans-Style Subs, 167
Pepperoni Pizza Casserole, 42
Roast Turkey Breast with Rosemary
  Gravy, 141
Slow-Cooked Herbed Turkey, 73
Slow-Cooked Turkey Sandwiches, 159
Southwest Turkey Casserole, 34
Turkey and Stuffing Pie, 214
Turkey, Gouda & Apple Tea Sandwiches, 155
Turkey Sausage Patties, 88
Turkey with Cranberry Sauce, 211

VEGETABLES (also see specific kinds)
Antipasto Salad, 236
Asparagus Cheese Triangles, 235
Balsamic Green Bean Salad, 99
Celery Root and Pear Slaw, 112
Cheesy Carrot Casserole, 98
Chicken Potpie, 137
Chicken Potpies, 123
Colorful Chicken Stew, 57
Cucumber-Stuffed Cherry Tomatoes, 13
Cucumber Tea Sandwiches, 165
Grilled Vegetable Medley, 104
Grilled Vegetable Sandwiches, 148
Hearty Minestrone, 160
Hearty Split Pea Soup, 148
Italian Orzo Salad, 117
Jalapenos with Olive-Cream Filling, 19
Layered Salad with Curry Dressing, 118
Lime Cucumber Salsa, 8
Magnificent Carrot Cake, 219
Parsnip-Asparagus Au Gratin, 222
Pistachio Lettuce Salad, 107
Roasted Fall Vegetables, 215
Roasted Vegetable Chili, 146
Rustic Autumn Soup, 166
Slow-Cooked Chicken Noodle Soup, 165
Slow-Cooked Vegetable Soup, 70
Summer-Fresh Quinoa Salad, 108
Veggie Potato Soup, 57
Veggie Potluck Salad, 104
Veggie-Sausage Cheese Soup, 50
Very Veggie Lasagna, 43

ALPHABETICAL RECIPE INDEX

A

Ambrosia Cupcakes, 183
Angel Food Cake with Berry Sauce, 200
Anise Fruit Bowl, 89
Antipasto Salad, 116
Antipasto Salad, 236
Apple Dumplings, 215
Apple Pork Roast, 143
Apricot-Apple Cider, 52
Apricot-Ricotta Stuffed Celery, 13
Artichoke Chicken Lasagna, 46
Artichoke Spinach Lasagna, 214
Asparagus Cheese Triangles, 235
Au Gratin Party Potatoes, 227

B

Bacon Cheeseburger Buns, 153
Bacon-Cheese Pinwheel Rolls, 228
Bacon Spinach Strata, 91
Baja Pork Tacos, 131
Baked Barbecued Brisket, 143
Baklava Tartlets, 190
Balsamic Green Bean Salad, 99
Barbecue Country Ribs, 56
BBQ Beef Sandwiches, 65
Beef & Tater Bake, 32
Beef Barbecue, 156
Berry 'n' Smoked Turkey Twirls, 246
Berry Surprise Cupcakes, 181
Big-Batch Marinara Sauce, 242
Biscuit Egg Bake, 87
Black Forest Cake, 188
Blond Butterscotch Brownies, 191
BLT Bruschetta, 15
Blue Cheese Date Wraps, 232
Blue Cheese Waldorf Salad, 112
Bow Tie Seafood Salad, 229
Brisket 'n' Bean Burritos, 128
Broccoli-Cauliflower Cheese Bake, 100
Broccoli Cheddar Brunch Bake, 91
Broccoli Chicken Supreme, 47
Broccoli Supreme, 105
Brunch Pizza, 94
Buffet Meatballs, 9
Butter & Herb Turkey, 134
Butterscotch Bliss Layered Dessert, 179
Butterscotch Peanut Bars, 171
Butterscotch Peanut Butter Fudge, 227

C

Cajun Chicken & Rice Soup, 147
Cajun Meat Loaf, 237
Candy Cookie Cups, 172
Caramel Marshmallow Treats, 181
Caramel Pear Pudding, 63
Caramel Praline Tart, 182
Caramel Pretzel Sticks, 185
Caribbean Crabmeat Salad, 109
Cauliflower Au Gratin, 116
Celery Root and Pear Slaw, 112
Champagne Baked Ham, 207
Cheddar-Veggie Appetizer Torte, 18
Cheese Enchiladas, 138
Cheesy Carrot Casserole, 98

Cheesy Chili Dip, 245
Cheesy Mushroom Morsels, 241
Cherry Baked Beans, 119
Cherry Chocolate Coconut
    Cupcakes, 189
Cherry Coffee Cake, 80
Cherry Oatmeal Cookies, 249
Chicago-Style Beef Sandwiches, 52
Chicken & Sausage Manicotti, 41
Chicken Artichoke Pizzas, 28
Chicken Bean Soup, 161
Chicken Little Sliders, 156
Chicken Potpie, 137
Chicken Potpie with Cheddar Biscuit
    Topping, 46
Chicken Potpies, 123
Chicken Salad Croissants, 160
Chicken Salad with a Twist, 111
Chicken Tater Bake, 37
Chicken Tetrazzini, 129
Chili Cheese Dip, 60
Chipotle-Rubbed Beef Tenderloin , 204
Chocolate Chip Cream Cheese Bars, 184
Chocolate Chip Raspberry Bars, 177
Chocolate Ganache Tarts, 192
Chocolate Macaroon Bars, 192
Chocolate Mint Wafers, 186
Chocolate Pudding Sandwiches, 237
Cinnamon Swirl Bread, 83
Coconut Almond Candies, 174
Coconut-Almond Fudge Cups, 230
Coconut-Pecan Brownies, 195
Coconut Rocky Road Treats, 247
Colorful Chicken Stew, 57
Confetti Pasta, 198
Cookie Dough Truffles, 233
Cornmeal-Coated Chicken, 127
Corny Chocolate Crunch, 27
Country Ribs with Ginger Sauce, 140
Crab Salad Tarts, 23
Crab-Stuffed Mushrooms, 15
Cran-Orange Relish, 242
Cranberry BBQ Turkey Sandwiches, 152
Cranberry-Glazed Ham, 124
Cranberry Jalapeno Cheese Spread, 17
Cranberry Turkey Crostini, 217
Cream Cheese Pound Cake, 193
Creamed Garden Potatoes and Peas, 99
Creamy Artichoke Dip, 62
Creamy Buffalo Chicken Dip, 238
Creamy Chicken Casserole, 39
Creamy Chicken-Rice Casserole, 43
Creamy Leek Soup with Brie, 157
Creamy Macaroni and Cheese, 59
Crepe Quiche Cups, 88
Crisp Lemon Cookies, 211
Crispy Chicken Wontons, 10
Crispy Snack Mix, 55
Crunchy Candy Clusters, 51
Crunchy Pomegranate Salad, 100
Cucumber-Stuffed Cherry Tomatoes, 13
Cucumber Tea Sandwiches, 165

D

Deli Beef Heros, 157
Deluxe Breakfast Bake, 90
Double-Cheese Macaroni, 36

E

Eggplant Muffuletta, 161
Enchilada Meatballs, 241

F

Fabulous Fruit Salad, 98
Family Gathering Potatoes, 233
Festive Broccoli-Cauliflower Salad, 209
Feta Breakfast Bake, 94
Fiesta Tuna Salad Sandwiches, 151
Five-Bean Salad, 113
Fresh Peach Lemonade, 185
Fresh Summer Salsa, 26
Fried Chicken Nuggets, 140
Frosted Pumpkin Bars, 205
Fruit Salsa, 24
Fruit Salsa with Cinnamon Chips, 29
Fruity Baked Oatmeal, 79

G

Gingerbread Cupcakes, 210
Glazed Kielbasa, 123
Glazed Pork Chops, 133
Gobbler Cobbler, 223
Granola-To-Go Bars, 83
Green Chili Beef Burritos, 61
Green Olive Dip, 56
Grilled Burgers, 202
Grilled Three-Potato Salad, 102
Grilled Vegetable Medley, 104
Grilled Vegetable Sandwiches, 148
Guacamole Appetizer Squares, 24

H

Ham & Cheese Potato Casserole, 37
Ham 'n' Cheese Squares, 82
Ham and Spinach Crepes, 93
Ham and Swiss Casserole, 220
Hash Brown Egg Breakfast, 59
Hawaiian Kielbasa Sandwiches, 55
Hearty Baked Beans, 103
Hearty Chili Mac, 152
Hearty Minestrone, 160
Hearty Pasta Tomato Soup, 65
Hearty Spaghetti, 129
Hearty Split Pea Soup, 148
Hearty Taco Chili, 66
Heavenly Filled Strawberries, 195
Herb 'n' Spice Turkey Breast, 142
Holiday Glazed Ham, 201
Holiday Pork Roast, 207
Homemade Guacamole, 21
Honey-Apple Turkey Breast, 128
Hot Chicken Salad, 38
Hot Cranberry Punch, 51
Hot Wing Dip, 10

I

Italian Orzo Salad, 117
Italian Pulled Pork Sandwiches, 151

J

Jalapenos with Olive-Cream Filling, 19

K

Kid-Pleasing Taco Pizza, 132

L

Lasagna Corn Carne, 32
Layered Salad with Curry Dressing, 118
Layered Tortellini-Spinach Salad, 113
Lazy Pierogi Bake, 42
Lemon Burst Tartlets, 178
Lemon Crumb Muffins, 78
Lemon-Poppy Seed Doughnut Holes, 93
Lemon Pudding Dessert, 182
Lemon Raspberry Jumbo Muffins, 85
Lemon Ricotta Cake, 208
Lemon Shortbread Cookies, 177
Lemon Tea Cakes, 171
Lime Chicken Tacos, 54
Lime Cucumber Salsa, 8

M

Macaroni Coleslaw, 119
Magnificent Carrot Cake, 219
Makeover Cheese-Stuffed Shells, 122
Makeover Peach Bowl Pizza, 184
Makeover Strawberry Cake, 176
Mandarin Chicken Bites, 23
Mango Cranberry Sauce, 202
Maple Pumpkin Cheesecake, 218
Marmalade Baked Ham, 141
Marshmallow Fudge, 245
Meat 'n' Cheese Stromboli, 166
Mediterranean Tomato Bites, 21
Mexican Roll-Ups, 248
Mini Barbecued Ham Sandwiches, 162
Mini-Burger Potato Bites, 28
Mini Burgers with the Works, 159
Mini Chicken Empanadas, 19
Mini Phyllo Tacos, 14
Mini Spider Bites, 218
Mint Chocolate Torte, 170
Moist & Tender Turkey Breast, 66
Moist Meat Loaves, 177
Mom's Meatballs, 244
Mom's Scalloped Potatoes and Ham, 73
Mushroom Pot Roast, 140

N

Nacho Party Cheesecake, 27
Nacho Rice Dip, 22
New Orleans-Style Subs, 167
No-Bake Cookie Balls, 235
Nutty Caramel Corn, 9

O

Omelet Casserole for 60, 80
Orange Cheesecake Breakfast Rolls, 77
Orzo Cheesecake Fruit Salad, 118

P

Parsnip-Asparagus Au Gratin, 222
Party Meatballs, 230
Peaches & Cream French Toast, 85
Peaches 'n' Cream Muffins, 78
Peanut Butter Easter Eggs, 201
Pearl Pasta Salad, 117
Pecan Butterscotch Cookies, 193
Pecan Candy Clusters, 212
Pecan-Raisin Cinnamon Rolls, 87
Pepperoni Pizza Casserole, 42
Pepperoni Pizza Dip, 70

Pesto Chicken Mostaccioli, 44
Pesto Pasta Medley, 105
Peter Pumpkin Cheese Puffs, 220
Picnic Sweet Potato Salad, 114
Pierogi Pasta Shells, 134
Pilgrim Hat Cookies, 217
Pineapple Orange Cake, 191
Pineapple-Pecan Cheese Spread, 29
Pistachio Lettuce Salad, 107
Pizza English Muffins, 249
Pizzawiches, 164
Pork and Cabbage Dinner, 132
Pork 'n' Shrimp Spring Rolls, 248
Pork Sandwiches with Root Beer
    Barbecue Sauce, 155
Pot Roast with Gravy, 142
Potato-Bar Chili, 138
Potato Chip Cookies, 180
Potatoes for a Crowd, 246
Presto Chicken Tacos, 124
Pretty Stuffed Spring Peas, 22
Puff Pastry Holly Leaves, 209
Pull-Apart Sticky Bun Ring, 77
Pumpkin Pie Dip, 188
Pumpkin Tiramisu, 212

R

Raspberry-Chipotle Glazed Ham, 136
Red Velvet Cookies, 240
Reuben Rolls, 239
Rhubarb Biscuit Coffee Cakes, 247
Ribbon Crispies, 179
Roast Turkey Breast with Rosemary
    Gravy, 141
Roasted Fall Vegetables, 215
Roasted Vegetable Chili, 146
Roundup-Day Beans, 228
Rustic Autumn Soup, 166

S

Santa Cupcakes, 223
Saucy Pork Chops, 137
Sausage Fettuccine Bake, 33
Savory Mediterranean Orzo, 110
Savory Mushroom Tartlets, 8
Scalloped Potatoes with Ham &
    Cheese, 34
Shredded Steak Sandwiches, 71
Simmered Smoked Links, 71
Slow-Cooked Chicken Noodle Soup, 165
Slow-Cooked Herbed Turkey, 73
Slow-Cooked Reuben Brats, 69
Slow-Cooked Turkey Sandwiches, 159
Slow-Cooked Vegetable Soup, 70
Slow Cooker Mexican Dip, 64
Slow Cooker Sloppy Joes, 61
S'more Drops, 176
Smoked Sausage Soup, 147
Smoky Potato Rounds, 17
Southwest Bean Soup, 158
Southwest Corn Bread Salad, 107
Southwest Turkey Casserole, 34
Southwestern Shepherd's Pie, 38
Spaghetti Ham Bake, 44
Spicy Barbecued Chicken, 199
Spicy Black Bean Soup, 167
Spicy Maple Chicken Wings, 12

Spicy Sausage Hash Browns, 50
Spinach Artichoke Dip, 68
Spinach Artichoke-Stuffed
    Mushrooms, 236
Squash Corn Bread, 222
Strawberry & Glazed Walnut Salad, 114
Streusel-Topped Blueberry Muffins, 84
Stuffed Baby Red Potatoes, 26
Stuffing from the Slow Cooker, 68
Summer-Fresh Quinoa Salad, 108
Sunny Morning Doughnuts, 84
Surprise Cupcakes, 175
Sweet 'n' Sour Appetizer Meatballs, 20
Sweet & Sour Chicken Wings, 18
Sweet-and-Sour Chicken Wings, 64
Sweet & Spicy Chicken Drummies, 131
Sweet Barbecued Pork Chops, 126
Sweet 'n' Moist Ham, 122
Sweet Pea Salad, 239
Swiss-Onion Potato Bake, 109

T

Taco Bean Soup, 150
Taco Casseroles, 41
Tangy Mashed Potatoes, 113
Tastes Like Eggnog Cake, 199
Texas Beef Barbecue, 63
Thick & Chunky Beef Chili, 164
Three-Meat Stromboli, 232
Toffee Malted Cookies, 229
Toffee Mocha Cupcakes, 186
Tomato Garlic Soup, 162
Trick-or-Treat Turnovers, 205
Tropical BBQ Chicken, 69
Truffle Chocolate Cupcakes, 172
Turkey and Stuffing Pie, 214
Turkey, Gouda & Apple Tea
    Sandwiches, 155
Turkey Sausage Patties, 88
Turkey with Cranberry Sauce, 211

V

Vanilla-Lime Fruit Salad, 103
Vegetarian Egg Strata, 89
Veggie Ham Crescent Wreath, 204
Veggie Potato Salad, 111
Veggie Potato Soup, 57
Veggie Potluck Salad, 104
Veggie-Sausage Cheese Soup, 50
Veggie Tortilla Pinwheels, 14
Very Veggie Lasagna, 43

W

Walnut-Cream Cheese Finger
    Sandwiches, 146
Warm Pomegranate Punch, 60
Warm Savory Cheese Spread, 226
Watermelon and Tomato Salad, 105
White Chocolate Cranberry
    Cookies, 175
Wild Rice Bread, 240

Y

Yellow Rice & Black Bean Salad, 108

Z

Zucchini Enchiladas, 136